The Great
Scandinavian

Baking Book

ON THE COVER

Gilded Butter Cookies

> 1 cup unsalted butter, at room temperature
> $^1/_2$ cup sugar
> $^1/_2$ tsp. salt
> 1 large egg yolk
> 2 $^1/_4$ cups all-purpose flour

In a large bowl, beat butter, sugar, salt, and egg yolk until smooth. Mix in flour. Form dough into a ball and flatten; wrap in plastic wrap and refrigerate, covered, overnight or for up to four days, so that flavors can blend. Divide chilled dough into four equal pieces. On a lightly floured surface, roll one piece of dough to 1/8-inch thickness. Cut into shapes using 2-inch cutters. Repeat with remaining dough. Bake on ungreased cookie sheets at 350° until edges are lightly browned, 9 to 12 minutes. Cool on wire racks.

For glaze, mix 1/2 teaspoon gold dust with a few drops of vodka or almond extract to make a paste. Brush lightly onto the cookies.

The Great Scandinavian

Baking Book

BEATRICE OJAKANGAS

Illustrated by Rudy Luoma

University of Minnesota Press
Minneapolis / London

First published in hardcover by Little, Brown and Company, 1988
First University of Minnesota Press edition, 1999

Published by the University of Minnesota Press
111 Third Avenue South, Suite 290
Minneapolis, MN 55401-2520
http://www.upress.umn.edu

Library of Congress Cataloging-in-Publication Data

Ojakangas, Beatrice A.
    The great Scandinavian baking book / by Beatrice Ojakangas;
    illustrated by Rudy Luoma.
        p. cm.
    Originally published: Boston : Little, Brown, 1988.
    Includes index.
    ISBN 0-8166-3496-3 (pbk.)
    1. Baking. 2. Cookery, Scandinavian.   I. Title.
TX763.O3326 1999
641.8'15—DC21   99-29064

Printed in the United States of America on acid-free paper

The University of Minnesota is an equal-opportunity educator and employer.

11 10 09 08 07 06 05   10 9 8 7

Now I first have praised the Master
I will praise our gracious hostess
She who has prepared the banquet
And has filled the table for us.
Large the loaves that she has baked us
And she stirred us up thick porridge
With her hands that move so quickly.

from the Finnish national epic, *The Kalevala*

Acknowledgments

*I*t is hard to know where to start thanking and acknowledging people for help and assistance that began years ago. The problem is that I am likely to omit some very important names. But I'll try not to:

Special thanks to my family, my husband Richard, and our children, Cathy, Greg, and Susanna, who have willingly tasted and evaluated successes and failures throughout the years.

Thanks to those friends of mine who have spent extended time in Norway, Sweden, and Denmark and generously shared information about foods and customs.

I wish to acknowledge contributions of recipes and hospitality from the Denmark Cheese Association, Maria Bogvald, and all her associates in Denmark. Thanks to the Norwegian Dairies, especially Ruth Marcussen Kielland and her staff, and to Marja Pekkala, home economist at Valio of Finland.

For personal encounters and inspired meals, thanks to Tello and Esa Anttila, Eija and Kaappo Vesander and their daughter Katja, Kaija Aarikka, and Leila Seppälä!

Jukka Marmo, a geologist and cohort of my husband, together with Sinikka, his wife, has sent innumerable ideas to me.

A special thanks to Sigrun Runolfsdottir in Iceland for sharing Icelandic recipes with me, and also to Kristjana Liefsdottir for her information and recipes. I also thank Inga Aaltonen of Kotiliese, and all the people of the Arabia company of Finland, and of Vaasan Mylly, the flour company of Finland. From these people I gained not only recipes but memories that are more colorful than any written account can ever be.

Contents

The Great
Scandinavian
Baking Book

Introduction

Scandinavians are master bakers. They love coffee and bake all kinds of good things to go with it, coffeebreads, pastries, cakes, and cookies, which they call little cakes. Because of their proximity to each other, the growing seasons and climates of Iceland, Norway, Denmark, Sweden, and Finland are similar. Consequently, the crops, including fruits and berries, are pretty much the same. Not only is the pulse of the season and year the same, but because all of the countries are basically Lutheran, the church year and religious holidays and celebrations share a historic commonality.

Scandinavians all know what it is like to have summer days with no night and winter days with no day. Their crafts and exquisite baked goods were developed during those long winters. How they could see to produce these works of art in the old days, with only dim candlelight, is a miracle in itself. Today, with plenty of light, they still bake and make attractive things but have less time and inclination to do so.

Scandinavians who immigrated to America brought with them tools, skills, and recipes for their favorite baked goods. Besides being of pure Finnish extraction myself, I grew up with Scandinavians all around me. Somewhat isolated in little villages and farms in northern Minnesota, we have seen to it that Scandinavian baking traditions

❖ 3

have been preserved. I have, as have many of my friends, traveled in the Scandinavian countries, and we have all brought back recipes and ideas that have become mingled with our grandmothers'.

On the farm in northern Minnesota where I grew up, we replicated the simplicity of the Finnish life. Our baking was practical, based on necessity. Life was simple but wholesome. We baked rye bread, cardamom "biscuit," and coffeecakes. Although we didn't use as much sugar as most, we didn't skimp on eggs, milk, and butter.

Our neighbors were Norwegians and down the road lived Danes and Swedes. My mother always said they were "real nice people," but we didn't "visit" them. Our visiting was usually with relatives or other Finns. Visiting was something we did on Sunday afternoon when we would get all dressed up and pile into the family car (Isä — father in Finnish — bought a new Ford right after the war) and drive to Aunt Esther's place, or to Uncle Edward's, or Uncle Jack's. Visiting consisted of drinking coffee and eating "biscuit" (as Minnesota Finns refer to the Pulla of this book) and cake. We children would be given fruit nectar and biscuit or cake and would be allowed to tear around outside with the children of the family we were visiting.

When we visited relatives with a cabin on "the lake" (which could be any of 10,000 in our near vicinity), it always smelled of boiling coffee. Always, there was biscuit, and there would usually be a white cake, with a caramel frosting, something like the Tosca Cake in the cake chapter.

When I decided to write this book, I thought it a good idea to include Iceland. It was, however, difficult to find information about Icelandic baking. Finally, my husband and I decided to take a trip to Iceland. We discovered on this wind-blown, rocky island-nation a heritage of baking all its own. I had expected pervasive Norwegian influence, and it was there, but with a great simplicity. A country that imports most of what it needs is naturally conservative in the use of such things as sugar. What Iceland seems to have in abundance are fresh air and hot water. Steam and hot water from geysers are used to warm homes, barns, swimming pools, and greenhouses. Bread is baked in special outdoor bakehouses with ovens heated by subterranean steam. It is a caramel-flavored black bread, 100% rye, that is baked for 24 hours.

Like Iceland, Finland is known for the simplicity of its food. Fancy breads and cakes depend on the dexterity and skill of the hand of the baker. The Danes, nearer continental Europe, bake wonderfully complex filled pastries. Swedes and Norwegians, especially those who are inland, lean heavily toward the art of baking and use lots of special tools to create beautiful baked goods. Tins and rolling pins, irons and molds are typical of Swedish and Norwegian baking.

My interest in and understanding of Scandinavian baking have developed through the years that I have been a food writer. I've traveled in Finland most extensively, and also in Sweden, Norway, Denmark, and, recently, in Iceland. In this collection are my favorite and most successful recipes. It would be impossible to include *every-thing* that is baked in these five countries, each heavily populated with superb home and professional bakers.

Ingredients

yeast: 1 package = 1/4 oz = 2 1/4 teaspoons

All of these recipes have been tested using standard measurements and standard ingredients in a home kitchen. There are some things that must be made with Scandinavian tools to achieve the right effect, and I've indicated when a special implement is necessary.

There are a few ingredients that need explanation:

FLOUR

When the recipe simply calls for "all-purpose flour," as in cakes, pastries, and cookies, you will achieve the best results if you use flour marked on the nutrition panel: protein, 11 or 12 grams per cup. This flour is not as good for a yeast dough because of the low gluten (protein) content, but makes a more tender product when leavened with baking powder or soda.

Yeast bread recipes may call for "bread flour or unbleached all-purpose flour." You will achieve the best results here if you use flour marked on the nutrition panel: protein, 13 or 14 grams per cup. This flour contains more gluten, which is necessary to create the proper elasticity for a yeast dough.

Recipes for cakes and certain pastries may call for cake flour. Cake flour contains only 8 grams of protein per cup and makes tender cakes and cookies, but it is no good for yeast doughs.

Some all-purpose flours sold in the South contain 8 or 9 grams of protein per cup; they are not good for yeast doughs, but are fine for cakes, cookies, and pastries.

BUTTER

People often ask me if I always use butter. I do. But I don't use *unsalted* butter exclusively. I have specified unsalted butter in those recipes where it makes a better product. Sometimes people ask, why use unsalted butter when you add salt later? The reason has to do with the blending quality of the butter. In some mixtures, the presence of salt in the butter tends to inhibit its blending quality. In those cases I call for unsalted butter. I have not tested the recipes with margarine, as I find the baking qualities of margarines vary among brands. If it is necessary for you to use margarine, be sure to use a high-quality unsalted margarine, rather than an economy brand.

EGGS

All the recipes have been tested with "large" eggs.

CARDAMOM

This is the favorite spice of Scandinavian bakers. Cardamom is a highly aromatic spice whose flavor dissipates very quickly. It is best to grind cardamom yourself, using a mortar and pestle, and use it immediately. Cardamom pods are white, papery, and nutlike in shape. The outer pod must be removed; only the little black seeds are used. When I was little, my mother gave me the tedious task of opening the pods and dumping the seeds into the mortar. Always ready to simplify procedures, I discovered that if you crush the whole pods, you can blow away the chaff and the aromatic seeds remain in the mortar, ready for crushing.

SAFFRON

This spice is the most expensive of all the spices used in Scandinavian baking. When I found out that saffron is the stigmas of a certain crocus grown in Spain and that it is hand harvested, I could understand its price! Saffron is available in tiny pouches as a powder, or in vials in threads. The powder dissolves into a liquid easily. The threads must be heated in a liquid. Some people strain them out, while others leave them in the dough.

SUGAR

When recipes call for "pearl" sugar, I mean a kind of sugar that is packaged and sold in Scandinavian countries and exported to the United States. Coarsely crushed sugar cubes can be substituted. Pearl sugar is used to decorate coffeebreads, coffeecakes, and cookies. You can find it in Scandinavian specialty stores and in well-stocked grocery stores, especially in Minneapolis and St. Paul.

CLOUDBERRIES AND LINGONBERRIES

These exotic berries grow near the arctic circle. They are exported to the United States in the form of preserves or jams and are available in Scandinavian food stores and in many well-stocked grocery stores, especially in the Twin Cities of Minneapolis and St. Paul.

Mail Order Sources

Some of the following have catalogues; others have lists of available Scandinavian cookware and specialty foods. If you write, be as specific as possible about which items or foods you desire.

BERGQUISTS IMPORTS
1412 Highway 33 South
Cloquet, Minnesota 55720

ERICKSON'S DELICATESSEN
5250 N. Clark Street
Chicago, Illinois 60640

INGEBRETSEN SCANDINAVIAN
CENTER
1601 E. Lake Street
Minneapolis, Minnesota 55407

MAID OF SCANDINAVIA CO.
3244 Raleigh Avenue
Minneapolis, Minnesota 55416
1-800-328-6722 (out of state)
1-800-851-1121 (in Minnesota)

NORWEGIAN & SWEDISH
IMPORTS
2014 London Road
Duluth, Minnesota 55812

SCANDINAVIAN DESIGNS
UNLIMITED
20 West Superior Street
Duluth, Minnesota 55802

WILLIAMS-SONOMA CO.
Mail-Order Department
P.O. Box 7456
San Francisco, California 94120

Baking Tips

HOW TO SCALD MILK

Heat the milk over direct heat or in a double boiler just until tiny bubbles form around the edges.

HOW TO RAISE BREAD DOUGH

The best time of year to get yeast bread dough to rise beautifully is in the summertime in an 85-degree kitchen! But the most appealing time to bake bread is in the middle of the winter when the kitchen is cold and everybody is shivering. However, even in the winter you can find toasty warm places for raising bread dough. Here are some ideas:

1. Heat rises. Check the highest spots in your kitchen — on top of the cabinets, above the refrigerator. Find a place where warm air is trapped; almost every kitchen has one.

2. Put dough to rise in a glass bowl and cover it with clear plastic wrap. If the sun is shining, place it in a sunny spot.

3. Do not place dough to rise over a radiator or heater. It can get so hot that it will kill the yeast.

4. To use the oven, place a pan of boiling water on the bottom rack of the oven. Turn the oven on to its highest setting for 2 minutes. Turn oven off. Cover the dough with a towel or plastic wrap and place in the oven above the pan of steaming water.

5. To use the microwave, place dough in a glass bowl. Set the bowl in a glass pie plate with hot water in it. Cover dough with waxed paper. Microwave at 10% power (Low) 4 minutes. Let stand 15 minutes. Repeat microwaving and standing until dough is doubled in bulk.

HOW TO COVER THE DOUGH FOR RISING

In the summer when bread dough rises quickly, I often cover the dough with a towel to allow air circulation around the dough and to minimize overheating. When the air is cooler, and when I want to minimize the loss of moisture from the top of the dough (in the winter the air is cooler *and* more dry), I cover the dough with plastic wrap.

These are not hard and fast rules. If I want to eliminate having to wash towels, I use plastic wrap. If I want to conserve plastic wrap, I use towels.

HOW TO TELL WHEN BREAD IS BAKED ENOUGH

The classic method is to tap the loaf with your finger; if it sounds hollow, the bread is done. This doesn't work when bread is very dense or has a soft crust. My favorite method is to insert a wooden skewer into the center of the loaf. When it comes back easily and is dry, the bread is done.

If the bread has browned and looks done, but does not test done, cover it with foil so it will not burn on the outside and continue baking. Bread that browns too quickly might indicate that your oven is baking a bit too hot. Reduce the temperature 25 to 50 degrees to finish baking.

ABOUT YEASTS

My favorite is active dry yeast. I buy it in bulk, but it is the same yeast I could buy in packages at the grocery store. I have tested these recipes also with the rapid-action yeasts or "quick-rise" yeasts, which are a completely different strain of yeast from the old-fashioned active dry. The recipes work fine. They may rise a little more quickly, maybe 10 or 15 minutes faster. Just check the dough a little earlier if you use rapid-action yeast.

It's best to dissolve yeast in water between 105°F and 115°F. It is easiest to dissolve the yeast in water, although some seasoned cooks dissolve it in warm milk. The temperature is critical because yeast is a living organism. Using liquid that is too cold is like pouring ice water on your houseplants. It stunts their growth. If you use water hotter than 115°F, you partially kill or stunt the growth of the yeast. Yeast makes bread rise because it produces carbon dioxide (just as a plant does) which rises and gets trapped in the meshwork of the flour and water mixture.

Yeast that comes in moist cakes works well, too. It is a little more sensitive to high temperatures and should be dissolved in liquid no more than 110°F. The only reason I don't use it more is that it isn't as easy to find in today's grocery store. When I do find it, I have to be sure to use it up before it gets moldy in the refrigerator. However, if you prefer cake yeast, you know all these problems, and it can be readily substituted for dry yeast in all the recipes in this book. One small cake of yeast is equal to 1 package of active dry yeast.

You will notice that I prefer to use the method of dissolving yeast first in liquid, then adding the remaining ingredients, rather than mixing dry yeast with a portion of the dry ingredients and *then* adding hot liquid. I do this because each time I make a yeast dough I want to check out the yeast action. Even when there is no sugar added to the yeast and water mixture, you can actually *see* the yeast beginning to work. It makes a little foam that starts to move around in the bowl. When I notice that action, I know my yeast is alive.

ABOUT DEEP-FAT FRYING

The classic Scandinavian fat for frying has always been lard. Many holiday pastries are deep fried because of the natural cycle. In the early part of December or late in the fall, the butchering took place on the Scandinavian farm. Every part of the animal was used. The hams were smoked and the bits and pieces of meat were made into cold cuts and sausages and other delicacies. The fat was rendered, clarified, and used as shortening and, because there was a lot of it, for deep frying of holiday pastries.

Many people today don't care for the taste of lard and prefer to use vegetable fats. I often use corn oil or safflower oil, or any other high-quality fat available in the market. If it is handled carefully, and you do not overheat it, the fat can be strained and kept refrigerated so it can be used more than once.

Breads for Meals

*I*t was five o'clock in the morning but already light. The bus took us to Reykjavik over what appeared to be a landscape under construction. The terrain, I thought, looked as though someone had bulldozed the whole country. My geologist husband corrected me. "No," he said, "that's lava, which cracks as it cools."

We checked in at the opulent Hotel Saga. After a soul- and body-warming bath in hot water that comes from the ground, we went down to breakfast.

Baskets of crusty, multi-grained bread with sesame and flax seed crusts were arranged across the breakfast buffet. I sampled every one. It was an unforgettable array, and already worth the whole trip!

That this book should begin with a chapter on breads is appropriate. Bread is the main item in the first meal of the day throughout Scandinavia.

Grainy rye and wheat breads, dense pumpernickels and black breads, rye breads aromatic with orange and spices, crispbreads of all thicknesses, soft or chewy flat breads, and rolled-up lefse comprise the repertoire. All my favorites are here, from sour Finnish rye to Swedish limpa to Danish pumpernickel, twice-baked rusks, and crisp crackerlike breads.

Although I can extoll the qualities of all Scandinavian breads, there is one for which I have no recipe. It is called "bark bread." My friend and neighbor Leona Larson, herself an avid bread baker, told me about it, as she learned the story from Ruth Andersen.

In the middle of the 1800s, when there was a severe famine in Europe, the Swedes and Finns made bread using pine bark, which was ground into a meal and baked into a flat waffle. The bark meal was mixed with a little wheat, oat, or rye meal, or whatever was available. Later, studies were done on the nutritional value of the bark, and it was found that it contained various forms of sugars, some minerals, and a small quantity of protein. During the famine many Finns and Swedes emigrated to the United States. My grandfather, an emigrant, was the only son in a family of five boys who did not starve to death in Finland during that terrible famine.

SWEDISH LIMPA
(*Rågsiktlimpör*)

*I*t's hard to know whether to call this bread Swedish or Norwegian, because the everyday breads in these two countries are so much alike. My Swedish and Norwegian friends make rye bread using light rye flour and various flavorings. Some bakers use only caraway, some only orange, and others a combination of orange with fennel, anise, or caraway seeds. The combination of all four flavors is the most deluxe and festive blend. In Finland, this deluxe bread is served during the Christmas holidays and is called *Joululimppu*. Because this bread is made with light or medium rye flour it has a fine texture.

The amount of rye flour and sweetness varies from recipe to recipe. This one can be made with an optional amount of sugar but we prefer the less-sweet option. I bake it in the wintertime in four-loaf batches, because baking several loaves is no more trouble than baking just one. In this method, the dough is simply mixed with a wooden spoon until most of the flour is blended in. I do this in the evening, and, because winter nights are cool, I can let it stand on the kitchen counter until morning without overproofing. In the morning the kneading is easy and the dough rises quickly. If your climate is warm, you can let the dough stand unkneaded as long as 3 to 4 hours. This delayed-kneading method gives the flour time to absorb liquid, the yeast time to "work" without developing a yeasty flavor, and the flavors of the ingredients time to meld together.

❖ Makes 4 loaves

1 package active dry yeast
$\frac{1}{4}$ cup warm water, 105°F to 115°F
$\frac{1}{2}$ to 1 cup light molasses or dark corn syrup
4 cups milk, refrigerator temperature
1 cup salad oil
$\frac{1}{2}$ to 1 cup light or dark brown sugar, packed
3 teaspoons salt
1 teaspoon each finely crushed caraway seed, fennel seed, and anise seed
grated peel of 1 orange*
1 cup uncooked rolled oats, regular or old-fashioned
2 cups light or medium rye flour
9 to 10 cups bread flour or unbleached all-purpose flour
warm molasses or dark corn syrup to brush hot loaves.

In a large bowl, dissolve the yeast in warm water and let stand 5 minutes. Stir in the molasses according to amount of sweetness desired, milk, oil, brown sugar to taste, salt, spices, and orange peel. Mix in the rolled oats and rye flour; beat well. Slowly stir in as much of the bread flour as possible to make a stiff dough. There should be no "dry" flour remaining in the bowl, but dough will be lumpy.

In cold climates, cover the bowl with plastic wrap and let stand at room temperature overnight. During this time the dough will rise to the top of the bowl. In warmer climates, or in the summertime, let stand 3 to 4 hours in a cool place.

Sprinkle top of dough with about $\frac{1}{4}$ cup all-purpose flour. With spatula, scrape down the sides of the bowl. Turn dough out onto floured surface and knead until smooth. If the batch is too big to handle, divide the dough into 2 parts and knead each part separately. Knead 5 to 10 minutes until smooth and satiny. Grease four 8- or 9-inch round cake pans or four 9 x 5-inch loaf pans. Divide kneaded dough into 4 equal parts. Shape each into a round or oblong loaf.

Place loaves in pans with smooth sides up. Cover and let rise in a warm place until almost doubled, about 1 hour.

Preheat oven to 375°F. Bake 35 minutes or until a wooden skewer inserted in the center comes out clean. If bread browns too rapidly while baking, cover with foil to finish baking. Remove from pans onto cooling racks. Brush hot loaves with warm molasses or dark corn syrup to glaze.

❖ You can grind the seeds and the orange zest (peeled with potato peeler) in an electric coffee grinder to make the job easier.

FINNISH RYE BREAD
(*Ruisleipä*)

*T*his is a nonsoured version of the classic Finnish rye bread, as we baked it in my youth, and as my mother and I still make it. We use half bread (or wheat) flour and half rye meal, the unsifted rye flour that includes some of the bran of the grain. This flour is sometimes called "rye meal," "dark rye," or "pumpernickel rye" on grocery shelves. For special occasions, I like to shape this bread in the traditional wheel with a hole in the middle. More often I shape it into fat rounds.

❖ Makes 2 loaves

> 1 package active dry yeast
> 1 tablespoon sugar
> 2 cups warm potato water,* 105°F to 115°F
> 1½ teaspoons salt
> 1 tablespoon melted shortening or lard
> 2 cups dark rye flour or rye meal or pumpernickel rye
> 3 to 4 cups bread flour or unbleached all-purpose flour
> 1 tablespoon melted butter

In a large bowl, stir yeast and sugar into warm potato water; let stand 5 minutes. Add salt and shortening. Add rye flour; beat until smooth. Adding 1 cup at a time, beat in enough bread or all-purpose flour to make a stiff dough. Turn out onto a lightly floured board. Cover with a dry cloth; let stand 5 to 15 minutes. Wash and grease bowl; set aside. Adding flour as necessary to prevent sticking, knead dough until smooth, about 10 minutes. Place in greased bowl, turning to grease all sides.

Cover and let rise in a warm place until doubled in bulk, about 2 hours. Lightly grease one large baking sheet or two 9-inch round cake pans. Turn dough out onto an oiled surface and divide into two parts. Shape each into a round loaf and place on the prepared baking sheet or in cake pans with the smooth side up.

Or, to shape a loaf with a hole in the center, press each loaf with moistened fingers into a flat round, 12 inches in diameter. With fingers, press a hole into the center of the loaf, then stretch a hole about 2 inches in diameter. Smooth out the edges.

Let loaves rise uncovered until almost doubled, about 30 minutes. Preheat oven to 375°F. Brush loaves with water and puncture tops with a fork in several places. Bake 30 to 35 minutes or until golden brown. Brush while hot with the melted butter; cool on a rack. To serve, cut round loaves in half, then set half with cut side down on board and slice. For the wheel, cut into wedges about 3 inches at the outside edge; split wedges horizontally.

◆ Save cooking water from mashed potatoes.

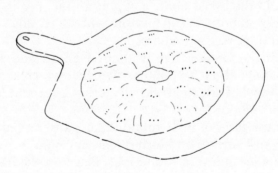

FINNISH CHRISTMAS BUTTERMILK RYE BREAD
(*Joululimppu*)

*F*innish Christmas rye bread is spicy with orange peel and caraway seed.

❖ Makes 3 loaves

2 packages active dry yeast
$\frac{1}{2}$ cup warm water, 105°F to 115°F
2 cups buttermilk❖
$\frac{3}{4}$ cup dark corn syrup or light molasses
$\frac{1}{4}$ cup softened or melted butter
2 tablespoons grated orange peel
1 teaspoon each *fennel seed and caraway seed*
2 teaspoons salt
2 cups dark rye flour
1 cup whole wheat or graham flour
4 to 5 cups bread or unbleached all-purpose flour

In a large bowl, dissolve the yeast in the warm water and let stand 5 minutes. Heat the buttermilk to lukewarm and add to the yeast mixture. Stir in the syrup, butter, orange peel, fennel seed, caraway seed, salt, and rye flour. Beat well. Stir in the whole wheat flour and beat again. Add the bread flour, a cup at a time, beating after each addition to keep smooth. When mixture will not readily absorb more flour, cover and let rest 15 minutes.

Turn dough out onto a lightly floured board and knead until smooth and satiny, about 10 minutes. Wash bowl, grease it, and add dough to the bowl. Turn to grease all sides. Cover and let rise until doubled, about 1 hour.

Lightly grease three 9-inch round cake pans or baking sheets. Lightly oil a work surface and turn dough out onto it. Divide into 3 parts and shape each into a round loaf. Place on the baking sheets with smooth sides up. Let rise, covered, in a warm place for about 45 minutes to 1 hour. Pierce loaves all over with a fork.

Preheat oven to 375°F. Bake loaves for 40 minutes or until a wooden skewer inserted in the center comes out clean. Remove from oven and pans and cool on racks.

❖ If you don't have buttermilk, use the same amount of fresh milk mixed with 2 tablespoons fresh lemon juice or vinegar.

SWEDISH CHRISTMAS DIPPING BREAD
(*Doppbröd*)

*O*n Christmas Eve, it is a ritual in many Swedish families to partake in the "dipping in the kettle." The custom stems back to the old days when the Christmas ham had to be simmered, which produced a lot of tasty stock in a pot. Every member of the family lowered slices of this rye bread into the pot and then enjoyed it with butter and slices of ham.

❖ Makes 2 loaves

1 package active dry yeast
$\frac{1}{4}$ cup warm water, 105°F to 115°F
2 tablespoons sugar
1 tablespoon each *fennel seed and anise seed,*
    crushed
1 teaspoon salt
2 tablespoons melted butter
2 cups buttermilk, ale, or beer, warmed
2 cups light or medium rye flour
3 to 3 $\frac{1}{2}$ cups bread flour or all-purpose flour
butter to brush hot loaves

In a large bowl, dissolve the yeast in the warm water; add the sugar and let stand 5 minutes until yeast foams. Add the fennel seed, anise seed, salt, butter, and buttermilk. Stir in the rye flour and beat well. Stir in bread flour until dough is stiff. Let it stand, covered, for 15 minutes.

Turn dough out onto a lightly floured board and knead for 5 minutes until smooth. Clean the bowl, lightly grease it, and add the dough to the bowl, turning to grease all sides. Cover with a towel and let rise in a warm place until doubled, about 2 hours.

Lightly grease 2 baking sheets.

Turn dough out onto a lightly oiled surface. Divide into 2 parts. Shape into 2 loaves and place on baking sheets with the smooth sides up. Let rise until almost doubled, about 45 minutes. Slash loaves, making a cross on the top using a sharp knife. Preheat oven to 375°F. Bake for 25 to 30 minutes or until loaves sound hollow when tapped. Brush with the melted butter while hot and cool on racks.

FINNISH BLACK BREAD
(*Hapanleipä*)

The traditional Finnish bread is baked in a big round, flat loaf with a hole in the center. In western Finland, this loaf was baked twice a year by farm wives, in the spring and again in the fall. It is a bread that relies for its flavor on the rye flour itself and the process of souring. Historically, souring the bread dough was the only means of leavening it, and every household guarded their "starter" carefully. The loaf owes its classic wheel shape to tradition. The farm wives, who labored to bake hundreds of loaves of bread at a time, would string them up on poles, slipping the pole through the center of the rather thin loaves, and store them in the granary or *aitta*. Finns are still fond of the shape, and you can buy the loaves with a hole in the center in bakeries today.

In other provinces of Finland, baking was done as often as every day, and the bread was not strung up on poles and stored, but was made into round, firm loaves. The method of mixing and souring the dough was very much the same for either shape.

I love this dense loaf, regardless of the shape, when it is cut into thin slices. You *do* need a sturdy, sharp knife and a bit of muscle to do it! It is delicious with a topping of pungent cheese, cold cuts, or smoked fish. We like it with fresh caviar from the herring or whitefish of our northern Minnesota waters, a product that is *exported* from Minnesota to the Scandinavian countries! My friend and fellow food writer in Finland, Tello Anttila, taught me how to serve it. Spread thin slices of rye bread with a thick layer of fresh golden caviar. Top that with sour cream, chopped onion, and freshly ground allspice. She served this as a first course along with iced Finnish vodka and Finnish ale.

When you make this bread you need to plan ahead. It takes 48 hours for the dough to sour. It slices best on the second day after baking.

To store the loaves, keep refrigerated for several months. You may also freeze them. According to Finns, this rye bread has a self-preserving quality, so it will not mildew. It will dry out, however, which, they claim, makes it good for the teeth. Finnish mothers give the heels of the bread to teething babies to chew.

❖ Makes 2 loaves

3 packages active dry yeast
4 cups warm water, 105°F to 115°F
7 to 9 cups dark rye flour
2 teaspoons salt (optional)
additional flour for shaping

In a large, preferably plastic bowl with a snap-on lid, dissolve the yeast in the warm water. Add 2 cups rye flour and beat to make a smooth mixture. Sprinkle the top of the dough with 1 cup rye flour. Cover tightly and let stand in a warm place for 24 hours. It will ferment and sour.

The second day, add 2 cups of the rye flour, stir, and let stand 24 hours more. The dough will have developed a pronounced sour aroma at the end of this period.

Stir in the salt and final amount of flour, but do not exceed 9 cups. Knead, preferably in a heavy-duty mixer, for 30 minutes. The dough should be very sticky. With damp hands and a dough scraper, shape dough into a ball and place in the bowl again. Sprinkle with just enough additional flour to make the top of the dough dry. Let rise 1½ hours in a warm place.

Turn dough out onto a lightly floured board. Divide into 2 parts. Lightly grease 2 baking sheets and cover with a thick coating of dark rye flour.

For a loaf with a hole in the middle, shape each half into a round loaf about 8 inches in diameter. With a floured finger, press a hole in the center of each loaf. Gently pull the hole until it is about 2 inches in diameter. With hands dipped in water, smooth out the edges and top of each loaf. Brush loaves generously with water and sprinkle with a generous coating of rye flour.

For round loaves, shape each part into a ball. Roll the ball around on a rye-flour covered board until it resembles a huge chocolate drop with a slightly pointed top, as shown in the illustration. Place loaves on the baking sheets with the point upward. You may put both loaves on the same sheet if it is large enough. Brush with water and sprinkle tops with more flour.

Place shaped loaves in a warm place until they have flattened out, spread apart, and the tops appear crackled, as sketched.

Place a large jelly roll pan on the bottom rack of the oven. Preheat oven to 350°F. Fill the jelly roll pan with boiling water and bake the loaves for 1 hour or until firm. Wrap baked loaves in towels or waxed paper to soften.

ICELANDIC STEAMED RYE BREAD
(*Rugbraud*)

*K*ristjana Liefsdottir and her husband, Thorsteinn Sigurdsson, live on a farm in northeastern Iceland. The treeless lava-flow landscape is craggy, and steam spews from a hole in the ground. A 2-inch pipe plumbed into the steam travels 500 feet to the house and runs into the hot-water tank, through the radiators, and into a heated swimming pool. The barn, with some fifty milking cows, is heated with water, and the cows drink warm water all winter long, which, son-in-law Bjorn claims, makes the cows produce more milk from less feed. Steam is piped into an outdoor oven where Kristjana bakes this classic Icelandic steamed rye bread. We later found this bread being sold in greenhouses around the country in areas where there are hot springs. (Hot-spring areas in Iceland abound with greenhouses, and vegetables, fruits, and flowers are luxuriously available the year round.) The steamed rye bread is baked for 24 hours in enclosed pans surrounded by thermal steam, during which time the sugar caramelizes and imparts a dark color and rich flavor to the bread. The bread is cut into bricklike squares, wrapped, and stored in a cold place. The bread slices much more easily after a few days.

I managed to duplicate this bread at home by creating a steam bath in my oven.

❖ Makes 1 loaf

> 1 package active dry yeast
> 2 cups warm water, 105°F to 115°F
> ½ cup dark brown sugar, packed
> 2 teaspoons salt
> 4½ cups dark rye flour

In a large bowl, dissolve the yeast in the water. Let stand 5 minutes. Add the sugar, salt, and rye flour and mix until dough is stiff. Turn out onto a lightly floured board and knead by hand or knead in a heavy-duty mixer for 10 minutes.

Grease a 9 x 5-inch loaf pan. Turn dough into the pan. Fold a piece of waxed paper and place it on top of the dough so the foil cover will not touch the bread. Cover with foil and crimp to seal well.

Place pan on a rack in a larger pan as shown. Add boiling water up to the level of the rack. Cover the entire thing with foil to seal it well.

Or, if you have a large roaster or casserole with a lid, top with the lid in addition to the foil.

Bake at 250°F for 24 hours. Check water level occasionally and refill if necessary.

Remove from oven, allow to cool completely, then unwrap and unmold from the pan. Wrap and chill for 24 hours before slicing.

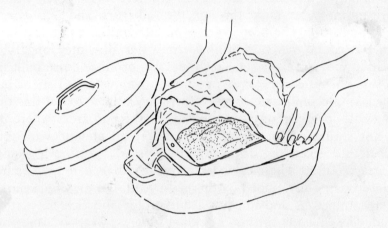

DANISH PUMPERNICKEL
(*Rugbrød*)

The Danes make this firm-textured pumpernickel to use as a base for their famous *smørrebrød*.

❖ Makes 2 loaves

2 cups coarse cracked wheat, 7-grain cereal,
  or dark rye flour
1 cup boiling water
2 packages active dry yeast
$\frac{1}{2}$ cup warm water, 105°F to 115°F
$\frac{1}{2}$ cup dark corn syrup or light molasses
3 tablespoons butter
2 tablespoons caraway seed
1 teaspoon salt
$3\frac{1}{2}$ to 4 cups bread flour or unbleached all-purpose flour

In a large bowl, combine the cracked wheat, cereal, or rye flour with the boiling water. Let stand until cooled to body temperature. In a small bowl, dissolve the yeast in the warm water and let stand 5 minutes.

Meanwhile, stir the molasses, butter, caraway seed, and salt into the grain mixture. When cooled, add the yeast mixture along with 1 cup of the bread flour. Beat until dough is smooth. Add more bread flour until dough is stiff. Cover and let stand 15 minutes.

Turn out onto lightly floured board and knead for 10 minutes or until dough is smooth. Wash bowl, grease it, and place dough in the bowl. Turn to grease all sides. Cover and let rise in a warm place until doubled in bulk, about 2 hours.

Grease two 9 x 5 x 3-inch loaf pans.

Punch down dough and divide into 2 parts. Shape each into a loaf. Place loaves with the smooth side up in pans. Cover and let rise until almost doubled, about 1 hour.

Preheat oven to 350°F. Brush tops of loaves with water, then bake 40 to 45 minutes or until loaves sound hollow when tapped. Turn out of pans; cool on rack.

RAISIN BEER BREAD
(Ølbrød)

*T*his is a bread made by both Swedish and Norwegian bakers. The addition of beer or ale gives a sourdough flavor to rye bread that is favored by many Scandinavians. The dough must rise overnight, so plan accordingly.

❖ Makes 3 loaves

2 cups milk
2 tablespoons butter
½ cup sugar
¾ cup dark molasses
1 (12-ounce) bottle dark beer or ale
2 packages active dry yeast
½ cup warm water, 105°F to 115°F
1 teaspoon ginger
1 teaspoon salt
½ teaspoon cinnamon
¼ teaspoon pepper
6 cups light or medium rye flour
1½ cups raisins
3½ to 4½ cups bread flour or unbleached all-purpose flour

In a saucepan, bring the milk to a boil. Measure the butter, sugar, and molasses into a large mixing bowl. Pour in the milk and add the beer or ale. Cool to lukewarm.

In a small bowl, dissolve the yeast in the warm water and add the ginger.

Stir the salt, cinnamon, pepper, and half the rye flour into the cooled liquids. Add the yeast and beat well. Add the remaining rye flour. Stir in bread flour until dough is stiff and will not absorb more. Cover with plastic wrap and let stand overnight.

Sprinkle flour lightly onto a board and turn dough out onto board. Sprinkle raisins over the top and knead the raisins into the dough.

Divide into 3 parts and shape each into a round loaf. Lightly grease 3 baking sheets and place dough onto the sheets. Let rise until almost doubled.

Preheat oven to 375°F, and bake for 45 minutes or until a wooden skewer inserted in the center of the loaves comes out clean. Place loaves on a rack to cool.

CURRANT RAISIN BREAD
(Rosinbrød)

*T*he success of this bread, as well as many others, depends on not allowing the dough to become too dry through adding too much flour. When you add an ingredient like raisins, which tend to break through the fiber of the dough, the dough becomes sticky. It is tempting then to add too much flour, but that will create a tough, dry loaf. In my recipe, I allow time for the dough to "pull itself together" by letting it rest for 15 minutes before kneading.

❖ Makes 1 loaf

> 2 packages active dry yeast
> $\frac{1}{2}$ cup warm water, 105°F to 115°F
> 1$\frac{1}{2}$ teaspoons sugar
> $\frac{1}{2}$ cup undiluted evaporated milk
> 1 egg
> 2$\frac{3}{4}$ to 3 cups unbleached all-purpose flour
> 1 tablespoon softened or melted butter
> $\frac{1}{2}$ teaspoon salt
> $\frac{1}{2}$ cup light or dark raisins
> $\frac{1}{2}$ cup currants
> butter to brush hot loaf
> sugar for topping

In a large bowl, dissolve the yeast in the warm water, add the sugar, and let stand 5 minutes until yeast foams. Stir in the milk, egg, and half the flour. With a wooden spoon beat by hand until smooth. Let stand 10 minutes. Add the butter, salt, raisins, currants, and more flour to make a stiff dough. Let stand 15 minutes, covered.

Turn dough out onto a lightly floured board and knead until smooth and springy, about 5 minutes. Clean the bowl, oil it, and return the dough to the bowl. Turn to grease all sides. Let rise, covered, until doubled, about 1 hour.

Grease and lightly flour a baking sheet. Turn dough out onto an oiled surface and shape into a fat, oblong loaf. Place on the baking sheet and let rise until puffy, about 45 minutes.

Preheat oven to 375°F. Bake for 25 to 30 minutes or until the loaf tests done. Brush with melted butter and sprinkle with sugar.

ICELANDIC MULTI-GRAIN BREAD
(*Grofarbraud*)

*L*oaves and rolls with a generous coating of sesame and flax seeds and light-textured centers are typical of Icelandic tables. The availability of natural steam, which is piped into commercial ovens, creates the wonderfully crusty exterior of the bread. You can reproduce this crustiness by baking the loaves or rolls on baking tiles set above boiling water. Place unglazed tiles on the top shelf of the oven. Place a large jelly roll pan or other wide pan on the bottom shelf of the oven. The tiles *and* jelly roll pan must be preheated with the oven. As you slip the risen bread onto the tiles on the top shelf, you pour water into the jelly roll pan, creating a burst of steam, which will give the bread a crusty and golden exterior. For the multi-grain cereal, check the supermarket or a health food store for a multi-grain cereal that needs to be cooked. One multi-grain cereal that I have found in a health food store contains cracked wheat, rye, cornmeal, flax, and millet. Cracked wheat or bulgur can be substituted for the cereal. You can purchase flax seed in most health food stores.

❖ Makes 2 loaves

> 1 cup multi-grain cereal or cracked wheat
> 3 cups boiling water
> 2 packages active dry yeast
> ¼ cup warm water, 105°F to 115°F
> 2 tablespoons light or dark brown sugar
> 3 teaspoons salt
> 2 tablespoons melted lard
> 5 to 6 cups bread flour or unbleached all-purpose flour
> flax seed, sesame seed, and sunflower seed for topping
> cornmeal for baking sheet

Measure the cereal into a large bowl. Add the boiling water, stir, cover, and let stand 1 hour.

In a small bowl, dissolve the yeast in the warm water. Add the sugar and let stand 5 minutes until foamy. Add to the cooled cereal mixture. Stir in the salt, lard, and half the bread flour. Beat until smooth. Add remaining flour, a cupful at a time, until dough is stiff. When you have added as much flour as the mixture will absorb easily, cover and let rest 15 minutes. Sprinkle board with some of the remaining flour. Turn dough out onto board and knead, adding flour as needed to relieve stickiness, until dough is smooth and springy in feel.

Wash the bowl and lightly grease it. Turn dough into the bowl, turn the dough in the bowl to grease top, cover with plastic wrap or a towel, and let rise in a warm place until doubled, 1 to 1½ hours.

Meanwhile, prepare the oven. Place upper rack in center of oven. Place second rack in the next position beneath it. Line upper rack with unglazed tiles or baking tiles (they need not cover the entire rack). Place a large pan on the bottom rack. Preheat oven to 400°F.

Cut a strip of foil about 18 inches long and place on a cookie sheet without sides. Sprinkle the foil with cornmeal to keep the bread from sticking to the foil and to allow it to brown evenly on top, sides, and bottom.

When dough has risen, dust lightly with flour while it is still in the bowl. Lightly oil a work surface or countertop. Turn dough out onto surface and divide into 2 parts. Lightly knead each part to expel air bubbles. Shape loaf into a fat oblong, about 4 inches in diameter and 14 inches long. Brush surface with water and sprinkle generously with a mixture of flax seed, sesame seed, and sunflower seed. Place loaves with smooth side up well apart on the strip of foil, placing loaves lengthwise, about 4 inches apart. Let rise until almost doubled. Slash crosswise in 3 or 4 places.

Slip loaves (still on the cornmeal-covered foil) onto preheated tiles in the oven. Pour 1 cup water into the hot pan beneath, creating a burst of steam. Bake for 25 to 35 minutes or until loaves sound hollow when tapped and exterior is golden and crusty. Remove from oven and cool on racks.

ICELANDIC THREE-GRAIN BROWN BREAD
(*Brunbraud*)

I first enjoyed this soda bread in a farm home in Iceland when Kristjana, in whose home we stayed, served it with the evening meal. It is a delicious dark bread that is a favorite because it is so quick and easy to make.

❖ Makes 2 loaves

½ *cup brown sugar, packed*
½ *cup softened butter*
1 *cup rolled oats*
1 *cup dark rye flour*
2 *cups whole wheat flour*
2 *cups all-purpose flour*
1 *teaspoon salt*
4 *teaspoons baking soda*
2½ *cups buttermilk**

Preheat oven to 350°F. Grease two 9 x 5 x 3-inch loaf pans.

In a large bowl, cream together the brown sugar and butter. Mix the rolled oats, rye flour, whole wheat flour, all-purpose flour, salt, and baking soda together in another bowl, then add to the creamed mixture along with the buttermilk. Mix until well blended. Divide the mixture between the two pans and smooth the tops. Bake 1 hour or until a wooden skewer inserted in the center comes out clean. Turn out of pans and cool on racks. This is excellent toasted.

❖ If you don't have buttermilk, measure the same amount of fresh milk and add 2½ tablespoons fresh lemon juice or vinegar.

DANISH OAT LOAF
(*Havrebrød*)

*T*his bread is a perfect counterpart to a bowl of thick pea soup.

❖ Makes 2 loaves

1 cup uncooked rolled oats
1 cup milk, heated to boiling
2 tablespoons butter
¼ cup dark brown sugar
1 teaspoon salt
1 package active dry yeast
1¼ cups water, 105°F to 115°F
4 to 5 cups bread flour or unbleached all-purpose flour

GLAZE AND TOPPING

1 slightly beaten egg
2 tablespoons milk
rolled oats

In a small bowl, combine the rolled oats with the milk. Stir to mix. Add the butter, brown sugar, and salt. In a large mixing bowl, dissolve the yeast in the warm water and let stand 5 minutes. When oat mixture is just warm to the touch, stir into the yeast mixture. Blend in 1 cup of the flour and mix until blended. Add the remaining flour a little at a time, beating to keep mixture smooth. When mixture is stiff, cover bowl with plastic wrap and let rest 15 minutes. Sprinkle board with flour, turn dough out onto floured board, and knead for 10 minutes until dough is smooth and satiny. Place dough in a greased bowl, cover, and let rise in a warm place until doubled, about 1 hour. Divide into 2 parts, shape into round loaves, and place in 2 greased 9-inch round pans. Let rise again until doubled.

Preheat oven to 375°F. Brush with egg mixed with milk and sprinkle with rolled oats. Bake for 25 to 35 minutes or until loaves sound hollow when tapped.

NORWEGIAN WHOLE WHEAT BREAD
(*Hvetebrød*)

*N*orwegians import most of their cereal grains and fruits but produce their own meat, dairy products, and vegetables. They produce a large amount of cheese, from the caramel-colored *gjetost*, the cheese that is made with the whey from goat's milk, to Jarlsberg, a well-known variety in the United States. One cheese that has not gained popularity here is *gammelost*, or "old cheese." It isn't really old, it just smells that way! When I was instructed how to approach it, I was told to spread whole wheat bread thickly with butter, then put a thin shaving of the smelly cheese on top, and to take *little* bites. This is one acquired taste I can live without! But hvetebrød is good as a base for other Norwegian cheeses, too.

❖ Makes 2 loaves

2 packages active dry yeast
2 cups warm water, 105°F to 115°F
¼ cup light molasses
¼ cup sugar
¼ cup melted shortening or butter
1½ teaspoons salt
2 cups whole wheat or graham flour
3 to 4 cups bread flour or unbleached all-purpose flour
butter to brush hot loaves

In a large bowl, dissolve the yeast in the water. Let stand 5 minutes. Add the molasses, sugar, shortening, and salt. Stir in the whole wheat flour. Add bread flour, 1 cup at a time, until dough is stiff. Let rest 15 minutes. Sprinkle breadboard with additional flour and turn dough out onto the flour. Knead 10 minutes until dough is smooth and springy. Wash bowl, grease it lightly, and add dough to the bowl. Turn over to grease top. Cover and let rise in a warm place until doubled. Punch down. Cover and let rise again until doubled. Punch down again and divide dough into 2 parts. Shape each into a round or oblong loaf. Lightly grease two round cake pans or two 9 x 5-inch loaf pans. Place loaves in the pans. Let rise until almost doubled.

Preheat oven to 375°F. Place loaves in the oven and bake 30 to 40 minutes or until loaves sound hollow when tapped or a wooden skewer inserted in the center comes out clean. Brush tops of loaves with melted butter.

DANISH SPICED WHEAT PUMPERNICKEL
(Nellike Brød)

*T*his old-fashioned bread is a heavy pumpernickel that is good served with butter and cheese or as a base for *smørrebrød*.

❖ Makes 2 loaves

> 2 packages active dry yeast
> $\frac{1}{2}$ cup warm water, 105°F to 115°F
> 1$\frac{1}{2}$ cups milk, scalded and cooled to lukewarm
> $\frac{1}{3}$ cup dark corn syrup
> 2 teaspoons salt
> 1 teaspoon ground cloves
> 1 teaspoon ground ginger
> 4$\frac{1}{2}$ to 5 cups whole wheat flour
> milk to brush loaves
> poppyseed for topping

In a large mixing bowl, dissolve the yeast in the warm water. Let stand 5 minutes. Add the milk and corn syrup. Stir in the salt, cloves, ginger, and half the flour. Beat until smooth. Stir in more flour until dough is stiff. Let stand 15 minutes.

Turn dough out onto a floured board and knead until smooth and elastic, about 10 minutes. Clean the bowl, oil it, and add the dough to the bowl. Turn over to oil the top of the dough. Cover and let rise in a warm place until doubled, about 1 to 1$\frac{1}{2}$ hours.

Grease two 9 x 5 x 3-inch loaf pans. Divide dough into 2 parts and shape into loaves. Place in pans. Let rise until about doubled. Brush loaves with milk and sprinkle with poppyseed.

Preheat oven to 375°F. Bake for 35 to 40 minutes until the loaves test done. Remove from pans and cool on rack.

DANISH WHEAT WALNUT WREATH
(*Valnøddekrans*)

*T*his bread is wonderful with cheese and flavored butter spreads. Add a bowl of fruit and it's sufficient for lunch!

❖ Makes 1 wreath

1 cup boiling water
⅔ cup whole wheat flour
2 packages active dry yeast
½ cup warm water, 105°F to 115°F
1 tablespoon dark corn syrup
2 teaspoons salt
1 cup unflavored yogurt or buttermilk
4½ to 5½ cups bread or unbleached all-purpose flour
½ cup coarsely chopped walnuts

In a small bowl, pour the boiling water over the whole wheat flour and let stand until room temperature.

In a large mixing bowl, dissolve the yeast in the ½ cup warm water. Let stand 5 minutes. Add the corn syrup, salt, and yogurt.

Add the cooled wheat flour mixture and beat with an electric mixer until smooth. (The whole wheat flour mixture may be lumpy.) Stir in bread or all-purpose flour 1 cup at a time, beating after each addition until dough is stiff. Let stand 15 minutes.

Turn out onto a lightly floured board and knead until smooth and elastic, about 10 minutes. Clean the bowl, oil it, and add dough to the bowl, turning to grease all sides. Let rise for about 1 hour or until doubled. Knead the walnuts into the dough.

Lightly oil a work surface and turn dough out onto it. Divide into 2 parts. Roll each part out to make a long strand, 26 to 30 inches long. Twist together to make a 2-strand rope.

Cover a baking sheet with parchment paper or lightly grease it. Place rope onto the baking sheet to form a wreath; pinch ends together. Let rise, covered with plastic wrap or a towel, until puffy, not quite doubled, about 45 minutes.

Preheat oven to 375°F. Bake for 30 to 35 minutes or until the loaf is lightly browned. Cool on a rack.

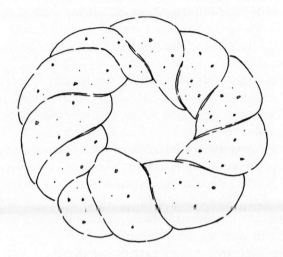

DANISH COUNTRY EGG BREAD
(*Landbrød*)

*T*his bread is pretty shaped in a 2-strand braid. Follow the directions, and you may be impressed with your own craft!

❖ Makes 2 loaves

> 2 packages active dry yeast
> 1½ cups warm water, 105°F to 115°F
> ¼ cup sugar
> 1 teaspoon salt
> 2 eggs
> ¼ cup vegetable oil
> 5 to 5½ cups unbleached all-purpose flour

In a large mixing bowl, dissolve the yeast in the warm water. Add the sugar. Let stand 5 minutes until the yeast foams. Beat in the salt, eggs, and oil. Stir in half the flour to make a loose batter and beat until satiny and smooth. Add flour to make a soft dough. Cover and let rest 15 minutes.

Turn out onto a lightly floured board and knead until dough is springy and satiny, about 10 minutes, adding just enough flour to prevent stickiness. Clean the bowl and oil it. Add dough to the bowl. Turn over to oil top of the dough. Cover and let rise until doubled, about 1 hour.

Lightly oil a work surface. Cut the dough into 2 parts. Working with 1 part of dough at a time, divide the part into 2 parts. Shape each into a long strand, about 30 to 36 inches long. To make a 2-strand braid, cross the strands and press in the middle of the join to seal the strands together, Step 1. Cross 2 opposite ends of strands over the join to the other side, Step 2. Then cross the other 2 strands over the join, Step 3. Repeat the crossing, Step 4; you will be making a braid "upward." When you come to the end of the strands, pinch them together, Step 5, and lay the entire thing on its side, Step 6. That's when you will see the "braid."

Try it again with the second part of the dough.

Cover baking sheets with parchment paper or lightly grease them. Place loaves on the baking sheets. Let rise until almost doubled, about 45 minutes, in a warm place.

Preheat oven to 375°F. Bake for 25 to 30 minutes or until golden and loaves test done.

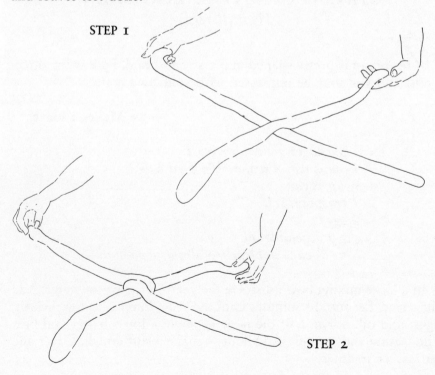

STEP 1

STEP 2

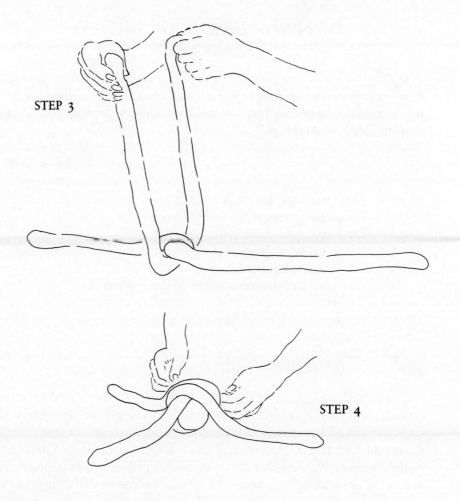

STEP 3

STEP 4

STEP 5

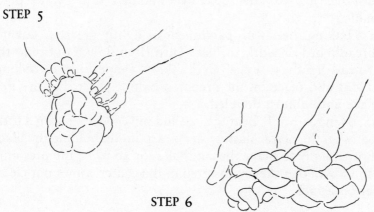

STEP 6

DANISH "FRENCH" BREAD
(*Franskbrød*)

*T*his is the most popular of the white breads in Scandinavia. It is not a real French bread, but Swedes, Norwegians, Finns, and Icelandics all call it *Franskbrød*.

❖ Makes 1 loaf

1 package active dry yeast
1 cup warm water, 105°F to 115°F
1 egg
4 teaspoons sugar
1 teaspoon salt
2½ to 3 cups unbleached all-purpose flour

GLAZE

1 egg
2 tablespoons milk

In a large bowl, dissolve the yeast in the warm water and let stand 5 minutes. Add the egg, sugar, and salt. Mix in half the flour and beat well. Slowly add enough of the remaining flour to make a stiff dough. Cover and let rest 15 minutes. Lightly flour a breadboard and turn dough out onto it. Knead 5 to 10 minutes until dough is springy and satiny. Wash and lightly grease the bowl. Place kneaded dough in the bowl; turn over to grease the top. Cover and let rise in a warm place until doubled.

Cover a baking sheet with parchment or lightly grease it. Lightly oil the breadboard or work surface. Turn risen dough out onto the board. Knead lightly to expel air bubbles. Shape into an oblong, rounded loaf and place on the prepared baking sheet. Let rise in a warm place until almost doubled.

Preheat oven to 400 °F. Beat the egg and milk together with a fork. Brush loaf with the glaze. Slash with a sharp knife, holding the blade almost horizontally to make the cut. Bake for 20 to 25 minutes until golden and a wooden skewer inserted in the center comes out clean. Cool loaf on a rack.

LEILA'S RYE BUNS
(*Leilan Pannuleipä*)

*M*y friend Leila wrote out her favorite everyday recipes when she learned of my interest in baking. Leila is a *puistotati* or "Park Auntie." In Finland each city park has a trained teacher who guides the activities and takes care of young children. Mothers drop off their young ones (from babies on up) at the park and are assured of responsible childcare while they do their errands. Leila is one of those caretakers. She doesn't work on Saturdays, her baking day. She makes a supply of this bread for her own family, along with other baked goods, which we often enjoyed during our stay in Finland.

❖ Makes 30 buns

> 2 packages active dry yeast
> ½ cup warm water, 105°F to 115°F
> 2 tablespoons light molasses or dark corn syrup
> 2 teaspoons salt
> 2 tablespoons melted butter or other fat
> 2 cups skim milk, scalded and cooled to lukewarm
> 2 cups light or dark rye flour
> 4 to 4½ cups bread flour or unbleached all-purpose flour

In a large bowl, dissolve the yeast in the warm water. Add the molasses and let stand 5 minutes until yeast foams. Add the salt, butter, milk, and rye flour and beat well.

Stir in the bread flour, a cupful at a time, until dough is stiff and will not absorb more flour. Let it rest, covered, for 15 minutes.

Sprinkle breadboard with flour. Turn dough out onto board and knead, adding more flour as necessary, until dough is smooth and satiny, about 10 minutes. Wash bowl, grease it, and add dough to the bowl. Turn over to grease the top. Cover and let rise until doubled, about 1 hour.

Cover baking sheets with parchment paper or lightly grease them.

Turn dough out onto a lightly oiled board and pat or roll out to about ¾-inch thickness. Cut into rounds using a glass or round cookie cutter. Place on prepared baking sheets. Let rise until puffy, 30 to 45 minutes.

Preheat oven to 400°F. Pierce each roll all over with a fork. Bake for 15 minutes until golden.

BUTTERHORNS
(*Smørhorn*)

*B*utterhorns are a "never-fail" favorite of many Scandinavian-American cooks. A Norwegian friend gave me this recipe. As she says in her instructions, "Chust mix them as you do for any rolls and then roll them into rolls!"

❖ Makes 2 dozen rolls

2 packages active dry yeast
½ cup warm water, 105°F to 115°F
¼ cup sugar
1 teaspoon salt
1 cup milk, scalded and cooled to lukewarm
3 eggs
½ cup softened butter
5 to 6 cups unbleached all-purpose flour
about ½ cup softened butter

GLAZE

1 egg
3 tablespoons milk

In a large bowl, dissolve the yeast in the warm water. Add the sugar. Let stand 5 minutes until the yeast foams. Stir in the salt, milk, eggs, and butter. Mix in 5 cups of the flour, 1 cup at a time, beating after each addition until smooth. Cover and let rest 15 minutes. Turn out onto lightly floured board and knead until smooth and satiny. Dough should feel quite soft, and the softer the dough you can handle the lighter the rolls will be. Clean the bowl and oil it lightly. Add dough to the bowl, turning over to oil the top. Cover and let rise until doubled, about 1 to 1½ hours in a warm place.

Cover baking sheets with parchment or lightly grease them.

Lightly oil a work surface. Turn risen dough out onto surface and divide into 3 equal parts.•

Roll one part out at a time to make a circle 12 to 14 inches in diameter. Rolling out yeast dough can be frustrating because it tends to shrink back. The trick is to roll it out, then give it a rest, roll out again and give it a rest, and in so doing you can roll it to the desired size.

Brush the circle of dough with softened butter, then cut into 8 equal wedges. Starting from the wide end, roll up toward the tip of the piece of dough, as sketched; tug slightly at the wide ends of the piece to exaggerate the width. Place rolls on the prepared baking sheets, about 2 inches apart, placing the tip beneath the roll so it won't pop up as it rises and bakes.

Repeat with remaining balls of dough. Let rise in a warm place until almost doubled. Preheat oven to 375°F.

Beat the egg with the milk to make a glaze and brush rolls lightly with the mixture. Bake for 15 to 18 minutes or until golden.

❖ The dough will seem very soft after rising, but resist the temptation to add more flour; instead, oil or butter your fingers to prevent stickiness. You may use a slight dusting of flour on the outside of the dough to keep it from sticking.

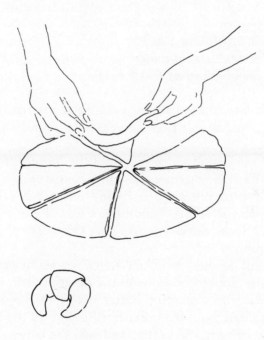

DANISH POPPYSEED ROLLS
(*Tebirkes*)

*T*he Danes enjoy these rolls freshly baked for breakfast.

❖ Makes 14 to 16 rolls

1 package active dry yeast
$\frac{1}{4}$ cup warm water, 105°F to 115°F
1 tablespoon sugar
1 cup milk, scalded and cooled to lukewarm
1 egg
$\frac{1}{2}$ teaspoon salt
1 cup butter, room temperature
4 cups all-purpose flour

GLAZE AND TOPPING

1 egg white
1 tablespoon water
2 tablespoons poppyseed

In a small bowl, dissolve the yeast in the warm water. Add the sugar, milk, egg, and salt to the yeast. Let stand 15 to 20 minutes until frothy.

In a large mixing bowl, rub $\frac{1}{2}$ cup of the butter into the flour with your fingers until the mixture resembles coarse crumbs. Add the yeast mixture and turn out onto a lightly floured board. Knead until smooth and elastic, about 5 minutes. Clean the bowl and lightly oil it. Place dough into the bowl, turn over to oil the top, and let rise for 20 to 30 minutes.

Cover a baking sheet with parchment paper or grease lightly.

On a lightly floured board, roll the dough out to make a 16-inch square. Spread the remaining butter over half the dough to within $\frac{1}{2}$ inch of the edge. Fold the unbuttered half over the buttered half of the dough, enclosing the butter, and seal the edges. Fold the dough again lengthwise and seal the edges to make a long roll 3 to 4 inches wide; it should stretch itself out to about 20 inches.

Place the dough on the prepared baking sheet. Mix the egg white and water to make a glaze and brush the top of the roll with the glaze. Sprinkle with poppyseed. Cut into 14 to 16 triangles. Separate the triangles slightly. Let rise until almost doubled, 30 to 45 minutes.

Preheat oven to 400°F. Bake for 15 minutes or until golden.

DANISH LUNCHEON BRAIDS
(Fletninger)

*T*hese 2-strand braids look like the typical 3-strand variety. If you are so inclined, follow the directions and master the technique. Otherwise, simply make these buns into a 2-strand twist.

❖ Makes 16 rolls

1 package active dry yeast
¼ cup warm water, 105°F to 115°F
⅓ cup milk
1 egg
¼ cup melted butter
1 tablespoon sugar
½ teaspoon salt
2 to 2½ cups all-purpose flour
1 slightly beaten egg white
sesame seed or poppyseed

In a large bowl, dissolve yeast in the warm water and let stand 5 minutes. Add the milk, egg, melted butter, sugar, and salt. Slowly beat in the flour until a stiff dough forms.

To shape, see illustrations for Danish Country Egg Bread. Divide dough into 16 pieces. Halve each piece. Roll each into a rope about 6 inches long. Take 2 of the ropes and place one over the other in the form of a cross. Press in the middle so that they stick together. Take 2 opposite ends and cross them over each other, then take the other 2 ends and cross them over the first 2. Continue to braid in this way upwards from the table until the ropes are all braided. Repeat for all of the rolls.

Cover baking sheets with parchment paper or lightly grease them. Place braids on the prepared baking sheet. Let rise 20 minutes. Brush with beaten egg white and sprinkle with sesame seed or poppyseed if desired.

Preheat oven to 375°F. Bake for 15 to 20 minutes or until golden and light. Do not overbake.

COPENHAGEN SALT STICKS
(*Saltstaenger*)

*C*rispy and salty, these sticks are typically served with soup. They can be made in quantity and will keep well when stored in an airtight tin.

❖ **Makes 40 sticks**

1 package active dry yeast
$\frac{1}{4}$ cup warm water, 105°F to 115°F
1 tablespoon sugar
$\frac{1}{2}$ teaspoon salt
$\frac{1}{4}$ cup softened butter
$\frac{1}{2}$ cup milk, scalded and cooled to lukewarm
1 egg
2 to 2$\frac{1}{2}$ cups all-purpose flour

GLAZE

1 slightly beaten egg white
1 tablespoon water
coarse (kosher) salt

In a large bowl, soften the yeast in the warm water; add the sugar and let stand 5 minutes until the yeast foams. Stir in the salt, butter, milk, and egg. Stir in the flour $\frac{1}{2}$ cup at a time until dough is stiff. Turn out onto floured board and knead until smooth and satiny. Wash bowl, grease it, and add dough to the bowl. Turn to grease all sides. Let rise in a warm place until doubled, about 1 hour.

Meanwhile, cover 1 large baking sheet with parchment or lightly grease it. Preheat oven to 350°F.

Lightly oil a work surface or countertop. Turn dough out onto the surface and knead lightly to expel the air bubbles. Divide into 8 equal parts. Between the palms of your hands and the work surface, roll dough out to make strands the length of your baking sheet, or about 16 inches long. Place on the prepared baking sheet, about 1 inch apart. Brush with a mixture of the egg white and water. Sprinkle with coarse salt. With a knife, mark off each strip to make 5 equal breadsticks, leaving the strands in place. Let rise 10 minutes, then bake for 30 minutes or until golden and crisp. Break apart.

HEALTHY RUSKS
(*Terveyskorput*)

$\mathcal{S}$candinavians in general love to keep rusks or "twice-baked breads" on hand. Rusks are a perfect base for cheese at breakfast; they are equally good for picnics or lunches, and in the summertime they keep well in a tin at a summer cottage. Vacation at the lake is *not* the time for baking! Rusks are made ahead at home or purchased in the wonderful home-style bakeries found all over Finland, as well as Sweden, Norway, Denmark, and Iceland.

❖ Makes 64 rusks

2 packages active dry yeast
$\frac{1}{2}$ cup warm water, 105°F to 115°F
2 tablespoons brown sugar
$1\frac{1}{2}$ teaspoons salt
$\frac{1}{2}$ teaspoon anise seed
$1\frac{1}{2}$ cups milk, scalded and cooled to lukewarm
$\frac{1}{2}$ cup dark rye flour
$\frac{3}{4}$ cup whole wheat flour
4 to $4\frac{1}{2}$ cups bread flour or unbleached all-purpose flour
$\frac{1}{4}$ cup softened butter

In a large bowl, dissolve the yeast in the warm water. Add the brown sugar and let stand 5 minutes until yeast foams. Stir in the salt, anise seed, milk, rye and whole wheat flour and beat until smooth.

Add the bread flour or all-purpose flour a cup at a time, beating between additions until dough is stiff and will not absorb more flour. Let stand, covered, 15 minutes.

Sprinkle breadboard with flour. Turn dough out onto board. Knead, adding flour to prevent stickiness, until dough is smooth and satiny, about 10 minutes. Knead in the softened butter.

Wash bowl and grease it. Add dough to the bowl and turn over to grease top. Cover and let rise in a warm place until doubled, about 1 hour.

Punch dough down and turn out onto an oiled surface. Cut the dough into quarters. Cut each quarter into quarters, then cut each piece of dough in half to make 32 pieces. Shape each into a small round roll. Place on a floured baking sheet. Cover with a towel and let rise until doubled, about 45 minutes.

Preheat oven to 425°F. Bake rolls 15 minutes until golden. Cool. Lower oven heat to 300°F. With 2 forks, split the rolls into halves horizontally, as illustrated. Place on baking sheet with cut side up. Bake until golden and dried, about 30 minutes. Remove from oven and cool on racks. Store in airtight container.

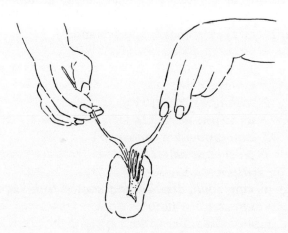

NORWEGIAN WHEAT RUSKS
(*Kavring*)

*H*ere is another classic twice-baked bread of Scandinavia, a summertime favorite when it is too warm to think of baking. Rusks keep well in airtight containers and are eaten as a substitute for freshly baked bread.

❖ Makes 64 rusks

1 package active dry yeast
¼ cup warm water, 105°F to 115°F
3 tablespoons sugar
2 teaspoons salt
3 tablespoons melted lard
2 cups warm water, 105°F to 115°F
4½ to 5 cups whole wheat or graham flour

In a large mixing bowl, dissolve the yeast in the ¼ cup warm water; add the sugar. Let stand 5 minutes until yeast foams. Stir in the salt, lard, and 2 cups warm water; add 2 cups of the flour. Cover and let rise until doubled, about 1 hour. Stirring batter, add more flour a cup at a time until dough is stiff and will not easily absorb more flour. Cover and let stand 15 minutes. Turn out onto lightly floured board and knead until dough is no longer sticky (a 100%-whole wheat dough will be "tacky," not sticky).

Wash bowl, grease it lightly, and add dough to the bowl. Turn over to grease the top. Cover and let rise again until doubled.

Meanwhile, cover baking sheets with parchment or lightly grease them. Lightly oil a breadboard or work surface and turn dough out. Knead lightly to expel air and divide in half. Divide each half into quarters, then again into quarters, making a total of 32 pieces of dough. Shape into smooth round rolls. Place rolls on prepared baking sheets. Cover with a towel and let rise in a warm place until almost doubled.

Preheat oven to 425°F. Bake for 12 to 15 minutes. Remove from oven, cool on racks, and with two forks, split each roll horizontally into two parts. Place on baking sheets again and bake at 250°F for about 1 hour or until dry and crisp.

FINNISH FLATBREAD
(*Rieska*)

I remember my grandmother talking about *rieska*, the classic Finnish quick bread. I also remember old Finnish ladies in my home town making something they called rieska. Some made it flat and unleavened, and some made flat yeast-leavened breads. Some used barley flour, others used rye flour, and still others used a mixture of grains in their breads. When we spent a year in Finland and I began to inquire about rieska, I also found many differences. The further north I went, the thinner the rieska. I found the local versions varied from a barley bread to an oat bread to a pancakelike bread to a bread that contained mashed potatoes. On the farm in western Finland where my mother's relatives came from, we had a yeast-raised, thin-batter rye bread in a free-form shape, which was called rieska.

I decided to include two kinds of rieska here. One is a barley quick bread. Barley flour can be purchased in health food stores. The other is a buttermilk multi-grain rieska, which is imprinted on the top with a decorative carved wooden mold before baking. It requires no kneading.

FINNISH FLAT BARLEY BREAD
(*Ohrarieska*)

*T*his is a quickly made rieska, or flatbread, that tastes best eaten while still warm and buttered. Finns serve this bread with any meal.

❖ Makes one 14-inch round flat loaf

3 cups all-purpose flour
2 cups barley flour
1 tablespoon sugar
1 tablespoon baking powder
2 teaspoons salt
½ cup lard or butter, firm, but not hard
2 cups buttermilk
1 teaspoon baking soda

Preheat oven to 425°F.

In a large bowl, combine the flours with the sugar, baking powder, and salt. With a fork or pastry blender, cut in the lard or butter until the mixture resembles coarse crumbs. Mix the buttermilk with the baking soda and stir into the dry ingredients until a soft dough forms.

Grease and flour a large pizza pan or cookie sheet. Pat dough out to about ½-inch thickness and pierce with a fork all over.

Bake for 20 minutes or until lightly browned but not hard.

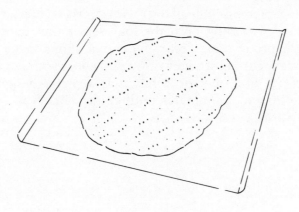

FINNISH FLAT MULTI-GRAIN BREAD
(*Rieska*)

nov 2006
no.

❖ Makes 1 large flatbread loaf

2 packages active dry yeast
½ cup warm water, 105°F to 115°F
1 cup warm buttermilk, 105°F to 115°F
1 teaspoon anise seed
1 teaspoon caraway seed
1 teaspoon salt
2 tablespoons dark corn syrup
1 cup whole wheat flour
1 cup dark rye flour
1 cup barley flour
melted butter to brush hot loaves

In a large bowl, dissolve the yeast in the warm water. Let stand 5 minutes. Stir in the buttermilk, anise seed, caraway seed, salt, and corn syrup. Beat in the whole wheat, rye, and barley flours to make a soft, smooth dough.

Cover and let rise in a warm place until doubled, about 1 hour. Grease a large cookie sheet and sprinkle with whole wheat or rye flour. Turn risen dough out onto the cookie sheet and flatten with floured hands to make an evenly thick, round loaf, about ¾- to 1-inch thick. Let rise 30 minutes.

Preheat oven to 400°F.

Before baking, pierce dough all over with a fork, or press a floured, decorative wooden carving onto the loaf, leaving an imprint. Or, using a heart-shaped or other decorative cookie cutter, make a design all over the bread, cutting straight through the loaf with the cutter in several places. (A ring of 6 or 7 hearts is a pretty design.) Bake immediately for 15 to 20 minutes until golden. Brush with melted butter. Serve warm, cut into wedges.

FINNISH BUCKWHEAT FLATBREAD
(*Tattarileipä*)

*I*n old Karelia, which is in the easternmost part of Finland, celebrations such as weddings and anniversaries were often events that lasted for days. There were bakers who were so good at making this bread that they would come to stay at private homes and bake this specialty, which is always served warm. Making the bread is a three-day process. It is not difficult, but there are long waiting periods between steps. It is a sourdough bread.

❖ Makes 1 flatbread, 15 x 10 inches

½ pound scrubbed potatoes
water to cover
½ teaspoon salt
2 cups potato water
1 package active dry yeast
¼ cup warm water, 105°F to 115°F
1 cup buckwheat flour
⅔ cup buttermilk
1 cup buckwheat flour
1 cup bread flour
1½ teaspoons salt
butter to brush hot bread

The day before you plan to make the bread, cook the potatoes in water to cover with the ½ teaspoon of salt. Peel and mash the potatoes and save 2 cups of the water in which the potatoes were cooked, adding it to the mashed potatoes. Let stand, covered, overnight.

The second day, in a large mixing bowl, dissolve the yeast in the warm water and let stand 5 minutes. Add the mashed-potato mixture. Stir in 1 cup of the buckwheat flour and let stand in a warm place overnight. This makes the sourdough. The next day, add the buttermilk, 1 cup buckwheat flour, bread flour, and salt. Beat well. The dough should be the consistency of cooked oatmeal.

Grease and flour a 15 x 10-inch jelly roll pan or cookie sheet with sides. Turn dough into the pan and smooth top.

Preheat oven to 450°F. Bake for 20 to 30 minutes until lightly browned. Brush with melted butter when loaf has baked 15 minutes. Remove from the oven and brush again with butter and serve warm.

FINNISH GRIDDLE-BAKED FLAT RYE BREAD
(*Sultsina*)

*S*ultsina is a thin rye bread that is baked on a dry griddle, much like tortillas or Norwegian Lefse. The sultsina are spread with a farina (Cream of Wheat) mixture before serving and are folded into a long, narrow sandwich.

The true sign of a folk recipe is that it has as many variations as there are cooks. This is such a bread. Not only does the bread itself vary from one cook to another, but each village tends to have its own variation. Some make it with all rye flour, some with a mixture. Some make the bread with barley flour. I learned to make sultsina in Koli, Finland, in a farm home. There, it was the only dish on the lunch menu, and individual bowls of cream and cinnamon sugar were offered with it. The children dipped their filled sultsina in cream, then in cinnamon sugar between bites.

❖ Makes about 15 sultsina

1 *cup cold water*
1 *teaspoon salt*
1 *cup rye flour*
1 *cup all-purpose flour*

FILLING

4 *cups milk*
¾ *cup farina*
1 *teaspoon salt*
butter

OPTIONAL FILLINGS

hot, seasoned mashed potatoes
hot, seasoned rice pudding

In a large bowl, mix the water, salt, and rye flour. Add the all-purpose flour and mix until dough forms. Knead until smooth, about 2 minutes.

Shape dough into a log. Cut into 15 equal parts.

On a lightly floured board, roll each part of dough out to make an 8-inch circle. Cover with plastic film to prevent drying.

Heat a cast-iron griddle until a drop of water sizzles on it. Bake the circles, without fat, one at a time, turning often, until the breads are browned in spots. Remove and stack, covered with a towel.

To prepare the farina filling, in a heavy saucepan, heat milk to boiling. Add the farina and salt and simmer until thickened. Add butter to taste.

To serve, spread 2 to 3 tablespoons of the hot farina mixture over the baked breads. Fold two opposite sides toward the center, then roll up as shown. Serve immediately.

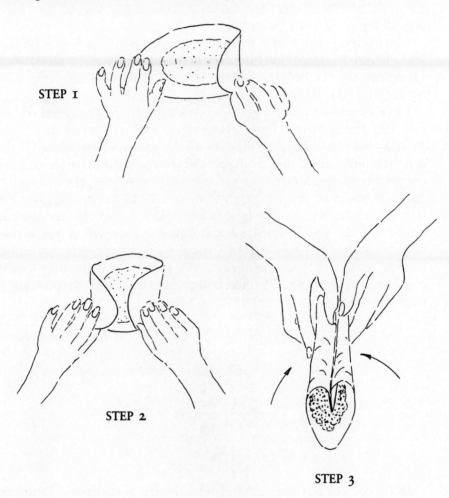

STEP 1

STEP 2

STEP 3

NORWEGIAN POTATO FLATBREAD
(*Lefse*)

Lefse is the deluxe flatbread of Norway, the bread made with tedious care for banquets, holidays, weddings, and all special occasions. Almost every district of Norway has its own favorite recipe for lefse, although it goes by different names in different areas. Most lefse recipes do not include yeast, but a few do. "*Krotakaker*" from the area of Hardanger, for instance, commonly known as "*Hardanger lefse*," is made with yeast.

This recipe is for a lefse that is made with potatoes and stays soft and pliable. Many of our Norwegian friends make this lefse in great quantities for the holiday season early in Advent. They wrap it in plastic and foil, folded, and freeze it.

Lefse has to be rolled paper-thin, using a specially carved rolling pin that has grooves. Early Norwegian settlers carved their own rolling pins out of hardwood, making the grooves lengthwise on the pin. Machine-tooled pins available today in Scandinavian shops have the grooves going around the pin instead. Either way, the rolling pin makes it easier to get the dough thin, and at the same time gives the lefse a surface pattern. The lefse is lifted with a thin wooden spatula onto a hot, dry griddle for baking. It is turned over with a special thin stick, and after baking is stacked and wrapped to preserve its moist, flexible texture. Experienced lefse bakers know that the best results come from preparing the lefse dough one day and refrigerating it until the next.

❖ Makes 20 lefse

> 4 cups pared, cooked, and diced russet potatoes
> $\frac{1}{4}$ cup butter
> $\frac{1}{2}$ cup whipping cream
> 2 tablespoons sugar
> 1 teaspoon salt
> $1\frac{1}{2}$ cups all-purpose flour

Drain cooked potatoes until absolutely dry. If necessary, return to dry saucepan and stir over medium heat until all moisture is gone. Put potatoes through ricer, or place in large mixing bowl and mash, using electric mixer. Beat in the butter, cream, sugar, and salt. Cover and refrigerate overnight. The next day, stir in the flour until well blended. Divide into 20 equal portions. Preheat lefse griddle, electric frypan, or pancake griddle to 400°F.

On floured surface, roll out the balls of dough until very thin, making circles about 10 to 12 inches in diameter. Using a long, thin spatula, transfer to heated griddle and cook on each side. Stack, separating lefse with waxed paper squares.

To serve, spread lefse with soft butter and fold into quarters or roll up. Some people like lefse sprinkled with sugar or cinnamon sugar. To serve on tray along with cookies, spread lefse with butter, sprinkle with cinnamon sugar, and roll up. Cut rolls into 1-inch pieces on the diagonal.

To freeze, fold lefse into quarters and wrap airtight in foil or plastic wrap. To serve, remove from freezer, thaw, and reheat in foil in a 300°F oven for 10 to 15 minutes.

HARDTACK
(Knäckebröd)

18 MAY 2006

*A*ll Scandinavians enjoy homemade crispbread, which we have come to know as hardtack. There are many varieties, and this is a favorite homemade, quick, crackerlike hardtack. It is made with oatmeal and has a nutty flavor and crisp texture. Hardtack is rolled paper-thin with a special knobby rolling pin. Many Scandinavians add hardtack pieces to their cookie trays. It is delicious eaten plain or with butter or a cheese spread.

❖ Makes 128 pieces

$\frac{1}{2}$ *cup vegetable shortening*
$\frac{1}{4}$ *cup butter, room temperature*
$\frac{1}{2}$ *cup sugar* *less*
2 *cups uncooked rolled oats*
3 *cups all-purpose flour*
$1\frac{1}{2}$ *teaspoons salt*
1 *teaspoon baking soda*
$1\frac{1}{2}$ *cups buttermilk*

In a large bowl, cream shortening, butter, and sugar until smooth. In a medium bowl, combine oats, flour, salt, and baking soda. Alternately add flour mixture and buttermilk to creamed mixture, blending until stiff like a cookie dough. Refrigerate 30 minutes. Grease a large baking sheet and sprinkle with rolled oats.

Preheat oven to 325°F. Divide dough into 8 equal portions. Shape each portion into a smooth ball. Return 7 balls of dough to bowl; cover and refrigerate. Place remaining ball of dough on prepared baking sheet. Flatten as much as possible with your hands, then use a rolling pin to roll dough to edges of baking sheet. Use a hardtack rolling pin to make pebbled imprints on top, or prick evenly with tines of fork to make a rough texture. With a pastry wheel, knife, or pizza cutter, score dough into 2-inch squares.

Bake 15 to 20 minutes or until crisp and golden. Cool 3 minutes on baking sheet, then place on a rack to finish cooling. Break into crackers where scored. Repeat with remaining dough, keeping dough chilled until you are ready to roll it out.

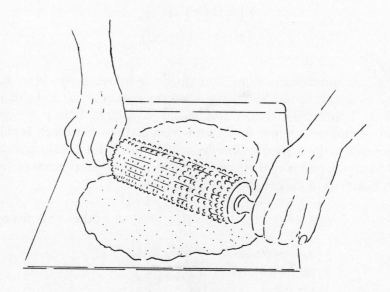

CHRISTMAS CRISPBREAD
(Julknäckebröd)

*O*f all breads, Swedes love crispbreads the most and they eat them at any time of day, especially during the Christmas holiday season. Many varieties are available on the market from thin to thick, and in shapes from squares to rectangles to a large round cake with a hole in the center.

The latter shape comes from the days when the breads were hung on poles in the kitchen and were simply lifted down and dusted off as needed. Fresh crispbread was always baked at Christmastime and was regarded as a *gudslän* or a "loan from God." For rolling the bread out you should have a rolling pin with hobnailed carving on it, which makes the dough stretch more easily. If you do not have one, use a regular rolling pin, but pierce the dough all over with a fork.

❖ Makes 8 dozen breads, about 2 x 4 inches

> 1 cup butter
> 1½ cups milk
> 2 packages active dry yeast
> ½ cup warm water, 105°F to 115°F
> 1 teaspoon sugar
> 1 teaspoon salt
> 1 teaspoon baking soda
> 2 cups whole wheat flour
> 3½ to 4 cups bread or all-purpose flour

In a saucepan, combine the butter and milk and heat just until the butter has melted. Cool to lukewarm.

In a large bowl, dissolve the yeast in the warm water, add the sugar, and let stand 5 minutes until yeast foams. Stir in the cooled butter and milk mixture, salt, baking soda, and whole wheat flour; beat until smooth. Add bread or all-purpose flour until dough is stiff. Cover and let stand 15 minutes. Turn dough out onto lightly floured board and knead 5 minutes until smooth and springy.

Divide dough into 4 parts and roll out each part right on a lightly greased 17 x 14-inch baking sheet until very thin, using a hobnailed rolling pin, or use a plain rolling pin and pierce the bread all over with a fork after rolling. Cut into 4 x 2-inch pieces using a pastry cutter or a straight-edged knife. Leave pieces in place on the baking sheet.

Preheat oven to 350°F. Bake for 25 minutes or until golden and crisp. Cool, break apart, and store in airtight tins.

ICELANDIC SNOWFLAKE BREADS
(*Laufabraud*)

*A*nyone who has ever made paper snowflakes will be familiar with this technique. The dough is rolled out thin, folded, and with a sharp knife the decorations are cut into each cake. They are then deep-fried until golden and served with smoked lamb — *hangikjöt* — at Christmas. As with most Scandinavian Christmas pastries, these are made early in the Advent season and stored in a cool place. (A "cool place" in Iceland — or Minnesota, for that matter — is not hard to find; it's usually a tin on the back porch!)

◆ Makes 32 rounds

4 cups all-purpose flour
1 teaspoon baking powder
1 tablespoon sugar
1 tablespoon melted butter
2 cups milk, heated to boiling
hot fat for frying
powdered sugar (optional)

In a bowl, combine the flour, baking powder, and sugar. Mix in the butter and hot milk until a stiff dough is formed. Turn out onto a lightly oiled surface and knead until smooth and cooled. Divide dough into four parts. Shape each into a ball. Divide each into 4 parts to make 16, then divide each of the resulting balls into 2 parts to total 32.

Cover baking sheets with waxed paper and dust the waxed paper lightly with flour.

On a lightly floured surface, roll out each part of dough to make a thin round about 8 inches in diameter. Place the rounds on the floured waxed paper. Chill 30 minutes.

In a skillet, heat 2 inches of fat to 375°F to 400°F. Vegetable shortening or corn or peanut oil may be used but the authentic fat is lard.

Fold the dough rounds, one at a time, into quarters, and, with a sharp-tipped knife, make little cuts and cut-outs in the dough. Fry the bread rounds, until golden brown, about 1 minute on each side. Remove and drain on paper toweling. Store in an airtight container in a cool place or in the freezer until ready to serve.

ICELANDIC WHEAT AND RYE HARDTACK
(*Hrökkbraud*)

A hobnailed wooden rolling pin is used to roll out the dough for this crispbread in thin circles, which are quickly baked. This bread greatly resembles one of the many varieties of Lefse made in Norway.

◆ Makes 20 rounds

1 package active dry yeast
½ cup warm water, 105°F to 115°F
2 cups lukewarm buttermilk
3 cups dark rye flour or pumpernickel rye flour
3 cups whole wheat flour
2 teaspoons salt
2 teaspoons crushed caraway seed
rye flour for rolling out the rounds

In a large bowl, dissolve the yeast in the warm water. Stir in the buttermilk. Combine the rye flour, whole wheat flour, salt, and caraway seed. Stir in 2 cups of the flour mixture and beat well. Gradually add the remaining flour mixture until dough is stiff. Let stand 15 minutes. Cover and let rise 1 hour until mixture is about doubled.

Preheat oven to 400°F.

Sprinkle top of dough with rye flour and scrape down the sides of the bowl with a spatula, cleaning the bowl as you go. Sprinkle a breadboard with rye flour. Turn dough out onto the board. Shape dough into a log and cut into 20 parts. Using a hobnailed hardtack rolling pin, roll out the dough to make rounds about 8 inches in diameter. Place on ungreased cookie sheets, 2 or 3 at a time.

Bake for 8 to 10 minutes until crisp and lightly browned. If, after removed from the oven and cooled, the hardtack is not crisp, return to the still-warm oven, placing the rounds directly on the oven racks, until crisp.

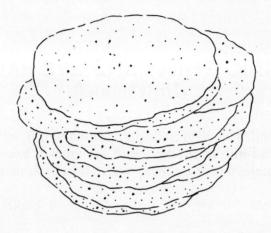

OATMEAL CRACKERS
(*Hafrakex*)

I first encountered oatmeal crackers made at home in Finland. Later, I discovered that the Swedes and Norwegians make them, too. I don't know about the Danes, but when I discussed them in Iceland, it seems that oatmeal crackers are a favorite there as well. The name *hafrakex* is Icelandic.

❖ Makes 60 crackers

1 cup old-fashioned rolled oats
1¼ cups milk, heated to boiling
¼ cup softened butter
¼ cup sugar
3 teaspoons baking powder
2 teaspoons crushed anise seed
¼ teaspoon salt
1¼ cups rye flour
1½ cups all-purpose flour

In a large bowl, mix the rolled oats and boiling milk. Let stand until cooled, about 1 hour. Stir in the butter, sugar, baking powder, anise seed, salt, and rye flour. Mix in the all-purpose flour slowly to make a stiff dough. Knead until blended.

Preheat oven to 425°F. Cut parchment paper to fit baking sheets, or lightly grease them.

Turn dough out onto a lightly floured breadboard and divide into two parts. Roll out one part at a time to make a 16 x 12-inch rectangle. Transfer to a sheet of parchment paper or prepared baking sheet. Using a ruler and pastry wheel, cut into 2 x 3-inch crackers and leave crackers in place. Repeat for second part of the dough.

Bake for 10 to 12 minutes or until golden. Cool on the sheet before removing. Store in airtight containers.

KARELIAN WATER RINGS
(Vesirinkilät)

*T*hese water-raised rolls resemble bagels. I remember women of my grandmother's era talking about water rolls, but for some reason it wasn't until we were entertained by a Karelian family that I was reminded of them. We enjoyed them every morning for breakfast, freshly baked and split, with butter and jam.

❖ Makes 16 rolls

2 packages active dry yeast
1¼ cups warm water, 105°F to 115°F
1 teaspoon salt
4 tablespoons melted butter
3 to 3½ cups bread or unbleached all-purpose flour

FOR RAISING

boiling water
2 tablespoons salt
1 teaspoon baking soda

In a large bowl, dissolve the yeast in the warm water. Let stand 5 minutes. Add the salt, butter, and half the flour, beating until smooth. Blend in flour until dough is stiff. Let rest 15 minutes, covered. Turn dough out onto a floured board and knead until smooth and satiny, 5 to 10 minutes. Clean the bowl, lightly oil it, and add dough to the bowl. Turn over dough to oil the top. Cover and let rise in a warm place until doubled, about 1 hour. (Dough may also rise in a cool kitchen overnight.)

Turn dough onto an oiled board. Divide into 16 parts. Shape each part into a strand 6 to 8 inches long. Turn into a ring and pinch ends together. Place on a sheet of lightly oiled waxed paper and let rise 30 minutes.

Preheat oven to 400°F. Cover a baking sheet with parchment paper and lightly spray with nonstick spray. Or, grease and flour a baking sheet.

Bring a wide pan (I use a 14-inch deep-frying pan) half-full of water to a boil; add the salt and soda. Lower the rings one at a time into the water and cook 30 seconds. Remove from water with pancake turner and place on prepared baking sheets.

Bake for 15 to 20 minutes until golden.

Breads for Coffeetime

offeetime makes up three of the six meals of the Scandinavian day. And what you eat with coffee, whether you are in Minnesota, Finland, Sweden, Denmark, Iceland, or Norway, is a coffeebread. Coffeebreads are not served with meals, but accompany morning coffee, afternoon coffee, or evening coffee. Normally, they are not buttered and, even if they are sweet, they are called coffeebreads, not coffeecakes.

On special occasions, such as after a club meeting or at church, coffeebreads are served with cookies, too. And on really fancy occasions (after a wedding, or during the Christmas season, or when you have special out-of-town visitors) a full-blown coffeetable is in order.

The coffeetable includes cardamom-flavored coffeebreads, plus other special sweet yeast breads, plain as well as frosted cakes, and a variety of cookies.

The formal Finnish coffeetable is like those I've experienced in Sweden, Norway, Denmark, and Iceland. It is served in three courses. The first course is always a sweetened yeast bread, often a braid, and often flavored with cardamom. With the first course you have a cup of coffee and sample a cookie or two. The second course is a pound cake or another unfrosted cake baked in a fancy tube pan. You sample the cake and a couple of cookies with another cup of coffee. The third course is a fancy filled cake, which you sample by itself, with a third cup of coffee. With the fourth cup of coffee, you sample anything you haven't already tasted, or go back for seconds. As with the flowers in the centerpiece, there should be an uneven number of choices on the table. Seven is considered perfect.

The recipes in this chapter are the first course of the coffeetable, the coffeebreads. Cakes and cookies follow in later chapters.

NORWEGIAN COFFEEBREAD
(*Hvetekake*)

*C*ardamom-perfumed, this cake brings back memories of Norway to those who have visited there. It is often cut into slices, spread with butter, sugar, and jam, or topped with *nøkkelost*, a favorite Norwegian cheese that is spiced with cloves. Or the bread may be topped with thin shavings of caramel-colored *gjetost*, another favorite Norwegian cheese. Gjetost is a sweet-tasting cheese made by slowly boiling off the liquid from the whey left from the manufacture of butter and cheese. The traditional version of gjetost was made entirely of goat's milk whey. Today, however, most of the gjetost exported from Norway is made largely of cow's milk whey with just a small percentage of goat's milk whey.

❖ Makes 2 round loaves

2 packages active dry yeast
½ cup warm water, 105°F to 115°F
1½ cups milk, scalded and cooled to lukewarm, or 1
*   (12-ounce) can undiluted evaporated milk*
¼ cup sugar
½ teaspoon salt
1 teaspoon freshly ground cardamom
3 tablespoons softened or melted butter
4 to 4 ½ cups unbleached all-purpose flour
melted butter to brush on loaves

In a large bowl, dissolve the yeast in the warm water. Let stand 5 minutes. Stir in the milk, sugar, salt, cardamom, and butter.

Stir in 3 cups of the flour and beat batter until glossy. Stir in 1 cup more flour. Let stand 15 minutes, covered.

Sprinkle board with some of the remaining flour. Turn dough out onto the board. Clean the bowl, lightly oil it, and set aside.

Knead dough until smooth and glossy, about 10 minutes. Place in the oiled bowl, turn over to oil the top of the dough, cover, and let rise in a warm place until doubled in bulk, about 1 hour.

Lightly oil a work surface. Turn dough out onto it and divide into 2 equal parts. Shape into smooth round loaves.

Dust baking sheets with flour (do not grease them), or cover with parchment paper. Place loaves on the baking sheets with the smooth sides up. Let rise in a warm place until almost doubled in bulk.

Preheat oven to 375°F. Brush loaves with melted butter. Bake for 30 to 35 minutes until golden and loaves sound hollow when tapped. Brush again with butter and cool on racks.

CARDAMOM COFFEEBREAD
(*Pulla*)

*A*lthough this bread is the basic yeast coffeebread of all Scandinavia, the name I give it is Finnish because of my own bias. The Swedes call it *vetebröd*, Norwegians call it *hvetebröd*, the Danes call it *hvedebrød*, and the Icelandics call it *hveitibraud*. All of these names mean "wheat bread."

The Finns who settled in the early 1900s in our country brought this recipe with them. At that time the Finnish word for wheat was *nisu* rather then *vehnä*, the modern name. (The Finnish language has been "Finnicized" since the early part of this century, and all words that were too "Swedish" such as nisu have been changed to more correct Finnish, which for wheat is "vehna.") But many American Finns still call this bread "nisu," and the debates become heated! Where I grew up, however, we called this bread "biscuit." Saturday was the day we baked biscuit so that it would be fresh for Sunday morning's coffee. My Finnish aunt, Ida Luoma, who was born and raised in Finland and emigrated to become the wife of my uncle Edward in about 1930, adamantly explains that "biscuit" is totally wrong. She says, "Ei se ole biskittiä, se on pulla!" (It isn't *biscuit*, it is *pulla!*) The name pulla, however, arises from the Swedish *bollar*, which is translated as "bun." But pulla is most often shaped into a braided loaf. All very confusing!

❖ Makes 3 loaves

2 *packages active dry yeast*
$\frac{1}{2}$ *cup warm water, 105°F to 115°F*
1 *teaspoon sugar*
$1\frac{1}{2}$ *cups (12-ounce can) undiluted evaporated milk*
$\frac{1}{2}$ *to 1 cup sugar*
2 *teaspoons salt*
$1\frac{1}{2}$ *teaspoons ground cardamom or seeds of 12 cardamom pods, crushed*
4 *eggs, room temperature*
7 *to 8 cups all-purpose flour*
$\frac{1}{2}$ *cup melted butter*

GLAZE

1 *slightly beaten egg*
2 *tablespoons milk*

In a large bowl, dissolve the yeast in the warm water; add the 1 teaspoon sugar, stir, and let stand for 5 minutes until yeast foams. Empty the milk into a pan and warm just to between 105°F and 115°F. Add milk, sugar according to sweetness desired, salt, cardamom, eggs, and half the flour. Beat with an electric mixer or spoon until dough is smooth and shiny. Beat in the melted butter. Add remaining flour 1 cup at a time until dough is stiff but not dry. Cover and let rest for 15 minutes. Turn out onto lightly floured board and knead until satiny and smooth, about 10 minutes. Wash bowl, grease it, and add dough to bowl, turning to grease top. Cover and let rise in a warm place until doubled, about 1 to 1½ hours. Turn risen dough out onto breadboard and divide into 3 portions.

Divide each portion into 3 parts. Roll out to make strands about 24 inches long. Make 3 braids, using 3 strands each as illustrated. Place on lightly greased baking sheets. Cover and let rise until doubled, about 1 hour.

Preheat oven to 375°F. Mix egg and milk to make glaze and brush braids with the mixture. Bake for 20 to 25 minutes until golden, or until a wooden skewer inserted in the center comes out clean.

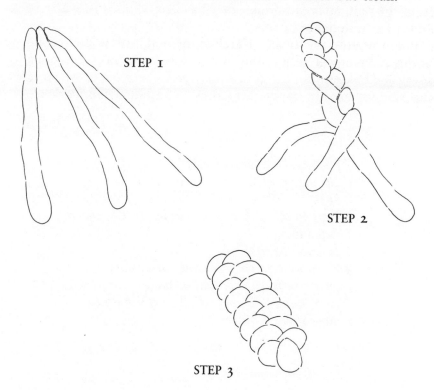

STEP 1

STEP 2

STEP 3

VIIPURI PRETZEL
(*Viipurinrinkeli*)

*T*he province of Karelia, in eastern Finland, once included the city of Viipuri; now called Viborg, it is within the borders of the Soviet Union. Many traditional Finnish foods are attributed to the heritage of the Karelians. This pretzel-shaped coffeecake is named after the city of Viipuri. Traditionally, the shaped pretzel is lowered into a pan of boiling water (as for bagels), then is allowed to rise 10 minutes before a quick bake in a hot oven.

Viipuri pretzel is traditionally baked on a bed of clean oat straw. According to an old Finnish cookbook, the purpose of the boiling is to give the baked loaf a beautiful sheen; the straw adds a smoky flavor to the bread.

A combination of cardamom and nutmeg gives the bread its flavor and combined with the smoky flavor from the oat straw will invoke nostalgic memories in those who remember the authentic bread. The straw fills another purpose, that of making the bread easy to remove from the pan, as bread dough that has been dipped in water sticks even to a well-greased pan.

If you wish to try the old Karelian method, follow the second set of directions in the recipe. But, if not, follow the first directions for rising and baking after the dough is shaped. Clean oat or wheat straw can be purchased in handicraft stores or Scandinavian markets.

❖ Makes 3 pretzels

1 package active dry yeast
$\frac{1}{4}$ cup warm water, 105°F to 115°F
2 eggs
2 cups milk, scalded and cooled to lukewarm
1 cup sugar
1 teaspoon salt
2 teaspoons freshly ground cardamom
$\frac{1}{2}$ teaspoon freshly grated nutmeg
5 to 5$\frac{1}{2}$ cups unbleached all-purpose flour
$\frac{1}{4}$ cup softened butter

1 slightly beaten egg
2 tablespoons milk
pearl sugar or crushed sugar cubes

In a large bowl, dissolve the yeast in the warm water. Let stand 5 minutes. Add the eggs, milk, sugar, salt, cardamom, and nutmeg and beat well until blended. Add 4 cups flour and beat until smooth. Stir in the butter and add flour until dough is stiff. Cover and let dough rest 15 minutes.

Turn dough out onto a lightly floured board. Knead, adding flour to prevent stickiness, until smooth and satiny, about 10 minutes. Wash bowl, grease it, and add dough to the bowl, turning it over to grease top. Cover and let rise in a warm place until doubled.

Cover 3 baking sheets with parchment paper or grease them and sprinkle with flour.

Turn dough out onto a lightly oiled work surface. Divide into 3 parts. Between hands and work surface, roll out each part of dough to make strands about 40 inches long. Place on the prepared baking sheets in the form of a pretzel. Cover with a towel and let rise until almost doubled, about 45 minutes.

Preheat oven to 400°F.

Mix the egg and milk to make a glaze. Brush pretzels all over with the glaze and sprinkle with the sugar.

Bake for 20 to 25 minutes until golden. Do not overbake. Remove from oven and cool on racks.

Cover 3 baking sheets with a layer of clean oat straw.

Heat 2 inches of water in an electric fry pan or in a large, rather deep skillet. Add 1 teaspoon baking soda to the water. Bring to a simmer.

Shape dough into 3 pretzels as directed above. Let stand 15 minutes after shaping. Pick up pretzels gently (it works best to hold the pretzels as you would to dip a cloth into water, with thumb and forefinger holding the place where the ends join the circle of dough). Drop into the water, one at a time, and let cook for 1 minute. Remove with a spatula. An easier way to handle the pretzels is to locate a cake rack that will fit into the skillet. Place the pretzel onto the cake rack and lower rack and bread into the simmering water. Lift out cake rack with bread using tongs or forks.

Place the pretzels on the baking sheet covered with straw. Omit the egg-milk glaze and sugar topping. Let rise 10 minutes.

Preheat oven to 400°F and bake pretzels for 15 to 20 minutes or until golden.

SWEDISH SAFFRON CHRISTMAS BREAD
(*Saffransbullar*)

*S*wedes are sentimental people, especially on December 13, when a beautiful blonde girl, dressed in a white robe, presides over the Lucia Day parade looking like a shimmering dream figure. Even the most reserved Swedish hearts melt.

There are many legends about who Lucia was and why she became so important to the Swedes. An old folk tale from Varmland, a province in western Sweden where there was a great famine, tells of a Lucia who suddenly appeared on board a ship and distributed generous amounts of food to the starving people.

Formerly, December 13 (*Lusse*) was believed to be the longest and darkest night of the year. Lusse marked the beginning of the Christmas season and the rule was that one should eat before dawn or it would be a bad Lusse. Today, it is customary in the Swedish home for the mother to be treated to breakfast in bed with hot coffee and St. Lucia's buns shaped in fancy twists. Swedish teachers, too, receive a similar tray, carried in by the "Lucia" of the classroom.

The golden butter-rich saffron bread has many traditional shapes that show up on coffeetables throughout the holiday season. Perhaps the most attractive is a braided wreath in which candles are sometimes stuck. Crowns, cats, chariots, and hearts are some others. This dough shapes easily because it is refrigerated and is simple to make because it requires no kneading.

❖ Makes 1 braided wreath
or about 24 buns

2 packages active dry yeast
$\frac{1}{2}$ cup warm water, 105°F to 115°F
$\frac{1}{2}$ cup sugar
$\frac{1}{2}$ cup melted butter
1 cup light cream
$\frac{1}{4}$ to $\frac{1}{2}$ teaspoon powdered saffron
2 eggs, room temperature
4 to 4$\frac{1}{2}$ cups unbleached all-purpose flour

1 egg
2 tablespoons milk

In a large mixing bowl, dissolve the yeast in the warm water. Add 1 tablespoon of the sugar and let stand until yeast foams, about 5 minutes. Add the remaining sugar, butter, cream, saffron, and eggs. Beat well. Stir in the flour, 1 cup at a time, beating well to keep mixture smooth and satiny. All of the flour should be moistened. Cover and refrigerate for 2 to 24 hours. To make buns, shape and bake as for Norwegian Coffee Buns.

To make a braided wreath, cut off $\frac{1}{3}$ of the chilled dough and reserve. Cut remaining dough into 3 parts. On a lightly floured board, roll each of the 3 parts out to make a strand 48 inches long and braid. Cover baking sheet with parchment paper or lightly grease it. Place braid in a wreath shape on the baking sheet; trim off about 1 inch of each end of the braid and fit cut ends together; pinch to seal. Reserve trimmings.

Divide reserved portion of dough into 3 parts. On a lightly floured board, roll into strands 24 inches long. Braid these also. Mix egg and milk together and brush large braid with glaze. Place small braid on top of large braid. Trim ends of small braid and fit together, pinching to seal.

On floured board, roll trimmings from dough to about $\frac{1}{4}$-inch thickness. Cut into leaf shapes using a knife or cookie cutter. With knife, score the leaves to decorate. Brush both braids with egg-milk glaze. Roll scraps out to make thin strands and twine the strands along the top of the braids. Decorate with the leaf cutouts. Brush with glaze. Let rise until doubled. Preheat oven to 375°F and bake for 25 to 35 minutes or until golden.

SOWING BREAD
(Såkaka)

*I*n old Sweden, it was a tradition to make an elaborately shaped loaf of bread encircled with a braid and decorated with curlicues, using grain from the past season. This fancy loaf became the centerpiece of the holiday table. It was not eaten. After the holidays were over, the bread was buried beneath the grain reserved for sowing in the springtime. At sowing time it was broken into pieces, soaked in a homemade beer, and distributed among all of the members of the household (including the family horse) to assure a rich harvest in the coming season. Today only the tradition of the fancy loaf remains, and it is an excellent choice for a holiday coffee party menu. The historic sowing loaf wasn't as rich and flavorful as this one.

❖ Makes 1 large loaf

2 packages active dry yeast
$\frac{1}{4}$ cup warm water, 105°F to 115°F
1 teaspoon sugar
$\frac{3}{4}$ cup light cream or half-and-half, scalded and
    cooled to room temperature
$\frac{1}{2}$ cup sugar
1 teaspoon salt
$1\frac{1}{2}$ teaspoons ground cardamom or seeds of 12
    cardamom pods, crushed
2 eggs, room temperature
$4\frac{1}{2}$ to 5 cups all-purpose flour
$\frac{1}{2}$ cup melted butter

GLAZE

1 slightly beaten egg
2 tablespoons milk
pearl sugar or coarsely crushed sugar cubes

ICING

1 cup powdered sugar
2 to 3 tablespoons brandy

In a large mixing bowl, dissolve the yeast in the warm water; add the teaspoon of sugar, stir, and let stand 5 minutes until yeast foams. Add cream, $\frac{1}{2}$ cup sugar, salt, cardamom, eggs, and half the flour. Beat with electric mixer until dough is smooth and shiny. Beat in the melted butter. Add remaining flour 1 cup at a time until dough is stiff but not dry. Cover and let rest for 15 minutes. Turn out onto lightly floured board and knead until satiny and smooth, about 10 minutes. Wash bowl, grease it, and add dough to bowl, turning over to grease top. Cover and let rise in a warm place until doubled, about 1 to $1\frac{1}{2}$ hours.

Turn dough out onto a lightly oiled work surface. Cut off $\frac{1}{3}$ of the dough and reserve. Knead remaining dough to make a smooth ball.

Cover baking sheet with parchment paper or grease lightly. Place smooth ball of dough onto prepared pan and press down until dough is no more than 1 inch thick, making a circle about 12 inches across. With tip of sharp knife, make cuts $1\frac{1}{2}$ inches into the circle and 1 inch apart around outside edge of the dough on the pan. Brush all over with egg mixed with milk.

Divide reserved dough into 3 parts. Between palms of hands and lightly floured board, roll each part out to make long, skinny ropes 30 to 34 inches long. Braid the ropes together. Lift braid onto dough on cookie sheet, forming a wreath about 2 inches in from the edge of the loaf. With sharp knife, trim ends of braid and pinch together to seal. Brush with egg glaze. Roll trimmings out to make strands 4 to 6 inches long, roll up into curlicues, and place in the center of the braid on top of the bread. Let rise in a warm place until loaf is puffy.

Preheat oven to 375°F. Before baking, brush loaf again with egg glaze, and sprinkle with the pearl sugar or crushed sugar cubes. Bake for 25 to 30 minutes or until loaf is golden. Remove from pan and cool on rack. While still hot, drizzle with a mixture of powdered sugar and brandy.

NORWEGIAN CHRISTMAS LOAF
(*Julekage*)

*N*orwegians cannot imagine a Christmas season without *Julekage*. Not unlike the Danish version and similar to the Icelandic, the Norwegian version is baked in a fat round loaf.

❖ Makes 3 loaves

2 packages active dry yeast
½ cup warm water, 105°F to 115°F
~~2 cups milk, scalded and cooled to lukewarm~~
½ cup sugar
½ cup softened butter
2 teaspoons salt
1 teaspoon freshly ground cardamom (optional)
2 eggs, beaten
7 to 8 cups all-purpose flour
1 cup golden or dark raisins
1 cup mixed candied fruits (optional)

GLAZE AND DECORATION

1 slightly beaten egg
2 tablespoons milk
pearl sugar, crushed sugar cubes and/or chopped almonds

ICING

1 cup powdered sugar
2 to 3 tablespoons heavy cream
½ teaspoon almond extract

In a large bowl, dissolve the yeast in the warm water and let stand 5 minutes. Blend in the milk, sugar, butter, salt, cardamom, and eggs. Beat well. Stir in half the flour and beat well. Add remaining flour, mixing to make a soft dough. Cover and let rest for 15 minutes.

Sprinkle board with a little flour and turn dough out onto it. Knead for 10 minutes or until dough is smooth and satiny. Last of all, knead in the fruits. Wash bowl, lightly grease it, and place dough in the bowl. Turn over to grease top of the dough. Cover and let rise in a warm place until doubled. Punch down and let rise again until doubled in bulk.

Butter three 8- or 9-inch round cake pans. Turn dough out onto a lightly oiled work surface. Divide dough into 3 equal parts. Shape each into a smooth round loaf and place loaves with the smooth side up in the baking pans. Cover and let rise until doubled.

Preheat oven to 375°F. Mix egg and milk to make a glaze. Brush tops of loaves with the glaze and sprinkle with sugar and/or almonds. Bake for 25 to 30 minutes until golden and loaves test done.

Top with almond glaze if desired. Mix powdered sugar with heavy cream and almond extract until smooth.

DANISH BUTTER CROWN
(*Smorkage*)

*T*o make this pastrylike bread you need a tube pan 10 to 12 inches in diameter.

❖ Makes 1 coffeecake

1¼ *cups chilled unsalted butter*
3 *cups all-purpose flour*
2 *packages active dry yeast*
¼ *cup warm water, 105°F to 115°F*
½ *cup milk, room temperature*
½ *teaspoon freshly crushed cardamom seed*
2 *eggs, room temperature*
1 *teaspoon salt*
¼ *cup sugar*

FILLING AND DECORATION

½ *cup sugar*
½ *cup unsalted butter, room temperature*
½ *cup almond paste*
1 *teaspoon almond extract*
½ *cup sliced almonds*
powdered sugar for topping

Cut butter into ¼-inch slices; add to flour in work bowl of food processor with metal blade in place. Process using on/off pulses until butter is the size of kidney beans, or with a fork or pastry blender cut butter into flour.

Turn mixture into a large bowl and chill. Measure yeast into a bowl. Add warm water; let stand 5 minutes. Add milk, cardamom, eggs, salt, and sugar and mix well. Pour liquid mixture over flour-butter mixture and fold together carefully just until flour is moistened. Cover and refrigerate 4 hours to overnight.

Turn dough out onto lightly floured board; dust with flour. Pound and flatten to a 20-inch square. Fold dough into thirds. Turn dough so short side faces you. Roll dough out a little and fold into thirds again. (Chill dough if necessary.)

To prepare filling, cream the sugar, butter, almond paste, and almond extract until blended. Spread dough with the filling and roll up. Cut into 8 equal slices.

Butter a 10-inch bundt pan or fancy tube pan. Sprinkle bottom of pan with sliced almonds. Place dough slices cut side down into the pan, spacing them evenly.

Let rise until almost doubled. Preheat oven to 375°F. Bake for 45 to 55 minutes or until golden. Dust with powdered sugar and serve warm.

ICELANDIC COFFEE WREATH
(*Fylltur Hveitibraudskrans*)

*T*he Icelandics have a practical and down-to-earth approach to all of their cooking and baking, but they are exceptionally skilled at making wonderful things to go with coffee!

❖ Makes 1 coffee ring

> 2 packages active dry yeast
> ½ cup warm water, 105°F to 115°F
> 1 egg
> ¼ cup butter
> ⅓ cup sugar
> ¼ teaspoon salt
> ⅓ cup sour cream
> 2½ to 3 cups unbleached all-purpose flour

1 *cup almond paste*
1 *egg*
2 *tablespoons sugar*
1 *tablespoon cinnamon*
1 *teaspoon vanilla*
½ *cup raisins*
1 *tablespoon grated orange peel*

GLAZE

1 *slightly beaten egg*
2 *tablespoons milk*
pearl sugar or crushed sugar cubes

In a large bowl, dissolve the yeast in the water and let stand 5 minutes. Add the egg, butter, sugar, salt, and sour cream. Beat in 2 cups of the flour to make a stiff dough. Cover and let rise in a warm place until doubled, about 1 hour.

Turn out onto lightly floured board and roll out to make a square about 20 to 24 inches across as illustrated.

To make the filling, blend the almond paste, egg, sugar, cinnamon, and vanilla. Spread this mixture over the rolled-out dough to within ½ inch of the edge of the dough. Sprinkle with the raisins and orange peel. Roll dough up, jelly-roll fashion, enclosing the filling, Step 1.

Cover baking sheet or a 16-inch pizza pan with parchment paper or lightly grease it. Place roll on the pan in the shape of a wreath and seal ends together, Step 2. With a pair of scissors, clip the wreath and lift the cut dough back over the wreath decoratively, Step 3. Let rise 1 hour or until puffy. Preheat oven to 400°F.

To make glaze, mix the beaten egg well with the 2 tablespoons milk. Brush wreath with the mixture and sprinkle with the pearl sugar. Bake for 20 to 30 minutes or until golden.

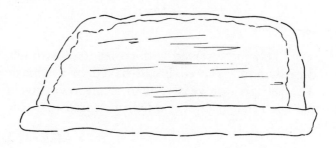

STEP 1

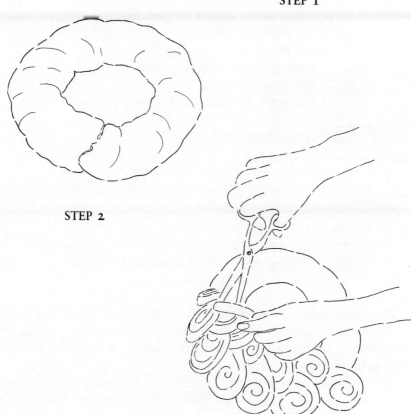

STEP 2

STEP 3

SWEDISH TEA RING
(*Vetekrans*)

*M*ore likely to be served with coffee than with tea, this cinnamon-and-cardamom-flavored bread baked in a wreath shape is a classic. The refrigerator yeast dough is my own invention. It is a no-knead dough that produces a light-textured yeast bread.

❖ Makes 1 large ring

2 packages active dry yeast
1 cup warm water, 105°F to 115°F
½ cup melted butter
½ cup sugar
3 slightly beaten eggs
1 teaspoon salt
1 teaspoon ground cardamom (optional)
4 to 4½ cups all-purpose flour
½ cup softened butter
½ cup sugar
1 tablespoon ground cinnamon
1 cup blanched almonds, finely chopped (optional)

GLAZE

1 cup powdered sugar
2 tablespoons hot coffee or milk
½ teaspoon almond extract

In a large bowl, dissolve the yeast in the warm water and let stand 5 minutes. Stir in the ½ cup melted butter, ½ cup sugar, the eggs, salt, cardamom, and 4 cups of flour until dough is smooth. Cover and refrigerate 2 to 24 hours.

Turn dough onto a floured board and roll out to make a 20- to 24-inch square. Spread with a thin layer of softened butter right to the edge. Mix ½ cup sugar and the cinnamon and sprinkle over the butter. Sprinkle the almonds over the cinnamon sugar. Roll up as for a jelly roll.

Grease a baking sheet and place the roll on the sheet, shaping it into a ring. Pinch ends together to close the circle. With scissors, cut almost through the ring at ½-inch intervals. Turn each piece so that the cut side is exposed. Let rise until almost doubled.

Preheat oven to 375°F. Bake for 15 to 20 minutes or until just golden. While ring bakes, mix the glaze ingredients. Brush while hot with the glaze.

SISTER'S COFFEECAKE
(*Søsterkage*)

"Sister cake" is sometimes translated as "nun's cake," a translation that is a bit misleading. A better translation of sister might be "deaconess," the Lutheran equivalent of nun. Although I have found a cake by this name in every Scandinavian country, there has been no consistency as to what the cake is actually like. The only similarity they have with each other is that they are all made with good ingredients and make wonderful eating! This variety is from Norway and is a cake made of cinnamon rolls baked side-by-side in a pan.

❖ Make 2 coffeecakes

2 packages active dry yeast
1 cup warm water, 105°F to 115°F
$\frac{1}{2}$ cup melted butter
$\frac{1}{2}$ cup sugar
3 slightly beaten eggs
1 teaspoon salt
$4\frac{1}{2}$ to 5 cups all-purpose flour

FILLING

$\frac{1}{2}$ cup softened butter
$\frac{1}{2}$ cup brown sugar, packed
1 tablespoon ground cinnamon

GLAZE

1 slightly beaten egg
2 tablespoons milk

In a large bowl, dissolve yeast in the warm water and let stand 5 minutes. Stir in the $\frac{1}{2}$ cup of melted butter, the $\frac{1}{2}$ cup of sugar, the eggs, salt, and $4\frac{1}{2}$ cups flour until dough is smooth. Cover and refrigerate 2 to 24 hours.

Sprinkle board with some of the remaining flour. Turn dough out onto the floured board and roll out to make a 24-inch square. Spread with a thin layer of soft butter right to the edge. Mix the brown sugar and cinnamon and sprinkle mixture over the butter. Roll up as for a jelly roll.

Grease two 9-inch square pans or 10-inch tube pans. Cut roll into 2-inch pieces and place them cut sides up in the pans evenly spaced, dividing the cut rolls between the two pans.

Let rise, covered, until almost doubled, about 45 minutes to 1 hour. Mix the egg and milk to make a glaze and brush the tops of each cake with the glaze.

Preheat oven to 375°F. Bake for 30 to 35 minutes or until a skewer inserted in the center comes out clean. Let stand 5 minutes in pan before unmolding. Serve warm.

BOSTON CAKE
(*Bostonkakku*)

*T*he Scandinavians seem to think that this cake is traditional to Boston. A Bostonian might not recognize it any more than an Austrian would recognize *Wienerbrød*.

❖ Makes 1 coffeecake

1 package active dry yeast
$\frac{1}{4}$ cup warm water, 105°F to 115°F
$\frac{1}{4}$ cup milk
2 eggs
$\frac{1}{3}$ cup sugar
$\frac{1}{2}$ teaspoon salt
$\frac{1}{4}$ cup softened butter
2 to 2$\frac{1}{2}$ cups unbleached all-purpose flour

FILLING

$\frac{1}{4}$ cup softened butter
$\frac{1}{2}$ cup sugar
1 tablespoon cinnamon

In a large bowl, dissolve the yeast in the warm water; add the milk, eggs, sugar, salt, and butter. Beat in the flour until dough is smooth and satiny. Cover and let rise in a warm place until doubled, about 1 hour.

Dust dough in bowl lightly with flour and gather into a ball. Turn out on lightly floured board and pat out to make a 14-inch square. Spread with soft butter. Mix the sugar and cinnamon and sprinkle over the butter. Roll up jelly-roll fashion.

Butter a 12-cup ring mold or bundt pan. Cut dough into 8 equal pieces. Place each cut piece with cut side down into the pan, spacing them evenly.

Cover and let rise until almost doubled. Preheat oven to 375°F and bake 25 to 30 minutes or until golden. Invert onto serving plate.

FINNISH COFFEEBREAD "PIZZA"
(*Peltileipä*)

*T*his old-fashioned quick and delicious coffeebread has been made by Finnish bakers for generations! The "pizza" part is my own idea because that's just how this coffeecake is made. The yeast dough is rolled out on a baking sheet, the toppings go on, it rises a bit and is baked. Saturday is usually baking day in a Finnish household. Often, a Finnish homemaker will take a portion of the Pulla dough and roll it out, spread it with toppings, and bake it for morning coffee. This recipe is perfect for a large crowd or coffee open house. It freezes well cut into squares and stacked in plastic containers ready to reheat and serve.

❖ Makes 2 coffeecakes, 16 x 12 inches

2 packages active dry yeast
$\frac{1}{2}$ cup warm water, 105°F to 115°F
1 egg
$\frac{1}{2}$ cup sugar
1 teaspoon salt
1 cup milk, scalded and cooled to lukewarm
$\frac{1}{2}$ cup softened or melted butter
4 cups unbleached all-purpose flour

TOPPING AND DECORATION

1 cup blanched almonds
$\frac{3}{4}$ cup sugar
$\frac{3}{4}$ cup softened butter
$\frac{1}{2}$ cup all-purpose flour
1 cup sliced or slivered almonds
1 cup powdered sugar
2 tablespoons milk

In a large bowl, dissolve the yeast in the warm water. Let stand 5 minutes. Add the egg, sugar, salt, and milk. Stir in the butter and 2 cups of the flour. Beat until smooth. Add the remaining flour and beat again until smooth. Cover and let rise in a warm place until doubled, about 1 hour.

To prepare the topping, grind the almonds in a food chopper with fine blade, or place in a food processor with steel blade in place.

Process until pulverized. Add the sugar, butter, and flour and process until mixture is a smooth paste.

Preheat oven to 400°F. Grease two 17 x 14-inch cookie sheets. Divide dough into 2 parts and place each on a cookie sheet. Pat out to rectangles 16 x 12 inches. Spread each with half the topping mixture. Sprinkle with additional sliced or slivered almonds. Bake for 20 minutes until crust is golden. Remove from oven and drizzle with icing made by mixing the powdered sugar and milk together. Serve immediately.

NORWEGIAN CREAM PUFF PRETZEL
(*Vandbakkelskringle*)

*O*ur Norwegian friends love to make a quick coffeecake this way. Often they spread cream-puff paste on a base of flaky pastry to make what they call "Danish." (This recipe omits the base pastry, which is found in the recipe for Walesbröd.) The paste is pressed through a pastry bag to make a pretzel, the shape of which on a storefront indicates to Scandinavians that baked goods are sold inside.

❖ Makes 12 servings

1 cup water
½ cup butter
1 cup all-purpose flour
4 eggs

FILLING (OPTIONAL)

⅓ cup finely pulverized almonds
⅓ cup chopped golden raisins
⅓ cup sugar

ICING

1½ cups powdered sugar
2 to 3 tablespoons fresh lemon juice
grated rind of 1 lemon
1 teaspoon softened butter

In a saucepan, bring water and butter to a boil. Remove from heat and add flour all at once. Stir quickly. Place back on heat and stir until it forms a ball. Beat in the eggs one at a time, remove from heat, and cool.

Combine the filling ingredients, if desired, and set aside.

Preheat oven to 425°F. Cover a baking sheet with parchment paper or grease generously.

Turn paste into a large pastry bag and press out onto a baking sheet in the form of a large pretzel. Or, using a spoon, you may drop spoonfuls in the design of a pretzel. If you choose to add the filling, press small, evenly spaced spoonfuls of it onto the top of the pretzel.

Bake for 20 minutes, reduce heat to 325°F, and bake 15 minutes longer, until the pastry is golden. Check for doneness by pressing to see if it feels firm. Do not overbake. Remove from oven and cool on a rack or serving plate. Drizzle with the icing while pretzel is still a little warm.

For the icing, combine the powdered sugar with enough lemon juice to make a smooth, rather thin mixture. Add the lemon rind and blend in the butter.

To serve, cut into chunks.

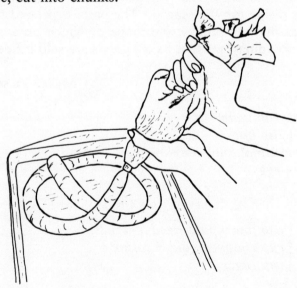

SWEDISH SAFFRON BATTER BREAD
(Saffronsbröd)

*F*or those who love the flavor of saffron but wish an alternative to shaping braids and twists from a kneaded dough, here is a Swedish batter bread. It appeals to me when I am busy and want a pretty, decorative bread in a hurry. Any fancy tube-type pan may be used to achieve an attractive bread with almost no effort.

❖ Makes one 10-inch fancy loaf

> 1 package active dry yeast
> $\frac{1}{4}$ cup warm water, 105°F to 115°F
> $\frac{1}{2}$ cup butter, room temperature
> $\frac{1}{2}$ cup sugar
> 3 eggs
> $\frac{1}{4}$ teaspoon salt
> $\frac{1}{2}$ cup milk, scalded and cooled to lukewarm
> $\frac{1}{4}$ teaspoon powdered saffron*
> 3 cups all-purpose flour
> $\frac{3}{4}$ cup golden raisins
> powdered sugar

In a small bowl, dissolve the yeast in the $\frac{1}{4}$ cup warm water. In a large bowl, cream butter and sugar and add eggs and salt; beat until smooth. Stir in milk, saffron, and yeast mixture. Gradually beat in the flour. When all the flour has been added, beat with electric mixer at medium speed for 5 minutes, scraping down the sides of the bowl occasionally. Mix in the raisins. Cover and let rise in a warm place until doubled, about $1\frac{1}{2}$ to 2 hours.

Meanwhile, generously butter a 10-cup kugelhopf, bundt pan, or other decorative tube-type mold. Dust lightly with flour. Stir down the dough and pour into the prepared pan. Cover and let rise in a warm place until the dough almost reaches the top of the pan, about 1 hour. Preheat oven to 350°F. Bake 40 to 45 minutes or until loaf is well browned and sounds hollow when tapped. Let cool in pan 15 minutes; invert onto rack to cool. Dust with powdered sugar.

❖ If you prefer, you may substitute 1 teaspoon grated lemon rind and $\frac{1}{2}$ teaspoon ground nutmeg for the saffron; flavor and color will be different but pleasant.

NORWEGIAN CINNAMON WREATH
(*Klippekrans*)

A rich, buttery dough is rolled up, filled with cinnamon and sugar, and made into a wreath. The wreath is slashed only about $\frac{1}{2}$ inch into the bread, just enough to expose a layer or two of cinnamon filling.

❖ Makes 1 large ring

2 packages active dry yeast
1 cup warm water, 105°F to 115°F
$\frac{1}{2}$ cup melted butter
$\frac{1}{2}$ cup sugar
3 slightly beaten eggs
1 teaspoon salt
1 teaspoon ground cardamom (optional)
$4\frac{1}{2}$ to 5 cups all-purpose flour

FILLING

$\frac{1}{2}$ cup softened butter
$\frac{1}{2}$ cup sugar
1 tablespoon ground cinnamon
1 cup dark raisins

GLAZE

1 egg
2 tablespoons milk

In a large bowl, dissolve the yeast in the warm water; let stand 5 minutes. Stir in $\frac{1}{2}$ cup melted butter, $\frac{1}{2}$ cup sugar, the eggs, salt, cardamom, and $4\frac{1}{2}$ cups flour until dough is smooth. Cover and refrigerate 2 to 24 hours.

Sprinkle board lightly with some of the remaining flour. Turn dough out onto a floured board and roll out to make a 20-inch square. Spread with a thin layer of softened butter right to the edge. Mix $\frac{1}{2}$ cup sugar and cinnamon and sprinkle over the butter. Sprinkle the raisins over the cinnamon sugar. Roll up as for a jelly roll.

Cover a baking sheet with parchment paper or lightly grease it. Place the roll on the sheet and pinch ends together to make a ring.

Let rise in a warm place until almost doubled. Mix egg and milk to make a glaze and brush ring with the mixture.

Preheat oven to 375°F.

With a sharp knife, make diagonal cuts spaced about 2½ inches apart, about ½ inch into the risen loaf.

Bake for 15 to 20 minutes or until just golden.

SWEDISH CINNAMON BUTTERHORNS
(*Kanelbullar*)

*T*hese are crescent-shaped rolls that are filled with cinnamon and butter.

❖ Makes 32 rolls

1½ *cups scalded milk*
½ *cup butter*
3 *eggs*
½ *cup sugar*
½ *teaspoon salt*
1 *package yeast*
¼ *cup warm water, 105°F to 115°F*
6 *cups all-purpose flour*

FILLING

½ *cup softened butter*
1 *cup sugar*
1 *tablespoon cinnamon*

GLAZE

1 *egg*
2 *tablespoons milk*
pearl sugar or crushed sugar cubes

In a large bowl, combine milk and butter; stir until butter is melted. Beat in eggs, sugar, and salt. In a small dish, dissolve the yeast in the warm water; let stand 5 minutes. Add to cooled milk mixture. Stir in flour, beating to make a smooth but thick batter. Cover and refrigerate 2 to 24 hours.

Divide dough into 4 parts. On floured surface roll each part out to make a 12-inch circle. Spread with softened butter. Mix cinnamon and sugar together and sprinkle over the dough evenly. Cut each circle into 8 wedges. Roll up each wedge, starting from the wide end, to make a crescent-shaped roll.

Cover baking sheets with parchment paper or lightly grease them. Place rolls on the prepared baking sheets. Let rise about 45 minutes until puffy. Beat the egg and milk together and brush rolls lightly with the mixture. Sprinkle with sugar. Preheat oven to 375°F. Bake 13 to 15 minutes until golden.

NORWEGIAN COFFEE BUNS
(*Hveteboller*)

*T*hese simple buns are served fresh with morning coffee.

❖ Makes 24 rolls

2 packages active dry yeast
$\frac{1}{2}$ cup warm water, 105°F to 115°F
$\frac{1}{3}$ cup sugar
1 teaspoon salt
$\frac{1}{2}$ cup melted butter
1 teaspoon pulverized cardamom seeds
2 cups milk, scalded and cooled to
    lukewarm
6 to 6$\frac{1}{2}$ cups all-purpose flour

GLAZE

1 slightly beaten egg
2 tablespoons milk
pearl sugar, plain sugar, or crushed sugar cubes
    for topping

In a large mixing bowl, dissolve the yeast in the warm water. Add a pinch of the sugar and let stand 5 minutes until yeast foams. Stir in the remaining sugar, salt, butter, cardamom, and milk.

Add half the flour and beat until smooth and satiny. Add the remaining flour slowly, stirring until mixture will not absorb more flour. Let stand 15 minutes.

Turn dough out onto a lightly floured board and knead until smooth and satiny, 5 to 10 minutes. Wash bowl, grease it, and place dough in bowl, turning to grease top. Cover and let rise until doubled, about 1 hour.

Turn dough out onto a lightly oiled surface. Divide into 24 parts. Shape into smooth balls.

Cover baking sheets with parchment or lightly grease them. Place dough on baking sheets and let rise until almost doubled, about 45 minutes. Preheat oven to 375°F.

Mix egg and milk and brush rolls with the mixture. Sprinkle with the sugar. Bake for 15 minutes or until golden.

DANISH CURRANT BUNS
(Teboller)

*T*hese buns are quick to make, require just one short rising, and are very rich and buttery.

❖ Makes 16 buns

1 package active dry yeast
¼ cup warm water, 105°F to 115°F
¼ cup milk
2 tablespoons sugar
1 egg
½ cup butter, room temperature
2 cups unbleached all-purpose flour
½ cup currants

GLAZE

1 slightly beaten egg
2 tablespoons milk

ICING

½ cup powdered sugar
2 to 3 teaspoons hot water or coffee
½ teaspoon almond extract

In a large mixing bowl, dissolve the yeast in the warm water. Let stand 5 minutes. Add the milk, sugar, egg, and butter. Mix in the flour and currants. Beat well by hand. The dough will feel smooth and rich. Turn it out onto a floured board and cut dough into quarters. Shape each quarter into a ball and cut again into quarters to make 16 pieces in all. Shape each piece into a smooth round bun.

Cover baking sheet with parchment paper or lightly grease it. Place buns on the baking sheet with the smooth side up and press with palms of hands to flatten slightly.

Mix egg and milk and brush buns with the mixture. Let rise for about 20 minutes until puffy but not doubled.

Preheat oven to 375°F. Bake for 13 to 15 minutes or until golden. To make the icing, mix the powdered sugar, water, and almond extract. Drizzle this mixture on the hot baked buns.

CARNIVAL BUNS
(*Fastelavnsboller*)

*T*he Danes take part in a European tradition of celebrating the season before the beginning of Lent with parties and games. "Carnival" is a time when caloric caution is thrown to the winds before the abstemious Lenten season. Just as an excuse for a coffee party, serve these on Shrove Tuesday. This handy refrigerator dough can be mixed up to 4 days in advance of shaping and baking; it handles best when thoroughly chilled.

❖ Makes 32 buns

1 package active dry yeast
$\frac{1}{4}$ cup warm water, 105°F to 115°F
1 cup whipping cream
$\frac{1}{4}$ cup undiluted evaporated milk
3 slightly beaten egg yolks
$3\frac{1}{3}$ cups all-purpose flour
$\frac{1}{4}$ cup sugar
$\frac{1}{2}$ teaspoon salt
$\frac{1}{2}$ cup butter, firm, but not hard
1 tablespoon melted butter

FILLING

$\frac{1}{2}$ cup golden raisins
$\frac{1}{2}$ cup mixed candied fruits
$\frac{1}{2}$ cup almond paste
2 to 3 tablespoons whipping cream

GLAZE

1 slightly beaten egg
2 tablespoons milk
pearl sugar or coarsely crushed sugar cubes

SYRUP

$\frac{1}{4}$ cup orange juice
$\frac{1}{4}$ cup sugar

In a small mixing bowl, dissolve the yeast in the warm water and stir. Let stand 5 minutes. Add the cream, milk, and egg yolks. In a large bowl, stir together the flour, sugar, and salt. Cut in $\frac{1}{2}$ cup butter with pastry blender or 2 knives until butter is in pieces the size of peas. Stir yeast mixture into flour mixture just to moisten. Brush the melted butter over the dough to prevent drying. Cover bowl with plastic and refrigerate overnight or up to 4 days.

Meanwhile, combine the filling ingredients in the food processor with the steel blade in place and process until chopped but not pureed, or chop in food chopper or by hand.

Mix the egg and milk to make a glaze.

Remove dough from refrigerator. Divide into 2 parts. Working with 1 part at a time, roll out on lightly floured board to make a 16-inch rectangle. Fold into thirds and roll out just enough to seal the layers. Fold in the opposite direction in thirds, which will result in a square of dough. Roll again to make a 16-inch square. Fold into thirds again to make a packet 16 inches long by about 5 inches wide. Roll out to 24-inch length by 6-inch width.

Cut lengthwise into two strips (each strip will be 3 inches wide). Cut into squares. You will have 16 squares. Place a teaspoon of the filling on the center of each square.

Fold the four corners of each square toward the center and press down well. Grease a baking sheet or cover it with parchment paper. Place squares on the paper with plenty of space between them. Brush with egg glaze and sprinkle with pearl sugar or crushed sugar cubes.

Repeat rolling out and shaping with the second half of the dough.

Let rise about 30 minutes until puffy.

Preheat oven to 350°F. Bake for 15 minutes or until golden brown. Meanwhile, combine orange juice and sugar; bring to a boil and boil just until sugar is dissolved. Brush hot buns with the orange syrup.

ICELANDIC ALMOND ROLLS
(*Möndlusnúdar*)

*I*celandics love their morning coffee and far prefer yeast rolls to other sweets. These sweet yeast rolls are filled with almond paste and cinnamon.

❖ Makes 30 rolls

2 packages active dry yeast
½ cup warm water, 105°F to 115°F
1½ cups rich milk, scalded and cooled to lukewarm
½ cup softened unsalted butter
½ cup sugar
1 teaspoon salt
2 eggs
6 to 6½ cups unbleached all-purpose flour

FILLING

1 cup almond paste
1 egg
2 tablespoons sugar
4 tablespoons unsalted butter
1 teaspoon vanilla

GLAZE AND DECORATION

1 cup powdered sugar
2 to 3 tablespoons cream
1 teaspoon almond extract
1 cup toasted chopped almonds*

In a large bowl, dissolve the yeast in the warm water. Let stand 5 minutes. Stir in the milk, butter, sugar, salt, and eggs. Add flour, beating well, until mixture will not readily absorb more flour. Cover and let dough stand 15 minutes. Turn out onto a lightly floured board. Knead, adding just enough flour to keep dough from sticking, until smooth and satiny, about 10 minutes. Wash bowl, lightly grease it, and turn dough into the bowl; turn dough over to grease top. Cover and let rise until doubled.

While the dough rises, prepare the almond filling. In food processor or bowl, blend the almond paste with the egg, sugar, butter, and vanilla until mixture is smooth and spreadable.

Line 30 muffin cups with paper cupcake liners.

Roll out the risen dough to make a rectangle about 24 inches long by 14 inches wide. Spread to within 1 inch of the edge with the almond filling. Roll us as for a jelly roll. Cut into 1-inch pieces. Place in paper-lined muffin cups with cut sides up.

Let rise in a warm place until about doubled.

Preheat oven to 400°F. Bake for 10 minutes or until golden. Mix the powdered sugar, cream, and almond extract to make a glaze, brush the hot rolls with the glaze, and sprinkle with toasted chopped almonds.

❖ To toast the chopped almonds, place in 300°F oven for 5 to 10 minutes.

MOM'S BISCUITS
(*Kanelipullat*)

*B*iscuit-baking day was always perfumed by the aroma of a coffee syrup boiling on the wood stove. The biscuits got a brush-bath of the syrup just as they came out of the oven. To make the lightest yeast dough, Mom always advocated keeping the dough as soft as possible—that is, avoiding the addition of too much flour.

❖ Makes 36 biscuits

2 packages active dry yeast
$\frac{1}{4}$ cup water, 105°F to 115°F
2 cups rich milk, scalded and cooled to lukewarm
$\frac{1}{2}$ cup sugar
$\frac{1}{2}$ cup melted butter
3 slightly beaten eggs
1 teaspoon salt
5 to 5$\frac{1}{2}$ cups all-purpose flour

FILLING

$\frac{1}{2}$ cup softened butter
1 cup white or packed brown sugar
1 tablespoon cinnamon

GLAZE

1 cup strong coffee
1 cup sugar

In a large mixing bowl, dissolve the yeast in the water. Add the milk and stir until blended. Let stand 5 minutes.

Stir in the sugar, butter, eggs, and salt. Beat in half the flour until the batter is smooth and satiny. Let stand 15 minutes. Slowly beat in enough flour to make a stiff dough.

Sprinkle breadboard with flour and turn dough out onto it. Cover with a bowl and let it stand again for 15 minutes. Knead 10 minutes until smooth and satiny, being stingy with the addition of the flour so as not to add too much. If dough gets sticky, let it sit and "relax" a few minutes. Then go back to kneading it.

Wash the mixing bowl, grease it, and add dough to the bowl,

turning to grease top. Cover and let rise in a warm place until doubled.

Roll out about half the dough at a time on a lightly oiled work surface to make a square about 20 inches on each side, sprinkling just lightly with flour, if necessary. Spread with softened butter to the edges. Mix the sugar and cinnamon and sprinkle over the butter. Roll up tightly jelly-roll fashion. Cut slices and place in buttered muffin tins, or close together in a buttered 13 x 9-inch baking pan, or slightly separated on buttered cookie sheets. Repeat procedure until all the dough is shaped into rolls.

Let rise until doubled. Preheat oven to 375°F. Bake for 15 minutes or until golden. While rolls bake, bring the coffee and sugar to a boil; boil 2 to 3 minutes.

Brush hot rolls with the coffee glaze. Cool.

FILLED DOUGHNUTS
(*Berlínarbollur*)

*W*hy these are named after Berlin, I don't know. They are known as Berlin doughnuts throughout Scandinavia. This version, from Iceland, has a rich vanilla filling.

❖ Makes 18 doughnuts

1 package active dry yeast
$\frac{1}{4}$ cup warm water, 105°F to 115°F
$\frac{1}{2}$ cup whipping cream
$\frac{1}{3}$ cup softened butter
2 tablespoons sugar
1 egg
2 cups all-purpose flour

FILLING

$\frac{2}{3}$ cup whipping cream
1 tablespoon all-purpose flour
1 tablespoon sugar
1 teaspoon vanilla
1 egg yolk

hot fat for deep frying
powdered sugar or cinnamon sugar

In a large bowl, dissolve the yeast in the warm water. Let stand 5 minutes. Stir in the whipping cream, butter, sugar, and egg. Add 1 cup of the flour and beat until smooth. Stir in the remaining flour gradually, beating until dough is smooth and satiny. Cover and let rest 30 minutes. Beat again until smooth. Let rest another 30 minutes.

Meanwhile, mix all the filling ingredients in a heavy saucepan. Stir over medium heat until mixture comes to a boil and thickens, about 5 minutes. Cool before using.

Turn out dough on a lightly floured board and shape into a smooth ball. Roll out to make an 18-inch square. Spoon 2 teaspoons of filling at a time onto the dough, spaced about 3 inches apart, over half of the dough, Step 1. Fold other half of dough over. Cut out the cakes with a cup or glass with a blunt rim, Step 2. (If a sharp cutter is used the puffs may open during frying and the filling run out.) With fingers, check to see that the edges are well sealed. Place puffs on a lightly floured piece of waxed paper to rise. Let rise until almost doubled, about 30 to 45 minutes.

Heat fat for frying to 375°F. (Lard or vegetable oil may be used.) Lower the puffs, a few at a time, into the hot fat and fry until golden brown on both sides. Remove and drain on paper toweling. Roll in powdered sugar or cinnamon sugar.

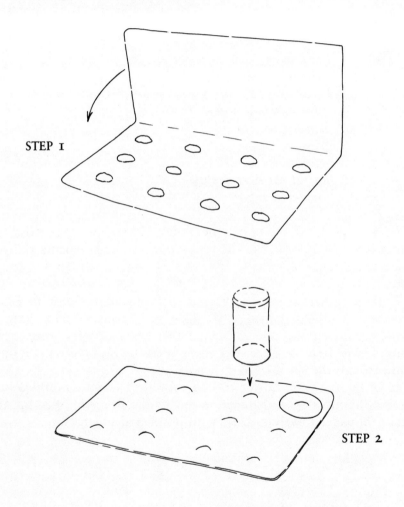

STEP 1

STEP 2

ICELANDIC CRULLERS
(*Kleinur*)

A favorite coffeebread in Iceland, these are served with morning coffee or afternoon "tea," which turns out also to be coffee. They are a fried bread shaped much like Norwegian *fattigman*.

❖ Makes about 48 crullers

4 cups all-purpose flour
4 teaspoons baking powder
1 teaspoon salt
2 teaspoons freshly ground cardamom
½ cup softened butter
⅓ cup sugar
1 egg
¾ cup milk
hot fat for deep frying
powdered sugar

In a large bowl, combine the flour, baking powder, salt, and cardamom. Make a well in the center of the dry ingredients and add the butter, sugar, egg, and milk. With a spoon, stir until a dough forms.

Turn dough out onto a floured surface and roll out to ⅛-inch thickness. Cut into strips ¾-inch wide and about 3 inches long to make parallelograms and cut diagonally, using a pastry wheel and a ruler. Make a slit in the center of each cruller and pull one pointed end through the slit. (See sketches.)

Heat fat to 375°F. Lower crullers into hot fat and fry until golden brown, about 1 to 2 minutes on each side. Remove from fat and drain on paper toweling. Dust with powdered sugar.

STEP 1

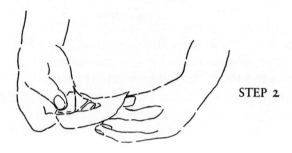

STEP 2

FINNISH SUNDAY ROLLS
(*Sunnuntaipyörykät*)

*T*hese are baked on Saturday so they will be fresh for Sunday morning's coffee. Rolls left from the previous week's baking are split and baked into rusks, which are then served during the week as "dunkers."

❖ Makes 3 dozen rolls

1 package active dry yeast
$\frac{1}{4}$ cup warm water, 105°F to 115°F
1 cup milk, scalded and cooled to lukewarm
1 cup sugar
1 teaspoon salt
2 eggs
$\frac{3}{4}$ cup softened butter
$5\frac{1}{2}$ to 6 cups unbleached all-purpose flour

GLAZE AND DECORATION

1 egg, beaten
$\frac{1}{2}$ cup sliced almonds
pearl sugar or crushed sugar cubes

In a large bowl, dissolve the yeast in the warm water. Let stand 5 minutes. Add the milk, sugar, salt, and eggs. Add the butter and 2 cups flour at one time, and beat until batter is satiny and smooth. Slowly stir in additional flour until dough is stiff and does not absorb more flour. Cover and let rest 15 minutes.

Turn dough out onto a lightly floured board. Knead, adding flour to prevent stickiness, for 10 minutes or until smooth and satiny. Wash bowl, grease it, and add dough to the bowl. Turn over to grease the top of the dough. Cover and let rise in a warm place until doubled, about 1 hour.

Lightly oil a work surface or breadboard. Turn dough out onto the prepared surface and cut into 36 equal portions. Shape each into a ball. Cover baking sheet with parchment paper or lightly oil it. Place shaped rolls onto the baking sheet with the smooth side up. With palm of hand flatten slightly. Let rise until puffy.

Preheat oven to 400°F. Brush risen rolls with beaten egg and sprinkle with sliced almonds and sugar. Bake for 10 to 12 minutes until golden. Do not overbake. Remove from baking sheet and cool on racks.

FINNISH SHROVE TUESDAY BUNS
(*Laskiaispyörykät*)

$\mathcal{S}$hrove Tuesday, the day before Ash Wednesday, the beginning of the Lenten season, is the day when these special buns are eaten. They are flamboyantly filled with rich and expensive ingredients—whipped cream and almond paste—as a reminder that in the season following food is to be simple, not rich. Shrove Tuesday buns are served for morning coffee, or for breakfast on top of a bowl of hot milk, or for dessert in a bowl of hot chocolate milk.

Shrove Tuesday, or *Laskiainen* in Finland, is a time for outdoor parties. Everybody lends a hand to build a toboggan slide, and children as well as adults take part in the fun. Lanterns and candles are hung in surrounding trees, and afterward everybody comes back into the house for pea soup and almond-filled Lenten buns for dessert.

❖ Makes 3 dozen rolls

1 recipe of the dough for Finnish Sunday Rolls

FILLING AND DECORATION

½ pound blanched whole almonds
1 cup powdered sugar
1 cup whipping cream
powdered sugar for garnish

Prepare the Sunday Rolls as directed.

For the filling, grind the almonds, or put into food processor with the steel blade in place and pulverize until finely ground. Add the powdered sugar and ½ cup whipping cream and blend until mixture makes a smooth paste.

When rolls are slightly cooled, cut a lid off the top about ½-inch down. Pull out a little dough to make room for a spoonful of the filling. Whip the remaining cream and slightly sweeten, if you wish, and put a spoonful on each roll. Replace the lid. Put powdered sugar into a sieve and dust over the rolls. Serve immediately.

NORWEGIAN FIGURE-8 CAKES
(*Kringla*)

Kringla may be anything from a yeast-raised bun to a cake that is shaped with a cookie press. This version is made with an anise-flavored yeast dough and is a favorite at Christmastime. The dough requires no kneading and is easy to shape because it is refrigerated.

❖ Makes 60 cakes

> 2 packages active dry yeast
> $\frac{1}{2}$ cup warm water, 105°F to 115°F
> $\frac{1}{2}$ cup sugar
> $\frac{1}{2}$ cup melted butter
> 1 cup light cream
> 1 tablespoon anise seed, crushed
> 2 eggs, room temperature
> 4 to 4$\frac{1}{2}$ cups unbleached all-purpose flour
> melted butter to brush baked kringla

In large mixing bowl, dissolve yeast in the warm water. Add 1 tablespoon of the sugar and let stand until yeast foams, about 5 minutes. Add the remaining sugar, butter, cream, anise seed, and eggs. Beat well. Stir in the flour, 1 cup at a time, beating well to keep mixture smooth and satiny. All of the flour should be moistened. Cover and refrigerate for 2 to 24 hours.

Cover a baking sheet with parchment paper or grease lightly.

Turn dough out onto a lightly floured work surface. Cut it into pieces the size of a large walnut. Roll out to strands about 8 inches long. Twist into figure-8s. Place on baking sheets. Let rise 1 hour until puffy.

Preheat oven to 400°F.

Bake for 15 minutes until golden. Brush baked kringla with melted butter. These are best served just out of the oven.

CARDAMOM RINGS
(*Herttaisetrinkilät*)

*T*his rich, cardamom-flavored yeast dough shaped into twisted rings to make individual portions is served in Finland for special-occasion coffeetables, such as one that might follow a baby's baptism. At the baptism a new child receives its first name. The baby may be two months old, but is known only as "baby" until this important occasion.

❖ Makes 32 rings

> 2 teaspoons freshly crushed cardamom seeds
> 1 cup milk
> 2 eggs
> ¾ cup sugar
> 1 teaspoon salt
> 2 packages active dry yeast
> ½ cup warm water, 105°F to 115°F
> 5 to 5½ cups unbleached all-purpose flour
> ¾ cup softened unsalted butter
> 1 egg, beaten, for glaze
> pearl sugar or crushed sugar cubes for topping

Combine the cardamom and milk and heat to lukewarm. In a large bowl, beat the eggs and sugar until frothy. Add the salt. In a small bowl, dissolve the yeast in the warm water. Let stand 5 minutes. Add the milk mixture to the eggs and sugar, then add the yeast and half of the flour. Beat until batter is satiny and smooth. Add all but the last ½ cup flour, and then add the butter, beating until smooth and satiny again. Dough will be quite stiff. Cover and let rise for 45 minutes until dough is puffy.

Turn dough out onto a lightly oiled surface. Divide into quarters. Divide each quarter into 4 equal parts to make 16 pieces of dough. Divide each into halves.

Shape each half into a ball and divide it into 2 parts. Between palms of hands and lightly oiled board, roll out each piece of dough to make a thin rope about 6 inches long. Wind 2 together and fasten ends to make rings.

Cover baking sheets with parchment or lightly grease them. Place rings on the baking sheets. Cover, and let rise about 45 minutes until puffy. Preheat oven to 400°F.

Brush rings with beaten egg and sprinkle with the pearl sugar. Bake for 7 to 10 minutes until golden.

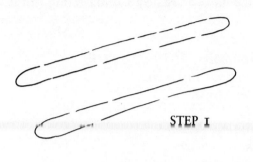

STEP 1

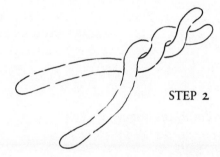

STEP 2

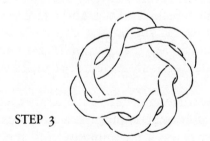

STEP 3

DANISH DREAM CREAM ROLLS
(*Cremeboller*)

*T*hese rolls are an easy version of Danish pastry, made with a refrigerated dough; they have a creamy vanilla filling in the center.

❖ Makes 20 rolls

$\frac{1}{4}$ *cup warm water, 105°F to 115°F*
1 package active dry yeast
1 tablespoon sugar
3 egg yolks
1 cup whipping cream
$\frac{1}{4}$ *cup milk, lukewarm*
3$\frac{1}{2}$ cups all-purpose flour
$\frac{1}{4}$ *cup sugar*
$\frac{1}{2}$ *teaspoon salt*
$\frac{1}{2}$ *cup firm butter*

FILLING

2 eggs
3 tablespoons sugar
3 tablespoons all-purpose flour
1 cup milk
1 teaspoon vanilla

GLAZE AND DECORATION

1 slightly beaten egg
2 tablespoons milk
pearl sugar or crushed sugar cubes
raspberry jam or strawberry jam

In a small bowl, combine the water, yeast, and 1 tablespoon sugar; stir and let stand a few minutes until the yeast foams. Add the egg yolks, cream, and milk; set aside.

In a large bowl, or in the work bowl of a food processor, combine the flour, sugar, and salt. Slice butter into $\frac{1}{4}$-inch pieces and add to the flour. With a pastry blender, or with on/off pulses of food processor, blend until butter is in pea-sized pieces. Pour liquid mixture over flour; blend just until flour is moistened. Cover and refrigerate 12 to 24 hours.

To prepare the cream filling, in a bowl, whisk together the eggs and sugar. In a saucepan, whisk together the flour and milk. Heat the milk to simmering, whisking all the time to keep the mixture smooth; cook until thickened and smooth. Whisk a portion of the hot milk mixture into the eggs, then return the entire amount to the saucepan; cook 1 minute longer. Cover and chill thoroughly. Add the vanilla.

Mix the egg and milk together to make a glaze.

Remove dough from refrigerator. Turn out onto floured board. With side of rolling pin, pound the dough until it is about 1 inch thick. Roll out as thin as possible and fold into thirds. Roll out again to make layers stick together. Fold into thirds again so that the dough makes a fat square.

Pound with side of rolling pin again to flatten dough. Roll out to make a rectangle 14 x 36 inches. Cut into 6-inch squares.

Spoon about 1 tablespoon of the cream filling onto the center of each square. Fold corners toward the centers of the squares, enclosing the filling within the packets.

Cover a baking sheet with parchment paper or lightly grease it. Place the filled squares on the baking sheet. Brush with beaten egg mixed with milk and sprinkle with pearl sugar or crushed sugar cubes. Let rise until puffy, 30 to 45 minutes. Preheat oven to 400°F. Bake for 15 minutes or until golden. Spoon jam on top of each hot roll.

CINNAMON EARS
(*Korvapuustit*)

*T*hese coffee rolls are a favorite in Finland. They are made of a simple sweet yeast dough filled with cinnamon and sugar. The refrigerated dough is easy to handle.

❖ Makes 24 rolls

2 packages active dry yeast
1 cup warm water, 105°F to 115°F
$\frac{1}{2}$ cup melted butter
$\frac{1}{2}$ cup sugar
3 slightly beaten eggs
$\frac{1}{2}$ teaspoon salt
1 teaspoon ground cardamom (optional)
$4\frac{1}{2}$ to 5 cups all-purpose flour

FILLING

$\frac{1}{2}$ cup soft butter
$\frac{1}{2}$ cup sugar
1 tablespoon ground cinnamon

GLAZE

1 slightly beaten egg
2 tablespoons milk
pearl sugar or crushed sugar cubes

In a large bowl, dissolve yeast in the warm water and let stand 5 minutes. Stir in $\frac{1}{2}$ cup melted butter, $\frac{1}{2}$ cup sugar, the eggs, salt, cardamom, and $4\frac{1}{2}$ cups flour until dough is smooth. Cover and refrigerate 2 to 24 hours.

Sprinkle board with some of the remaining flour. Divide dough into 2 parts. Turn out onto the lightly floured board, and roll each part out to make a rectangle about 12 inches by 24 inches long. Spread each half with half the butter and sprinkle with half the sugar and cinnamon. Roll up, starting from a 24-inch side. Cut each roll diagonally into 12 pieces. Each piece will be about $\frac{1}{2}$ inch on one side and 3 inches thick on the other. With two thumbs, press down the middle of the side of each roll. In so doing the two cut edges will be forced upward. The rolls will resemble two "ears."

Cover 2 baking sheets with parchment or lightly grease them. Place cinnamon ears on prepared baking sheets. Let rise until puffy. Mix the egg and milk to make a glaze. Brush rolls with the glaze and sprinkle with the pearl sugar.

Preheat oven to 400°F. Bake for 8 to 10 minutes or just until golden.

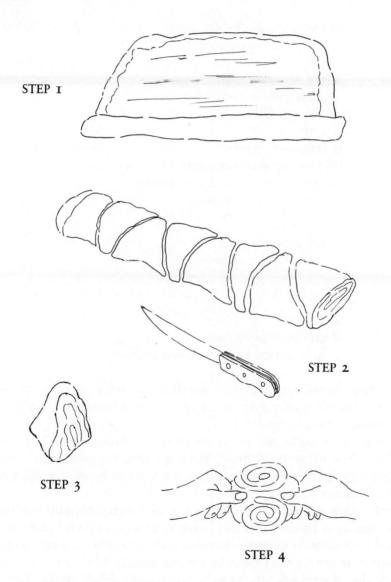

STEP 1

STEP 2

STEP 3

STEP 4

DANISH ALMOND CINNAMON ROLLS
(*Mandel-Kanelboller*)

*D*anish bakers love to roll butter into any dough to make it extra rich, extra good, extra light.

❖ Makes 24 rolls

2 packages active dry yeast
½ cup warm water, 105°F to 115°F
¼ teaspoon salt
2 tablespoons sugar
2 tablespoons butter
¾ cup scalded milk
2 eggs
¼ teaspoon nutmeg
3½ cups all-purpose flour
½ cup butter, room temperature

FILLING

4 tablespoons sugar
2 teaspoons cinnamon
¼ cup finely ground almonds

ICING

1 cup powdered sugar
2 to 3 teaspoons strong hot coffee

In a large bowl, dissolve the yeast in the warm water. Let stand 5 minutes. Add the salt, sugar, and 2 tablespoons butter to the scalded milk; cool to lukewarm.

Add milk mixture to the yeast mixture; beat in the eggs and nutmeg. Mix in 3½ cups flour, beating until dough is satiny and smooth and rather soft. Scrape down sides of the bowl. Let rise until doubled, about 1 hour.

Dust dough with additional flour. Scrape down sides of bowl. Rub work surface with oil and turn dough out onto it. Dust lightly with flour if necessary to prevent stickiness on the surface of the dough. Pat out to make a rectangle 10 by 12 inches.

Spread half of the ½ cup butter along one long half of the dough.

Fold unbuttered side over the dough. Press edges together. Transfer onto an oiled baking sheet and chill for 1 hour.

Without removing dough from the baking sheet, pat out to 10 by 16 inches. Spread center third with the remaining butter. Fold one side of dough over the buttered center, then fold other side over to make 3 thicknesses of dough. You should end up with close to a square shape. Chill 1 hour longer.

On a lightly floured board, roll dough out to make a 16-inch square. Combine the 4 tablespoons sugar with the cinnamon and ground almonds. Sprinkle over the dough. Roll up as for a jelly roll. Cut into 24 slices.

Lightly grease 24 muffin cups or line with paper cupcake liners. Place one slice of dough with cut side up into each. Let rise until puffy, about 45 minutes.

Preheat oven to 375°F. Bake for 15 to 20 minutes until golden. Mix the powdered sugar with the coffee and drizzle on hot rolls.

Cookies and
Little Cakes

A little table covered with a creamy white, embroidered, lace-edged linen cloth. Coffee cups, a little larger than demitasses, set on saucers; the saucers set on plates with coffee spoons nestled next to the cups and pretty napkins pulled through the handles. A plate of three kinds of buttery cookies in the middle of the table. This scene was set for a simple afternoon coffee during our visit in Norway.

On another occasion, I happened into a bank in Stockholm to cash a traveler's check. It was the bank's anniversary and they were serving coffee, cardamom bread, and ginger cookies. Of all cookies, scalloped, thin, spicy ginger cookies (which are called *pepparkakor*) are by far the favorite. They are served year-round, but at Christmastime there are special ones, which are richer and even spicier. I have a cookbook from Finland with 100 different recipes for *"pipparkakku"*! People often wonder why the recipe for pepparkakor, to use the Swedish name, does not include pepper as an ingredient. In old Swedish, the word *peppar* was used for *all* spices, including cinnamon, nutmeg, and cloves.

Bakery browsing is one of my favorite activities when traveling; while others find every cathedral and museum, I never miss a *pâtisserie* or a *Konditorei!* The varieties of cookies I have found could fill a volume. "One of this," "one of that" are phrases that I think Berlitz should include in books for travelers like me!

The cookies I've eaten throughout Scandinavia are replicated in this chapter down to the last crumb, and I offer as many as possible from the amazing variety. The selection here includes favorites from everyday gingersnaps to fanciful rolled cones.

Many of the cookies here are specialities that are favorites for holidays and special celebrations. Cookie baking heads the list, and Scandinavian bakers worth their salt will not put their rolling pins down until every available container is filled and stashed away. One woman I know has as a goal to have baked twenty-four different kinds of cookies by Christmas Eve. She packs them up for special gifts to family, friends, and shut-ins.

Gingerbread cookies are among the favorite cookies in all of Scandinavia. They are important for holiday baking, too, and are cut into whimsical shapes. I first became aware of them when we spent a year in Finland. At the beginning of the Advent season, piggy-shaped gingerbread cookies marked with the name *nissu-nassu* appear in shops wherever baked goods are sold. These cookies signal children that the special season leading to Christmas is beginning. Hearts, stars, gingerbread boys, and other animal shapes are traditional, too.

I was curious about the use of animal shapes, not only in baked goods, but also in Christmas decorations. Scholars believe that the tradition goes back to pagan times, when animals were slaughtered to appease the gods. Poor people who had no animals to offer substituted animal-shaped baked goods at their harvest festivals. After Christianity was introduced, Christmas came at the time of the traditional harvest festival. Baked goods were naturally important, and animal shapes were carried over to modern times.

GINGERBREAD HOUSE
(*Pepparkakstuga*)

*T*he gingerbread house is a tradition not restricted to the Scandinavian countries. But Scandinavians, having a bent toward architecture, turn out some creative structures. Inspired by my neighbor Barbara Collins, who makes a new gingerbread house every year at Christmastime, adding to and elaborating on it more and more each time, I spent about five years following the tradition. Sometimes I made the standard house, and at other times altered the structures to make a complete Bethlehem scene, complete with the inn on one side and a stable on the other.

In the directions that follow, the standard measurements are given. Alter them any way you wish to make your own creative house or scene. The basic dough is very spicy, so it will add a fragrant aroma to the area in which you place the house. It is, of course, 100 percent edible!

❖ Makes 1 house

1 cup butter, room temperature
1 cup brown sugar, well packed
2 tablespoons cinnamon
4 teaspoons ginger
3 teaspoons ground cloves
2 teaspoons baking soda
$\frac{1}{2}$ cup boiling water
5 cups all-purpose flour

FROSTING AND SUGAR SYRUP

1 egg white
3 cups powdered sugar
1 teaspoon white vinegar
1 teaspoon almond extract
2 cups sugar

In a large bowl, cream the butter and sugar until blended. Add the cinnamon, ginger, and cloves. Mix the baking soda with the boiling water and add to the dough along with the flour. Mix to make a stiff dough. If necessary add more water, a tablespoon at a time. Chill 2 hours or overnight.

Cut patterns for the house, making patterns for the roof, front walls, gabled walls, chimney, and door out of cardboard.

Roll the dough out on a large, ungreased baking sheet and place the patterns on the dough. Mark off the various pieces with a knife, but leave the pieces in place.

Preheat oven to 375°F. Bake for 12 to 15 minutes until the cookie dough feels firm. After baking, again place the pattern on top of the gingerbread and trim the shapes, cutting the edges with a straight-edged knife. Leave to cool on the baking sheet.

Prepare the frosting by mixing the egg white with the powdered sugar, vinegar, and almond extract until smooth. Put mixture into a pastry bag and pipe through a fine tip onto the pieces of the house, making the decorations on the parts before assembling the house. Let the frosting harden.

To glue the house together, first place the 2 cups sugar in a wide, heavy skillet. Place over low heat and stir until the sugar melts but does not burn. Dip the edges of the house pieces into the syrup as you put the house together. The sugar hardens quickly, so you need to work rapidly.

Finally, put the house on a tray or board and surround it with cotton for snow, evergreen twigs, and figures.

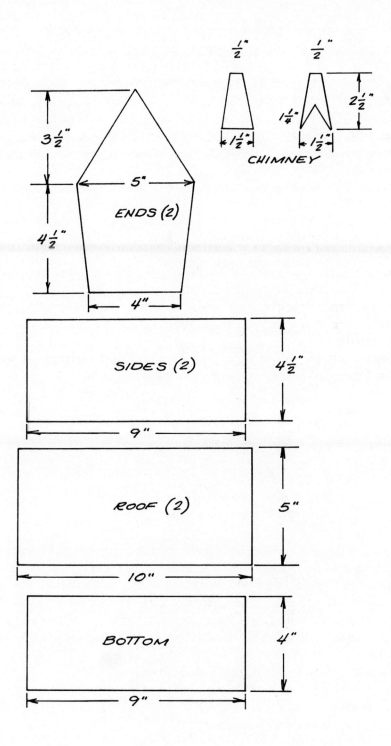

$\frac{1}{2}$"

$\frac{1}{2}$"

$2\frac{1}{2}$"

$1\frac{1}{4}$"

$1\frac{1}{2}$"

CHIMNEY

$3\frac{1}{2}$"

5"

ENDS (2)

$4\frac{1}{2}$"

4"

SIDES (2)

$4\frac{1}{2}$"

9"

ROOF (2)

5"

10"

BOTTOM

4"

9"

CHRISTMAS GINGER COOKIES
(*Julpepparkakor*)

*G*ingersnaps are by far the favorite Scandinavian cookie, and at Christmastime they are cut into fanciful shapes and elaborately decorated. Hearts, stars, angels, grandmas and grandpas, boys and girls, horses, roosters, pigs, cats, and manger animal cut-outs are the favorites.

❖ Makes about 8 dozen cookies

1 cup softened butter
1½ cups sugar
1 egg
1½ tablespoons grated orange peel
2 tablespoons dark corn syrup
1 tablespoon water
3¼ cups all-purpose flour
2 teaspoons baking soda
2 teaspoons cinnamon
1 teaspoon ginger
½ teaspoon cloves

ICING FOR DECORATION

1 egg white
3 to 4 cups powdered sugar
1 teaspoon almond extract

In a large bowl, cream the butter and sugar together. Add the egg and beat until light and lemon colored. Stir in the orange peel, syrup, and water. Combine the flour with the soda, cinnamon, ginger, and cloves. Stir into the creamed mixture until a dough forms. Gather into a ball and chill several hours or overnight.

Cover baking sheets with parchment paper or lightly grease them. Preheat oven to 325°F.

Turn dough out onto a lightly floured board and roll out to about ⅛-inch thickness. Cut into shapes using cookie cutters. Place on prepared baking sheets and bake for 8 to 10 minutes until cookies are set but not overly browned. Cool.

Mix the egg white with the powdered sugar and almond extract to make a thin icing. Turn into a pastry bag with a writing tip and press icing onto cookies to decorate.

DANISH PEPPERNUTS OR "BROWN BREADS"
(*Pebernødder* or *Brunbrød*)

*T*his is a cookie that starts arguments! First the name. Some call it "brown bread" or *brun brød;* to others it is a "peppernut," or simply a "ginger nut." The name and the recipe vary from one Scandinavian baker to another and from one household to another, from one area of a country to another, and even from one country to another. Every Dane insists that the only person who really knew how to bake them was Mother, Grandma, or Aunt Brigitte. I like to bake these little nut-sized cookies by the hundreds and serve them in baskets as "nibblers." It sounds like a lot of work, but I've simplified the procedure. I just roll the dough into $\frac{1}{2}$-inch-thick strips and cut them into $\frac{1}{2}$-inch-long pieces with scissors, dropping the dough bits right on a cookie sheet. I can fit a hundred or so on one baking sheet! This sounds like a huge quantity, but when you bake them in such tiny bits, it isn't so enormous an amount after all.

❖ Makes about 600 cookies

1 cup butter, room temperature
1 cup light or dark brown sugar, packed
1 egg
1 cup pulverized filberts or almonds
$2\frac{1}{2}$ cups all-purpose flour
1 teaspoon baking powder
$\frac{1}{2}$ teaspoon baking soda
1 teaspoon freshly ground cardamom
$\frac{1}{2}$ teaspoon each *cinnamon, cloves, allspice, and nutmeg*

Preheat oven to 375°F. In a large mixing bowl, cream the butter with the sugar. Add the egg and pulverized nuts. Mix the flour with the baking powder, soda, cardamom, cinnamon, cloves, allspice, and nutmeg and blend into the creamed mixture until a stiff dough forms. Shape dough into a ball. Cut off a portion of the dough at a time and roll between hands and work surface to make a slim, pencil-shaped strand about $\frac{1}{2}$-inch thick. Dip scissors in water and snip off $\frac{1}{2}$-inch pieces of the dough at a time. Place on ungreased cookie sheet. Bake for 8 minutes or until cookies are lightly browned. Remove from oven and cool.

FINNISH WEDDING RINGS
(*Avioliittopikkuleipä*)

*D*elicate and buttery, these cookie rings are sandwiched together with strawberry jam. If you use a doughnut cutter for the rings don't reroll the centers; rather, bake them and sandwich them together, too. This way you get two different shapes of cookies at once.

❖ Makes 20 sandwiched rings
and 20 sandwiched "holes"

$\frac{1}{2}$ cup butter, room temperature
$\frac{1}{2}$ cup sugar
1 egg white
$\frac{1}{4}$ teaspoon salt
$1\frac{1}{4}$ cups all-purpose flour
strawberry jam, strained

In a mixing bowl, cream the butter and sugar. Whip the egg white with the salt until stiff and blend into the butter mixture. Add the flour to make a stiff dough. Chill 30 minutes.

Cover baking sheets with parchment paper or lightly grease them. Preheat oven to 375°F.

On a lightly floured board, roll the cookie dough out to about $\frac{1}{16}$-inch thickness. With a doughnut cutter, cut out rings and place rings and center cutouts on the prepared baking sheets. Bake for 6 to 8 minutes until lightly browned. Spread half the cookies with strained strawberry jam and top with the second half of the cookies.

SWEDISH RYE COOKIES
(Ragkåkor)

*T*hese are made in Finland, too, where they are called *ruiskakut*. They are little buttery cookies made with rye flour and baked with a hole in the center to simulate the large loaves of rye bread that are eaten all year long.

❖ Makes 4 dozen cookies

1 cup butter, room temperature
$\frac{1}{2}$ cup sugar
1 cup light rye flour
$1\frac{1}{4}$ cups all-purpose flour
2 to 3 tablespoons ice water

In a large bowl, cream the butter with the sugar until smooth. Add the rye flour, then the all-purpose flour, and mix until well blended. Blend in the ice water (adding more if necessary). Gather into a ball and chill.

Cover baking sheets with parchment paper or lightly grease them. Preheat oven to 350°F.

Pinch off small pieces of dough and knead lightly to make them workable. Roll out on a lightly floured surface to $\frac{1}{8}$-inch thickness. Cut into $2\frac{1}{2}$-inch rounds and pierce all over with a fork. With a small bottle cap, cut a hole in the center of each cookie.

Bake for 8 to 10 minutes or until firm and beginning to brown on the edges. Cool on parchment paper, or remove from cookie sheets and cool on racks.

FINNISH BARLEY COOKIES
(*Ohrapiparit*)

*B*arley flour makes a light, slightly nutty-flavored and delicate cookie. Barley is a grain that can be grown in Arctic climates because it ripens quickly. It is low in gluten, and therefore makes tender cookies.

❖ Makes about 4 dozen cookies

1 egg
½ cup sugar
½ cup melted butter
1½ teaspoons ground cinnamon
1½ cups barley flour
½ teaspoon baking soda

In a large bowl, whip the egg and sugar. Add the melted butter and cinnamon. Combine the flour and baking soda and mix in until a smooth dough forms. Chill until firm.

Cover baking sheets with parchment paper or lightly grease them. Preheat oven to 400°F.

On lightly floured surface, roll dough out to about ⅛-inch thickness. Cut into 2-inch or 3-inch rounds, then cut each round into halves to make half-circles. Place on prepared baking sheet and bake until lightly browned, about 8 to 10 minutes.

ICELANDIC JEWISH CAKES
(*Gydingakökur*)

*W*hy the name Jewish cakes, I don't know. Every Icelandic cook I talked to said that these *must* be on the Christmas cookie tray! They are rolled out very thin and result in a delicate, crisp cookie that is topped with pearl sugar or crushed sugar cubes and chopped almonds.

❖ Makes 48 cookies

2 cups all-purpose flour
2 teaspoons freshly ground cardamom seeds
$\frac{1}{8}$ teaspoon baking powder
$\frac{3}{4}$ cup firm butter
1 egg
2 teaspoons lemon juice
2 to 4 tablespoons water
cold strong coffee to brush cookies
pearl sugar or crushed sugar cubes
chopped blanched almonds

In a bowl, or in the work bowl of a food processor fitted with the steel blade, combine the flour, cardamom, and baking powder. Cut in the butter or process until the mixture resembles coarse crumbs. Beat the egg with the lemon juice and 2 tablespoons water. Mix into the dry ingredients until dough holds together, adding more water if necessary, a tablespoon at a time. Gather into a ball and chill for 30 minutes to 1 hour.

Cover baking sheets with parchment paper or lightly grease them. Preheat oven to 375°F.

On a lightly floured board, roll dough out to about $\frac{1}{8}$-inch thickness. Cut out 3-inch rounds. Place on prepared baking sheets and brush with coffee; sprinkle with sugar and almonds.

Bake for 10 to 12 minutes or until golden.

NORWEGIAN ALMOND COOKIES
(*Mandelflarn*)

*T*hese cookies spread out thin and crisp as they bake, with pale centers and crisp, golden edges.

❖ Makes 24 cookies

½ cup softened unsalted butter
½ cup sugar
1 egg
1 teaspoon almond extract
½ cup all-purpose flour
⅔ cup sliced almonds
1 tablespoon water

Cover baking sheets with foil and grease the foil. Preheat oven to 350°F. Cover a stick, dowel, or long spoon handle with foil.

In a mixing bowl, cream the butter and sugar. Add the egg and almond extract. Beat in the flour until light. Stir in the sliced almonds and water.

Spoon 1 rounded tablespoonful of dough at a time onto the baking sheet, spacing the cookies 4 inches apart. Flatten with spoon dipped in water to about 3-inch diameter. Bake 5 to 7 minutes just until edges begin to brown and cookies have spread out. Remove from oven. With a thin spatula, loosen cookies. Lift onto rack to cool or drape cookies over the foil-covered stick so cookies bend into a U shape as they cool.

DANISH LACE COOKIES
(*Kniplingskager*)

*T*hese are thin and lacy and are made with uncooked rolled oats.

❖ Makes 3 dozen cookies

> ½ *cup butter*
> 1½ *cups uncooked old-fashioned rolled oats*
> ¼ *teaspoon ground ginger*
> 1 *egg*
> ⅔ *cup sugar*
> 1 *teaspoon baking powder*
> 1 *tablespoon all-purpose flour*

Grease baking sheets generously and dust with flour. Preheat oven to 350°F.

Melt the butter and stir in the rolled oats and ginger. Beat the egg with the sugar until foamy. Mix the baking powder and flour and stir into the egg mixture along with the oatmeal mixture. Drop a level tablespoonful at a time onto the prepared baking sheets, 2 to 3 inches apart.

Bake for 8 to 10 minutes or until golden. Cool about 1 minute, then remove cookies with a spatula onto a rolling pin. You may prefer to keep these cookies flat. If you bend them too much they crack into pieces—a slight bend is all they need. Store in an airtight container.

DANISH ROCKS
(*Rokkekager*)

*T*hese are drop cookies studded with fruits, nuts, and spices. In my home, these are known simply as "Christmas cookies" when candied fruits and nuts are added. At other times of year, we replace the pineapple and cherries with extra raisins, dates, and nuts.

❖ Makes about 8 dozen cookies

1 cup butter, room temperature
1½ cups light or dark brown sugar, packed
3 eggs
2½ cups all-purpose flour
½ teaspoon salt
1 teaspoon baking soda
1 teaspoon cinnamon
½ teaspoon nutmeg
¼ teaspoon cloves
1 teaspoon vanilla
3 cups mixed candied pineapple and cherries or raisins
2 pounds pitted dates, cut up
1 cup whole filberts
1 cup whole pecans
1 cup coarsely chopped walnuts

Cover baking sheets with parchment paper or lightly grease them. Preheat oven to 350°F.

In a large bowl, cream the butter and sugar. Add eggs and vanilla and beat well. Combine the flour, salt, baking soda, cinnamon, nutmeg, and cloves. Add to the creamed mixture to make a smooth dough. Mix in the fruits and nuts. Drop by teaspoonfuls onto the prepared baking sheets about 2 inches apart. Bake 8 to 10 minutes until lightly browned. Remove from baking sheets and cool on racks. Store in an airtight tin. These cookies keep well.

DANISH SUGAR DROPS
(*Zuckerkager*)

*W*hen you remove these cookies from the pan they are soft and thin; they become crisp as they cool.

❖ Makes 8 dozen cookies

1½ cups butter, room temperature
2 cups sugar
2 eggs
1 teaspoon vanilla
3 cups cake flour
½ teaspoon cream of tartar

Cover baking sheets with parchment paper or lightly grease and flour them. Preheat oven to 400°F.

In a large bowl, cream the butter and sugar until smooth and light. Beat in the eggs and vanilla. Mix the flour with the cream of tartar and add to the creamed mixture.

Drop by teaspoonfuls onto the prepared baking sheets, about 2 inches apart. Bake for 8 minutes or until cookies have a golden brown edge but are not completely browned in the center. If using parchment paper, allow to cool right on the paper. If not, remove cookies while hot and cool on rack.

LEMON WAFERS
(*Citronsmåkager*)

"*White* on white" foods are common in Scandinavia, and these cookies are an example. They should not be browned or they will lose their delicate flavor. The lemon icing has no color either, but the taste is novel.

❖ Makes 5 dozen cookies

$\frac{1}{2}$ *cup unsalted butter, room temperature*
1 cup sugar
4 eggs
2$\frac{1}{4}$ cups all-purpose flour
2 teaspoons lemon extract

GLAZE

1 cup powdered sugar
1 tablespoon fresh lemon juice

Cover baking sheets with parchment paper or lightly grease them. Preheat oven to 350°F.

Cream the butter and sugar. Add the eggs and beat until well mixed. Add the flour and beat until mixture is light. Blend in the lemon extract. Drop by rounded teaspoonfuls onto the prepared baking sheets, about 2 inches apart. Bake 6 to 8 minutes until cookies feel firm and are just lightly browned around the edges.

Mix 1 cup powdered sugar with 1 tablespoon fresh lemon juice and enough water to make a thin glaze. Drop a half-teaspoonful of the lemon glaze on each hot cookie.

SARAH BERNHARDT CAKES
(*Sarah Bernhardt-Kager*)

Sarah Bernhardt, the great French actress, captured Danish hearts to such an extent that they named these special chocolate-mousse-topped meringue cakes after her.

❖ Makes 12 cakes

1 egg white
$\frac{1}{2}$ cup sugar
1 (2$\frac{1}{2}$-ounce) package blanched slivered almonds, pulverized
1 tablespoon cornstarch
1 teaspoon almond extract

TOPPING AND DECORATION

1 cup (6 ounces) semisweet chocolate chips
$\frac{1}{3}$ cup butter
1 egg
1 teaspoon grated lemon rind
1 teaspoon sugar
1 teaspoon vanilla
12 blanched almonds

Cover a baking sheet with parchment paper or grease and flour it. Preheat oven to 350°F.

In a large bowl, whisk the egg white until foamy; add the sugar, and beat until mixture holds soft peaks. Fold in the almonds, cornstarch, and almond extract.

Spoon into 12 mounds evenly spaced on the prepared baking sheet, allowing plenty of space between them. Bake until top is dry and cakes are a creamy color, about 10 minutes. Remove from sheet and cool on rack.

Melt $\frac{1}{2}$ cup of the chocolate chips in a small bowl over hot water. Melt the butter in another pan. Whip the egg with the lemon rind, sugar, and vanilla until light and fluffy. Mix the cooled chocolate and butter together and add the egg mixture. When this has thickened, spread it over the base of the cakes, allowing the mixture to set.

Melt the remaining chocolate and pour over the firm chocolate layer. Decorate each cake with an almond.

AUNT HANNA'S COOKIES
(*Hannatädinkakut*)

*T*his favorite everyday Finnish cookie can be found year-round in supermarkets in Finland. I usually make them for my holiday cookie tray.

❖ Makes 6 dozen cookies

$\frac{1}{2}$ *cup softened butter*
$\frac{1}{2}$ *cup sugar*
2 cups cake flour
2 teaspoons baking powder
$\frac{1}{2}$ *cup whipping cream*
almond halves or glazed cherries for decoration

Cover baking sheets with parchment paper or lightly grease them. Preheat oven to 350°F.

In a mixing bowl, cream the butter and sugar until blended. Mix the flour with the baking powder and add to the butter mixture, a little at a time. Blend in the cream until a stiff dough forms. Chill if necessary.

Using 1 teaspoonful of dough at a time, roll into small balls. Place on the prepared baking sheets. Press a halved almond or a halved glazed cherry into each cookie.

Bake for 10 minutes or until very light golden and set. Cool on the baking pan. Store in an airtight tin or freeze.

NORWEGIAN BERLIN RINGS
(*Berlinerkranser*)

*A*lthough these cookies are known throughout Scandinavia, I associate them with Norwegians, who first introduced them to me. Rich with butter and eggs, the cookies are shaped into little strands, then bent into rings, topped with pearl sugar, and baked.

❖ Makes 48 cookies

2 hard-cooked egg yolks
2 uncooked egg yolks
1 cup sugar
2½ to 3 cups all-purpose flour
1 cup butter

GLAZE

2 egg whites
¼ cup pearl sugar or crushed sugar cubes

In a mixing bowl, mash the hard-cooked yolks with the uncooked yolks and add the sugar.

In a large mixing bowl, or in the work bowl of a food processor with the steel blade in place, measure the flour and slice in the butter. With pastry blender or fork, mix until butter is cut into the flour, or using on/off pulses of the food processor process until mixture is crumbly. Add the egg yolk mixture and mix until a stiff dough forms.

Gather dough into a ball and refrigerate 4 to 8 hours.

Cover baking sheets with parchment paper or lightly grease them. Preheat oven to 350°F.

Working with a part of the dough at a time, roll between palms of hands and lightly floured board into ropes ½-inch thick. Cut into 3-inch sections and turn into little wreaths, pinching ends together. Dip into unbeaten egg white and then into the sugar. Place on prepared baking sheets. Bake for 10 to 12 minutes or until lightly browned.

SWEDISH WALNUT-CINNAMON COOKIES
(*Kanelkakor*)

*T*hese delicate cookies are coated with walnuts, which toast during baking.

❖ Makes 2 dozen cookies

> $\frac{1}{3}$ *cup butter, room temperature*
> $\frac{2}{3}$ *cup sugar*
> *1 egg*
> *1 teaspoon vanilla*
> *1$\frac{1}{4}$ cups all-purpose flour*
> *1 teaspoon baking powder*
> *1 teaspoon cinnamon*
> $\frac{1}{4}$ *cup finely chopped walnuts*
> *2 tablespoons cinnamon*
> *2 tablespoons sugar*

In large bowl, cream butter and sugar. Beat in the egg and vanilla until light. Sift flour with baking powder and 1 teaspoon cinnamon. Add to the creamed mixture, blending well. Chill dough 30 minutes.

Cover baking sheets with parchment paper or grease lightly. Preheat oven to 350°F.

Mix the walnuts, 2 tablespoons cinnamon, and 2 tablespoons sugar in a small bowl.

Shape chilled dough into balls the size of walnuts. Roll each ball in the walnut-cinnamon mixture. Place on prepared baking sheets about 3 inches apart. Bake 10 to 12 minutes until golden and set. Do not overbake.

DANISH FILBERT BUTTER COOKIES
(*Hasselnødssmakåger*)

*T*he hazelnut is the fruit of the cobnut bush, which grows all over Europe. It is a rich-tasting nut and is popular in Europe as well as in the Scandinavian countries. Filbert is another name for hazelnut, and it gets the name because the nut ripens about August 22, St. Philbert's Day.

❖ Makes 4 dozen cookies

$\frac{2}{3}$ *cup butter, room temperature*
$\frac{1}{2}$ *cup sugar*
1 egg
1$\frac{1}{2}$ cups all-purpose flour
$\frac{1}{2}$ *teaspoon baking powder*
1 cup filberts or hazelnuts, toasted and pulverized*

In a mixing bowl, cream the butter and sugar until blended. Mix in the egg. Add the flour and baking powder and beat until fluffy. Add the filberts. Chill dough until firm enough to shape, about 30 minutes.

Cover baking sheets with parchment paper or lightly grease them. Preheat oven to 400°F.

Shape into balls about the size of small walnuts. Press tops of the cookies with a fork, making a crisscross pattern. Bake for 7 to 8 minutes until lightly browned.

❖ To toast nuts, spread on cookie sheet. Bake at 300°F 5 to 10 minutes until toasted.

DANISH VIENNA FINGERS
(*Wienerstänger*)

*A*lthough I like to make these colorful and buttery cookie strips for my holiday cookie tray, in Scandinavia they are available in bakeries all year.

❖ Makes 45 cookies

$\frac{2}{3}$ *cup butter*
$\frac{1}{2}$ *cup sugar*
1 egg
1 teaspoon grated lemon rind
1$\frac{1}{2}$ cups all-purpose flour
1 teaspoon baking powder
$\frac{1}{2}$ *cup strawberry or raspberry jam or jelly*

ICING

1 cup powdered sugar
1 tablespoon lemon juice

Cover a baking sheet with parchment paper or lightly grease it. Preheat oven to 375°F.

In a large mixing bowl, cream the butter and sugar. Add egg and beat until light. Add the lemon peel, flour, and baking powder to make a dough. Chill 30 minutes. Divide into 4 parts. Roll each part into strips 15 inches long. Place on baking sheet 2 inches apart. Press a groove in the center the length of each strip.

Bake 10 minutes. Spoon jam or jelly along each groove. Return to oven and bake 10 minutes or until pale gold on the edges.

Mix the powdered sugar and lemon juice. Add enough water to make an icing. Drizzle the cookie strips with the icing when you take them from the oven. Cut diagonally into $\frac{3}{4}$-inch cookies.

NORWEGIAN BROWNED BUTTER COOKIES
(Drømmer I Ørkenens Sand)

*T*hese are also called "dream" cookies and are flavored with butter that has been browned and cooled.

❖ Makes 36 cookies

1 cup butter
⅓ cup sugar
½ teaspoon vanilla
1 egg yolk
¼ teaspoon cream of tartar
2 cups cake flour

In a heavy skillet, melt the butter over medium heat and cook, stirring, until the butter is golden brown but not burned. Pour into a bowl and let stand at least 8 hours.

Stir butter with a fork and add the sugar, vanilla, and egg yolk. Mix the cream of tartar with the flour and add to the butter-sugar mixture, stirring until a stiff dough forms. Shape into balls the size of small walnuts.

Cover a baking sheet with parchment paper or lightly grease and flour it. Preheat oven to 375°F.

Place cookies on the baking sheet. Bake for 15 to 20 minutes or until golden.

DANISH SUGAR PRETZELS
(*Kringler*)

$\mathcal{T}$he pretzel is the trade sign of the Danish baker. Danes use this shape for all kinds of baked goods, including cakes, pastries, breads, and cookies.

❖ Makes 130 cookies

> 3 cups all-purpose flour
> 1 cup butter, firm, but not hard
> 1 teaspoon baking powder
> 1 egg
> $\frac{1}{2}$ cup heavy cream
> pearl sugar or crushed sugar cubes for topping

Cover baking sheets with parchment or grease them. Preheat oven to 350°F.

In a bowl, or in the work bowl of a food processor, combine flour, butter, baking powder, egg, and heavy cream. Mix with hand mixer or process until dough forms. Chill 30 minutes. Using pieces of dough the size of a small walnut, roll into thin strips about 6 inches long. Turn into pretzel shapes and dip tops in pearl sugar or crushed sugar cubes. Place on prepared baking sheets with sugar side up. Bake for 10 to 12 minutes until golden.

FINNISH TEASPOON COOKIES
(*Lusikkaleivät*)

*B*rowned butter gives these cookies a nutty flavor. They are shaped in teaspoons before baking and sandwiched with strawberry jam after baking. These classic, old-fashioned cookies have been made in Pohjanmaa, the western province of Finland, for several generations. Very delicate and tender, they are a little fussy to make, but the effort is well worth while!

❖ Makes 4 dozen cookies

1 cup unsalted butter
¾ cup sugar
3 teaspoons vanilla
2 cups all-purpose flour
1 teaspoon baking soda
1 egg yolk
strawberry jam
powdered sugar

In a small, heavy saucepan, brown the butter over medium to low heat until it is a pale tan color. Cool. Pour into a mixing bowl. Stir in the sugar and vanilla. Combine flour and baking soda and gradually add to the butter mixture. Stir until the mixture is uniformly crumbly. Blend in the egg yolk and knead until dough is smooth.

Preheat oven to 325°F. Cover baking sheets with parchment paper. Uncovered sheets need not be greased.

To shape a cookie, press dough firmly into a teaspoon. Tap side of spoon onto the cookie sheet to gently remove the shaped cookie. Bake for 6 to 8 minutes until just barely browned. Allow to cool right on the baking parchment.

Spread jam on the flat side of one cookie. Add a second cookie to form an almond-shaped sandwich. Using a sieve, dust the cookies with the powdered sugar. The flavor improves after the cookies have been stored at least 2 days, and they can be frozen.

PRESSED BUTTER COOKIES
(*Spritz*)

*T*o make these cookies you need a spritz cookie press, which comes with a number of plates, so you can shape many different kinds of cookies, from camels to Christmas trees, stars, or snowflakes. Unsalted butter and cake flour make these cookies delicate and tender.

❖ Makes about 5 dozen cookies

1½ *cups unsalted butter, room temperature*
¾ *cup sugar*
3 egg yolks
3 cups cake flour
1 teaspoon vanilla
¼ *teaspoon almond extract*

In a large bowl, cream the butter and sugar until smooth. Add the egg yolks and beat until light. Gradually mix in the flour until dough is smooth; blend in the vanilla and almond extract.

Fit cookie press with your choice of plate. Fill with the dough. Press cookies out onto ungreased cookie sheet.

Preheat oven to 350°F. Bake cookies for 12 to 15 minutes or until just barely golden.

DANISH VANILLA WREATHS
(*Vanillekranse*)

*T*hese are the best known of the Danish cookies, as they are sold in tins in this country. Of course, cookies that have been baked months ago and shipped long distances hardly resemble the freshly baked product!

❖ Makes about 8 dozen cookies

$\frac{3}{4}$ *cup sugar*
$\frac{3}{4}$ *cup butter, room temperature*
1 egg
$\frac{1}{4}$ *cup finely minced almonds*
1 teaspoon vanilla
1$\frac{3}{4}$ cups all-purpose flour

In a bowl, cream the sugar and butter until blended. Add the egg, almonds, vanilla, and flour and mix until dough is smooth. Chill 30 minutes. Cover baking sheets with parchment paper or lightly grease them. Preheat oven to 350°F.

Put the dough into a cookie press or pastry bag with a star tip and about $\frac{1}{2}$-inch opening. Press out into long strips. Cut into lengths of 3 inches and shape into rings. Or press out into rings about 2 inches in diameter right on the prepared baking sheets. Bake for 8 to 10 minutes until golden.

SWEDISH FARMER COOKIES
(*Bondkakor*)

*T*his refrigerator cookie dough is shaped into a roll, chilled, then sliced and baked.

❖ Makes 5 dozen cookies

2 cups all-purpose flour
1½ teaspoons baking powder
¾ cup sugar
1 cup slivered almonds
1 tablespoon dark molasses
⅔ cup softened unsalted butter
1 egg
2 tablespoons water

Combine all the ingredients in a bowl or food processor. With electric mixer or with steel blade of food processor, mix until dough forms.

Divide dough into 3 parts and shape each into a roll, about 1½ inches in diameter. Roll in plastic wrap or waxed paper and chill until firm, 1 to 2 hours or longer.

Cover baking sheets with parchment paper or lightly grease them. Preheat oven to 400°F. Slice cookies ¼-inch thick and place on baking sheets. Bake for 8 to 10 minutes until barely browned.

DANISH VANILLA SLICES
(*Vaniljesmåkager*)

*T*hese are cookies that will keep well in an airtight tin, or they can be frozen to keep for several months. The dough is shaped into a log that can be refrigerated at least 2 weeks or frozen for several months.

❖ Makes 3 dozen cookies

> 1 cup butter, room temperature
> ¾ cup sugar
> 1 egg
> 3 cups all-purpose flour
> 1 teaspoon baking powder
> 2 teaspoons vanilla extract
> powdered sugar

In a large bowl, cream the butter and sugar until smooth. Blend in the egg and beat until light. Mix the flour and baking powder and blend along with the vanilla into the creamed mixture until a stiff dough forms. Knead lightly and divide into 2 parts. Roll each part to make a 2-inch-diameter log. Wrap in waxed paper and foil and chill at least 1 hour or up to 2 weeks.

Cover baking sheets with parchment paper or lightly grease them. Preheat oven to 375°F. Cut dough into ¼-inch-thick slices. Place on baking sheet about 2 inches apart. Bake for 10 to 12 minutes until golden. Allow to cool on the baking sheets, then dust with powdered sugar. Store in an airtight container.

SWEDISH CHOCOLATE-FROSTED ALMOND BARS
(*Mazarinkakor*)

*T*he name "mazarin" indicates that an almond filling is part of the pastry. You can step into any pastry shop any time of year in almost any Scandinavian country and add these to your coffee or tea tray! They may be baked in fancy tins, but I often make them into a bar cookie.

❖ Makes 48 bars, about 1 x 2 inches.

2 cups all-purpose flour
$\frac{1}{4}$ cup sugar
1 egg
1 cup softened butter

FILLING

$\frac{1}{3}$ cup softened butter
$\frac{3}{4}$ cup sugar
2 eggs
$\frac{3}{4}$ cup blanched almonds, finely chopped

ICING

1 cup milk chocolate or semisweet chocolate chips

Preheat oven to 375°F.

In the large bowl of an electric mixer, combine the flour, sugar, egg, and butter. Mix at low speed until mixture is crumbly. Press mixture into a 13 x 9-inch pan, working it up the sides of the pan about $\frac{1}{2}$ inch. Bake 20 minutes until pale golden.

For the filling, cream the butter and sugar. Add the eggs, beating until light and fluffy, scraping sides of the bowl. Mix in the almonds. Spread filling over the pastry and bake another 10 minutes until filling is set. Remove from oven and cool.

Put the chocolate chips into a small, heavy-duty plastic bag with a zip-type closure. Place in a bowl of hot tap water until chips are melted. Knead bag to be sure chips are completely melted. Wipe bag dry with paper toweling. With scissors, cut a small opening across one of the bottom corners of the bag. Squeeze out a thin stream of chocolate, crisscrossing the top of the bars.

NORWEGIAN TOSCA SQUARES
(*Toscabakelser*)

*T*raditionally these squares are baked in little individual tins that are lined with pastry and filled with the almond filling. Scandinavian-Americans, however, are more likely to turn the recipe into bar cookies. They're just as tasty, even though the shape isn't as "European."

❖ Makes 16 squares

$\frac{1}{3}$ cup butter, room temperature
3 tablespoons sugar
1 egg yolk
1 cup all-purpose flour

FILLING

$\frac{2}{3}$ cup blanched almonds
5 tablespoons soft butter
$\frac{1}{2}$ cup sugar
1 whole egg
1 egg white

ICING

$\frac{1}{4}$ cup butter
$\frac{1}{4}$ cup sugar
$\frac{1}{2}$ cup chopped or slivered almonds
1 tablespoon all-purpose flour
1 tablespoon milk

Lightly butter a 9-inch square baking pan or a $7\frac{1}{2}$ x 11-inch pan. Preheat oven to 400°F.

In the large bowl of an electric mixer, cream the butter with the sugar until smooth. Blend in the egg yolk and flour until dough forms. Press into the baking pan evenly and build up the edges about $\frac{1}{2}$ inch. Bake 15 minutes.

Meanwhile, pulverize the almonds in the food processor or in a food chopper. Blend almonds with the butter and sugar. Beat the egg and egg white until fluffy and fold into the butter and almond mixture. Pour into the partially baked crust.

Bake 10 to 15 minutes until the filling is set.

Meanwhile, to make the topping, melt the butter in a small saucepan. Add the sugar, almonds, flour, and milk. Heat, stirring until thickened. Simmer 3 to 4 minutes, then remove from the heat. Spread mixture over the baked cake. Cool and cut into squares.

ALEXANDER'S TARTS
(*Alexanterintortut*)

*C*zar Alexander II of Russia ruled Finland in the eighteenth century. He was a kind man and was well liked by the Finnish people. It was he who first acknowledged the Finnish language and made it a second official language. (The official language had previously been Swedish.) Czar Alexander II has a street in Helsinki named after him (Alexanterinkatu), as well as these little sweet tarts that are sold in coffee shops throughout the year and are often served on the coffeetable. I sometimes like to cut them into tiny, 1-inch squares.

❖ Makes 36 tarts, 1 x 2 inches

1⅓ cups all-purpose flour
¼ teaspoon baking powder
¼ cup sugar
½ cup butter, room temperature
1 egg yolk
2 to 4 teaspoons water
½ cup raspberry jam

FROSTING

1 cup powdered sugar
2 teaspoons cornstarch
2 to 3 tablespoons hot water
½ teaspoon almond extract

In a mixing bowl, combine the flour, baking powder, and sugar. With a fork or pastry blender, cut in the butter until mixture resembles coarse crumbs. Blend the egg yolk and 2 teaspoons water and mix into the crumbs. Press together to make a dough, adding a bit more water if necessary. Chill 30 minutes.

Preheat oven to 350°F. Cover a baking sheet with parchment paper or lightly grease it.

Divide dough into 2 parts. Roll each part out to make an 8-inch square. Trim edges. Place the 2 squares on the prepared baking sheet and bake until pale golden, 12 to 15 minutes. Cool on the sheet. Spread 1 square with jam and place second square on top of the jam-spread square to make a sandwich.

Mix the powdered sugar, cornstarch, water, and almond extract to make a rather thin frosting. Spread evenly over the square and let stand until frosting has hardened. With a thin, sharp knife, cut into 1 x 2-inch rectangles.

ALMOND TARTS
(*Mandelformer*)

*A*nother name for this cookie that is baked in a tin is *sandbak-kelser*, a must on the holiday cookie tray. They are made in special little fluted tins, which are available in many different sizes. A practical size is about 2 inches in diameter, as the tart shells baked in this size are small enough to serve like cookies, but large enough to fill with a dab of jam, jelly, or whipped cream.

❖ Makes about 4 dozen tarts

$\frac{3}{4}$ *cup unsalted butter, room temperature*
$\frac{2}{3}$ *cup sugar*
1 cup blanched almonds, pulverized or ground
1 teaspoon almond extract
1 egg
2 cups all-purpose flour

In a large bowl, cream the butter and sugar until light and fluffy. Blend in the pulverized almonds, almond extract, and the egg. Stir in the flour. Turn dough out onto a lightly floured surface and knead until smooth. Add a bit more flour if needed to make a stiff dough. Gather into a ball. Chill 30 minutes.

Preheat oven to 375°F. Lightly butter fluted tart molds, $2\frac{1}{2}$ to 3 inches in diameter. Pinch off parts of the dough and, using your thumbs, press into the tart pans to make a thin, even layer. Bake for 12 to 15 minutes or until golden.

To remove from molds while still warm, turn molds upside down and tap gently with a spoon to loosen, or place a cold, wet towel over the inverted molds. Remove molds from tarts and cool.

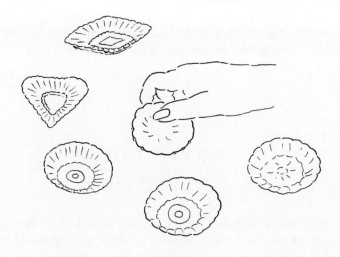

SWEDISH OATMEAL TARTLETS
(*Havreformar*)

These buttery little pastry shells are baked in fancy fluted tins and served either with the bottom side up to show off their shape or filled with jam and whipped cream. Scandinavian cooks use sandbakkel tins, and they usually have a variety of sizes on hand.

❖ Makes 40 2-inch tartlets

1 cup uncooked quick-cooking rolled oats
1½ cups all-purpose flour
⅛ cup sugar
¾ cup butter
1 egg

Lightly grease 40 tartlet pans. Preheat oven to 400°F.

In a large mixing bowl, or in the work bowl of a food processor with the steel blade in place, combine the rolled oats, flour, and sugar. Slice the butter into ½-inch chunks and add to the dry ingredients. Cut in with a knife or pastry cutter, or process until the mixture resembles coarse crumbs. Add the egg and mix until the dough holds together; if necessary, add water, 1 teaspoon at a time. On a work surface, roll dough into a strip and cut into 40 equal pieces. Press dough, using your thumb dipped in flour, into the tartlet pans, making the shell thicker at the edges than at the base. Place tins on a baking sheet. Bake for 12 to 15 minutes until pale golden. Cool and remove from pans by tapping on the bottom of each mold.

FINNISH KING'S CAKES
(*Korinttikakut*)

My friend Leila makes these cardamom-spiced currant cakes whenever there is a special occasion. She bakes them in little fluted molds.

❖ Makes 2 dozen cakes

$\frac{1}{2}$ *cup butter, room temperature*
$\frac{1}{2}$ *cup sugar*
4 eggs
1 teaspoon freshly crushed cardamom
$\frac{1}{2}$ *cup currants*
1 cup all-purpose flour

Butter 24 small 2-inch fluted sandbakkel tins or any other tiny fluted molds. Preheat oven to 375°F.

In a mixing bowl, cream the butter and sugar until blended. Whisk in the eggs one at a time until mixture is well blended. Add the cardamom, currants, and flour, and beat until light and fluffy.

Spoon the mixture into the tins, filling them about $\frac{3}{4}$ full. Place tins on a baking sheet and bake for 12 to 15 minutes until golden. Remove cakes from tins and cool on paper toweling.

RUNEBERG CAKES
(*Runebergintorttut*)

*F*ebruary 5 is the birthday of Finland's national poet, J. L. Runeberg. The flag flies on this day, commemorating his birth, and these little cakes are served in his honor. Most people buy them in bakeries.

❖ Makes 12 cakes

$\frac{1}{2}$ *cup butter, room temperature*
$\frac{1}{2}$ *cup sugar*
2 eggs
1$\frac{1}{2}$ cups cake flour
$\frac{1}{2}$ *teaspoon baking powder*
$\frac{1}{2}$ *cup finely pulverized blanched almonds*
currant jelly

FROSTING

$\frac{1}{2}$ *cup powdered sugar*
1 teaspoon lemon juice
2 to 3 teaspoons hot water

Preheat oven to 350°F. Butter 12 runeberg molds, baba molds, timbales, or cupcake tins. (The authentic mold has straight sides; it is about 2 inches in diameter and 2½ inches deep.)

In a mixing bowl, cream the butter and sugar. Add the eggs and beat until light. Mix the flour and baking powder; beat into the creamed mixture until light and fluffy. Mix in the almonds.

Pour into the prepared molds, filling about ⅔ full. Bake for 15 to 20 minutes or until pale golden brown. Remove from pans and cool. Dot each tart with about ½ teaspoon currant jelly. Mix the powdered sugar, lemon juice, and hot water to make a smooth frosting. Drizzle cakes with the frosting.

CRISPY KRUMKAKE
(*Krumkake*)

*B*oth the Norwegians and Swedes make *krumkake*, the thin, crisp cookie that is baked in a special krumkake iron. The iron is heated on top of the range on a burner and looks something like a waffle iron without deep grids. Krumkake irons usually have a fancy, swirled design that imprints on the cookie. It takes special skill to eat these fragile cookies as well as patience to make them! But it isn't Christmas without them in a Scandinavian household.

❖ Makes 2 dozen cookies

> *1 cup sugar*
> *½ cup softened butter*
> *2 eggs*
> *1 cup milk*
> *1½ cups all-purpose flour*
> *water if necessary*

In a medium bowl, cream the sugar with the butter. Beat in the eggs until mixture is light and lemon colored. Beat in the milk and flour until blended and smooth. Let stand 30 minutes.

Preheat krumkake iron over medium heat on top of range until a drop of water sizzles when dropped on top.

Open iron; lightly brush inside top and bottom with shortening, oil, or melted butter. Spoon 1 tablespoon batter onto center of hot iron. Close iron. Bake about 1 minute on each side until cookie is lightly browned. Insert tip of a knife under cookie to remove from iron; roll hot cookie into a cigar or cone shape. Cook on rack. Cookies become crisp as they cool. Repeat with remaining batter. Batter will thicken as you use it; add water a tablespoon at a time as necessary to thin it to the consistency of thick cream. Store baked cookies in airtight containers. You can also keep them frozen for several months.

DANISH STRAWBERRY CONES
(*Kraemmerhuse*)

*T*hese crisp cookies are shaped into cones while they are still warm. They can be made ahead and stored in an airtight tin. Just before serving, fill them with whipped cream and fresh strawberries.

The cookies spread out in a crazy way while they bake, especially if your cookie sheet warps and bends with heat. Simply separate and loosen the thin cookies while still hot and as they cool you can turn them into cones. The darker the cookie, the more quickly it will become brittle; if it hardens, slip it back into the oven until soft, then remove and turn into a cone shape.

❖ Makes 24 cones

$\frac{1}{2}$ *cup butter, room temperature*
$\frac{1}{2}$ *cup sugar*
$\frac{1}{2}$ *cup all-purpose flour*
2 egg whites
1 teaspoon vanilla
1 cup whipping cream, whipped
fresh strawberries, whole or halved

Heavily grease 4 baking sheets. Preheat oven to 400°F.

In a mixing bowl, cream the butter and sugar together until light and fluffy. Blend in the flour. Whip the egg whites until stiff and blend into the mixture along with the vanilla.

Using a teaspoon, place 2 to 3 rounds of the mixture well apart on each cookie sheet; as the mixture spreads use a butter knife or spatula dipped in cold water to shape the mounds into 3-inch rounds.

Bake one sheet at a time for 5 to 6 minutes until edges of the cookies are just beginning to brown. Quickly remove each from the sheet with a thin wet spatula. Shape into a cone and place each in the neck of a bottle to set. When cones have set, transfer them to a cake rack to cool.

To serve, fill each cone with a spoonful of whipped cream and decorate with a whole or half strawberry. You may keep the cones upright by placing them in about 1 inch of sugar in the bottom of the serving bowl.

ROSETTES
(*Struvor*)

*T*hese are fragile and pretty deep-fried pastries; you need a special rosette iron to make them. Rosette irons in various shapes are available in specialty shops and department stores. The trick to making good rosettes is to preheat the iron in the fat, and to be sure not to dip the iron so deeply into the batter that it coats the top of the iron. If you fry the tops, the pastries will not slip off the iron at all!

❖ Makes 60 rosettes

2 eggs
1½ teaspoons sugar
1 cup milk
1 cup all-purpose flour

hot fat for frying
powdered sugar

In a large bowl, beat the eggs, then add the sugar. Mix in the milk and flour just until batter is smooth and free of lumps. It should be the consistency of thick cream. Have batter in a container just wide enough to permit easy dipping with the irons.

Heat fat to 370°F. (Vegetable oil, lard, or shortening may be used.) Place rosette iron into the fat to preheat. Dip into batter and return to fat for 20 to 35 seconds or until the rosette is lightly browned. Lift up and drain over the fat a few seconds, and using a sharp knife or fork remove the rosette and let drain on paper towels. Sprinkle with powdered sugar.

NORWEGIAN FANCY STICKS
(Hjortebakelse)

*T*his traditional fried Christmas cookie is twisted into knots, cut into sticks, or twisted into a ring and slashed around the outside edges, before cooking.

❖ Makes 36 cookies

$\frac{1}{4}$ *cup softened butter*
$\frac{1}{2}$ *cup sugar*
2 eggs
$\frac{1}{2}$ *teaspoon cream of tartar*
$\frac{1}{2}$ *teaspoon freshly ground cardamom*
2 cups all-purpose flour

hot fat for frying
powdered sugar

In a bowl, cream the butter and sugar together; add the eggs and beat until light. Blend in the cream of tartar and cardamom. Add flour to make a stiff, smooth dough. Chill until firm, about 1 hour.

Using 2 tablespoonfuls of the dough at a time, shape dough into strands about 5 inches long. Shape into knots, or make into circles and slash the outside edges. Or shape into 3-inch sticks and slash alternately on one side and then the other.

Heat fat to 375°F. (Vegetable oil, lard, or shortening may be used.) Fry the cookies until golden, turning once. Drain. Dust with powdered sugar.

DANISH SMALLS
(*Klejner*)

*S*wedes and Norwegians call these fried cookies *fattigman,* or poor men, although today we see nothing really poor about them! Shaped like the Icelandic Kleinur (which is made with an entirely different dough), this cookie dough is rolled out thin, cut into diamonds, slashed in the center, and twisted into a knot. Some call them "lover's knots."

❖ Makes about 60 cookies

2 cups all-purpose flour
$\frac{1}{4}$ cup sugar
$\frac{1}{2}$ teaspoon baking powder
$\frac{1}{2}$ cup butter
5 to 6 tablespoons heavy whipping cream
1 egg
1 teaspoon freshly crushed cardamom seeds

hot fat for frying
powdered sugar

In the work bowl of the food processor with the steel blade in place, or in a mixing bowl, combine the flour, sugar, and baking powder. Slice the butter and add to the dry ingredients. Process or blend until the mixture resembles coarse crumbs. Add 5 tablespoons of cream, egg, and cardamom and mix until a dough forms. Add more cream if necessary to moisten the dough. Chill 30 minutes.

On a lightly floured board, roll dough out to $\frac{1}{8}$-inch thickness and cut into strips about $1\frac{1}{4}$ inches wide. Cut the strips diagonally into diamonds about $3\frac{1}{2}$ inches long. Make a lengthwise slash through the center of each with the point of a knife. Pull one end of the piece through the slash to form a half-knot.

Heat fat (vegetable oil, lard, or shortening) to 375°F. Drop knots into the fat and cook until golden on both sides, turning once or twice. Remove from fat and drain on paper toweling. Dust with powdered sugar. Store in an airtight tin in a cool place.

HALF-MOONS
(Hálfmánar)

A prune-filled cookie is included in the Scandinavian holiday tradition. In Iceland, they're called half-moons, the pastry being a rich cardamom-scented butter dough.

❖ Makes 48 cookies

8 ounces (2 cups) pitted prunes
1 cup water
2½ cups all-purpose flour
2 teaspoons baking powder
1 teaspoon freshly ground cardamom seeds
1 cup firm butter
⅔ cup sugar
1 egg, beaten
1 tablespoon lemon juice
2 to 3 tablespoons ice water

In a saucepan, cook the prunes in the water until soft, about 15 minutes. Puree and cool.

In a large bowl, or in the work bowl of a food processor with the steel blade in place, combine the flour, baking powder, and cardamom. Cut in the butter or process until the mixture resembles coarse crumbs. Add the sugar. Mix together the egg, lemon juice, and 2 tablespoons ice water. Blend into the flour mixture just until dough holds together. Press into a ball and chill 1 hour.

Cover baking sheets with parchment paper or lightly grease them. Preheat oven to 375°F.

On a floured board, roll dough out to about ⅛-inch thickness. With plain round 3-inch cookie cutter, cut out rounds. Spoon 1 scant teaspoon of the prune puree onto the center of each round. Fold and press edges together firmly to seal. Place on prepared baking sheets. Bake for 10 to 15 minutes until golden.

FINNISH CHRISTMAS STARS
(*Joulutortut*)

*T*raditionally in Finland, holiday baked goods are not served until Christmas Eve or, at the earliest, the eve of Christmas Eve. That's when these prune-filled stars come out, signaling the beginning of the Christmas holidays. The day after Christmas is a day for visiting and comparing the quality of the stars from one household to the next! Each baker has his or her own favorite recipe, varying from a flaky puff pastry to a rich and tender butter pastry like this one.

❖ Makes 36 stars

2 cups (8 ounces) pitted prunes
water to cover
2 tablespoons lemon juice
½ cup sugar
3 cups all-purpose flour
1 teaspoon baking powder
1½ cups heavy cream, whipped
1 cup softened butter

GLAZE

1 slightly beaten egg
2 tablespoons milk
pearl sugar or crushed sugar cubes for garnish

Cover the prunes with water and simmer slowly until very soft. Puree and add the lemon juice and sugar. Cool.

For the pastry, mix the flour and baking powder. Stir into the whipped cream and knead in the softened butter. Shape dough into a ball and chill 1 hour.

On a floured board, roll out pastry to ¼-inch thickness. Fold dough into thirds, folding first one third over the center, then the opposite third over the center. Roll out to seal the layers. Turn dough and fold again into thirds, making the dough into a perfect square. Roll out, retaining the square shape, to make an 18-inch square. Cut into 3-inch squares. With a sharp knife, make cuts from the corners toward the centers of the squares, each about 1½ inches long. Place a spoonful of the prune filling onto the center of each square. Shape into pinwheel stars by lifting every other split corner toward the center onto the filling.

Cover baking sheets with parchment paper or lightly grease them. Preheat oven to 400°F.

Place filled stars on the prepared baking sheets. Mix the egg and milk and brush stars with the glaze. Sprinkle with pearl sugar or crushed sugar cubes.

Bake 7 to 10 minutes or until lightly browned.

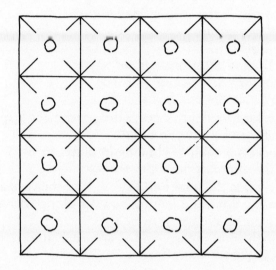

SWEDISH ALMOND RUSKS
(*Mandelskorpor*)

*A*lmonds and butter are two basics in Scandinavian cookie baking. Almond rusks are baked into long sticks, which are cut into diagonal slices after baking, then rebaked until crisp.

❖ Makes 45 rusks

$\frac{1}{2}$ *cup blanched almonds*
$\frac{1}{2}$ *cup butter, room temperature*
$\frac{1}{2}$ *cup sugar*
2 eggs
2 cups all-purpose flour
1 teaspoon baking powder

Cover one large baking sheet with parchment paper or lightly grease it. Preheat oven to 375°F.

In food processor with steel blade in place, or on a board with a knife, chop the almonds until coarse.

In a bowl, cream the butter and sugar; add the eggs and beat until fluffy. Stir in the flour and baking powder along with the almonds. Mix until a smooth dough is formed.

Divide dough into 3 parts and shape each into a 15-inch rope. Place on baking sheet about 2 to 3 inches apart.

Bake 12 to 15 minutes or until cookie strips are golden. Reduce oven temperature to 300°F. Cool cookie strips on baking sheet for 10 minutes. With sharp knife, cut into $\frac{3}{4}$-inch wide pieces on the diagonal. Separate them from each other. Return to oven and bake 20 to 30 minutes or until totally dry.

HAZELNUT TOASTS
(*Knassandi Hnetuskorpur*)

I first ate these delectably flavored melba-toast-shaped rusks in Iceland. Because they're a bit sweet and studded with filberts, I don't know whether to call them a bread, a coffeebread, or a cookie, even though they are, technically, a twice-baked bread.

❖ Makes 25 pieces

2 *eggs*
$\frac{3}{4}$ *cup sugar*
1$\frac{1}{4}$ *cups all-purpose flour*
2 *cups whole filberts*

Preheat oven to 300°F. Grease an 8 x 3-inch loaf pan and line with waxed paper.

Beat eggs and sugar together until light and fluffy. Combine the flour and filberts, then blend into the egg mixture.

Turn into the loaf pan. Bake for 60 to 70 minutes until golden and loaf tests done. Remove from pan immediately and peel the paper from the loaf. Turn loaf upside down and, with a thin, sharp knife, cut into $\frac{1}{4}$-inch slices. The loaf and nuts slice more easily while still hot. Place the slices on a baking sheet.

Increase oven to 450°F. Bake for 3 to 5 minutes until slices are toasted and crisp. Remove from oven and allow to cool on the pan. Store in an airtight tin.

Cakes and Tortes

On a sunny day in June, I attended a retirement party at the Arabia porcelain factory in Helsinki. The room was filled with famous people. A long table, covered with a yellow cloth, held flowers in bright summer colors in a centerpiece fully three feet in diameter.

On this important occasion there were three kinds of fancy cakes on the coffeetable, as well as several coffeebreads, cookies, filled pastries, and unfrosted cakes. Guests were offered Finnish champagne and sparkling fruit juice. After champagne toasts we were ushered to the coffee and the delectable choices on the table.

Other occasions on which Scandinavians are likely to be honored with such a lavish coffeetable are birthdays, name days, and anniversaries. Scandinavian cakes and tortes all grace the coffeetable as star attractions, and a major celebration with many guests might call for as many as three (for example, Opera Torte, Danish Othello Cake, and Swedish Almond Butter Torte). However, these rich cakes and tortes are rarely served after a meal.

Some cakes must play supporting roles. In this category are buttery pound cakes and apple cakes. I have included a few chocolate cakes, although Scandinavians generally prefer to eat their chocolate out of hand rather than cook with it. Cakes that support the beloved fresh berries of summer have a special place, and I've included the simplest cheesecake ever (it has only 2 tablespoons of sugar!). This is just a sampling of Scandinavian cakes. So many cakes, so little space!

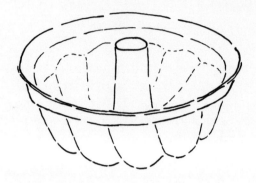

SWEDISH SUGAR CAKE
(*Sokerkaka*)

*T*his cake is meant to be served without a frosting or icing and with just a dusting of powdered sugar. On the fancy Scandinavian coffeetable, it belongs as the "middle" course, to be taken with the second cup of coffee. For the best flavor, pulverize fresh cardamom seeds rather than purchasing ready-ground cardamom.

❖ Makes 12 servings

>   2 cups all-purpose flour
>   1¼ cups sugar
>   2 teaspoons baking powder
>   1 teaspoon freshly pulverized cardamom seed
>   ½ teaspoon salt
>   3 eggs
>   1½ cups whipping cream
>   vanilla wafer crumbs for coating pan

Measure flour, sugar, baking powder, cardamom, salt, eggs, and whipping cream into large mixer bowl. With an electric mixer, blend for 30 seconds on low speed, scraping bowl often. Beat 3 minutes at medium speed. Butter a 9-inch tube-type fancy mold and dust with vanilla wafer crumbs. Pour batter into pan. Bake at 350°F for 55 to 60 minutes or until a toothpick inserted in the center comes out clean. Remove from pan immediately; cool on wire rack.

SWEDISH BRANDY BUTTER POUND CAKE
(*Sandkaka*)

*A*lthough the name is literally translated "sand cake," this cake is really not dry and sandy but is rich and buttery with an even crumb. The original recipe is made with potato flour, but I tried it with cake flour, which resulted in a delicately textured, smooth-grained pound cake.

❖ Makes 12 servings

fine dry bread crumbs for coating pan
1 cup butter, softened or at room temperature
1 cup sugar
4 eggs
2 tablespoons brandy
2 cups cake flour
2 teaspoons baking powder
4 tablespoons water
powdered sugar

Butter a 9-inch fancy tube-type pan. Dust with breadcrumbs. Preheat oven to 350°F.

In a large bowl, cream the butter and sugar until smooth and blended. Add the eggs and brandy and beat until light and lemon colored. Combine the flour and baking powder. Mix into the cake batter and beat until smooth and light, adding water a tablespoon at a time. Pour into the prepared pan. Bake for 45 to 50 minutes or until a skewer inserted in the center comes out clean. Remove from oven, let cool in the pan for 5 minutes, then turn out onto a rack and cool completely. Dust with powdered sugar before serving.

SWEDISH SOFT SPICE CAKE
(*Pepparkaka*)

*T*his cake belongs on the Christmas coffeetable, which traditionally includes highly spiced baked goods. A special elongated, fluted mold is used for this cake; however, you can bake it in a fancy tube-type pan.

❖ Makes 12 to 16 servings

vanilla wafer or zwieback crumbs for coating pan
½ cup butter
1 cup sugar
3 eggs
1 teaspoon cinnamon
1 teaspoon ginger
½ teaspoon cloves
1¾ cups all-purpose flour
1 teaspoon baking soda
⅔ cup dairy sour cream

Preheat oven to 350°F. Butter a 9-inch fancy tube-type pan or Swedish spice cake pan and dust with vanilla wafer crumbs or zwieback crumbs.

In the large bowl of an electric mixer, cream the butter and sugar until smooth; add the eggs and spices and beat until light and fluffy. Mix in the flour, baking soda, and sour cream until batter is smooth. Pour into the prepared pan and bake for 20 to 30 minutes or until the cake tests done. Cool 5 minutes in the pan, then turn out onto a rack and finish cooling.

FRUITCAKE
(*Hedelmäkakku*)

*S*candinavians in general are not fond of fruitcake that is chockful of fruit. They prefer a simple pound cake with raisins and perhaps a few pieces of candied fruit.

❖ Makes one 10-inch cake

> *vanilla wafer crumbs for coating pan*
> *1 cup unsalted butter, room temperature*
> *1 cup sugar*
> *5 eggs*
> *2 cups all-purpose flour*
> *2 teaspoons baking powder*
> *½ teaspoon salt*
> *1⅓ cups golden raisins*
> *3 tablespoons finely chopped candied orange peel*
> *2 tablespoons finely chopped candied fruit-cake fruits*
> *¼ cup finely chopped blanched almonds*

Butter a 10-inch fluted tube-cake mold and dust lightly with vanilla wafer crumbs. Preheat oven to 350°F.

In a large mixing bowl, cream the butter and sugar until blended; add the eggs and beat until light and fluffy.

Mix the flour, baking powder, and salt. In a small bowl, combine the raisins, orange peel, cake fruits, and almonds. Add 1 tablespoon of the flour mixture to the fruits and toss to coat each piece well.

Blend the flour into the creamed mixture, then add the raisin mixture, blending well. Turn into the prepared cake pan and smooth out the batter.

Bake for 50 to 60 minutes or until a wooden skewer inserted in the center comes out clean. Cool 5 minutes before removing from the pan.

NORWEGIAN CARAMEL-ALMOND TOSCA CAKE
(*Toscakage*)

*A*lthough Puccini's opera may have had some influence on the name originally, *Tosca* means to Scandinavians a layer of caramel and almonds staged atop a gold sheet cake.

❖ Makes 10 servings

3 eggs
1 cup sugar
1 teaspoon vanilla
1½ cups all-purpose flour
1½ teaspoons baking powder
¾ cup butter, melted
3 tablespoons milk

TOPPING

⅓ cup butter
½ cup slivered blanched almonds
½ cup sugar
½ cup whipping cream

Beat the eggs until foamy. Add sugar and beat until light and lemon colored; add vanilla. Mix flour with baking powder and fold into the egg mixture until blended. Mix the melted butter and milk and stir into the flour and egg mixture until batter is smooth and blended. Turn into a buttered 10-inch springform pan or an 11- or 12-inch tart pan with a removable bottom. Bake at 350°F for 35 minutes. Meanwhile, prepare the topping. Melt butter in an 8- or 9-inch frying pan. Add almonds, and stir over medium heat until almonds are toasted and golden. Stir in the sugar and cream. Turn heat to high and bring to a vigorous boil, stirring constantly. Boil for 2½ minutes just until mixture begins to become slightly darker tan and thickens slightly. Pour hot topping over cake and place under broiler until topping is bubbly and lightly browned.

SWEDISH FILBERT CAKE
(*Hasselnötskaka*)

*T*his cake is also made with pecans and walnuts, especially by Swedish-Americans. It is delicious served with whipped cream and fresh fruit.

❖ Makes one 9-inch
square or tube cake

zwieback crumbs for coating pan
4 eggs
1¼ cups sugar
2 cups filberts, pulverized or ground
1⅓ cups all-purpose flour
2 teaspoons baking powder
½ cup melted butter
1 cup light cream or half-and-half

Butter a 9-inch fancy tube-type pan or a square pan and dust with zwieback crumbs. Preheat oven to 350°F.

In the large bowl of an electric mixer, beat the eggs until frothy; slowly add the sugar and beat until light and lemon colored, at high speed, about 5 minutes. Fold in the nuts. Sift the flour and baking powder over the mixture and fold in, using a rubber spatula. Blend in the melted butter and cream. Pour into the prepared pan and bake for 45 to 50 minutes until the cake tests done.

SWEDISH CHOCOLATE POUND CAKE
(*Chokladkaka*)

*A*lthough this cake is supposed to be served unfrosted, it is delectable sliced and topped with berries and whipped cream.

❖ Makes one 9-inch cake

vanilla wafer crumbs for coating pan
1¼ cups cake flour
1 teaspoon baking powder
⅓ cup softened butter
¾ cup sugar
2 eggs, separated
1 teaspoon vanilla extract
½ cup semisweet chocolate chips or 4 ounces semisweet
*   chocolate, melted*
½ cup heavy cream

Butter a 9-inch fancy ring mold. Dust evenly with vanilla wafer crumbs. Preheat oven to 300°F.

In a small bowl, stir the flour and baking powder together. In a large mixing bowl, cream the butter with the sugar; add the egg yolks, vanilla, and chocolate; beat until light and fluffy. Add the cream alternately with the flour mixture. Whip the egg whites until stiff and fold into the mixture. Pour into the prepared cake pan. Bake for 50 minutes or until the cake tests done. Let cool in pan 5 minutes, turn out onto a rack, and finish cooling.

NORWEGIAN STRAWBERRIES AND CREAM CAKE
(*Bløtkake*)

*T*his is basically a wonderfully light and eggy sponge cake that absorbs the juices of fresh strawberries and the rather thin custard in its filling. Literally translated the name means "wet cake." Although we call this "Norwegian," it is popular throughout Scandinavia when fresh strawberries are in season. The layers are split and filled with custard, jam, and berries. Whipped cream is piled on top in a cloudlike drift. Scandinavian cooks sink a few beautiful fresh strawberries into the topping for a final garnish.

❖ Makes about 16 servings

¾ *cup cake flour*
1 teaspoon baking powder
6 eggs, separated
1 cup sugar

FILLING

3 egg yolks
2 tablespoons butter
2 tablespoons cornstarch
1½ cups half-and-half
¼ *cup sugar*
2 teaspoons vanilla extract
½ *cup strawberry or apricot jam, warmed and strained*
1 pint fresh strawberries

TOPPING

1½ cups whipping cream
2 tablespoons powdered sugar
1 teaspoon vanilla

Blend flour with baking powder; set aside. In large bowl, whip egg whites until fluffy; gradually add sugar, and beat until stiff and meringuelike. In small bowl, beat egg yolks until frothy. Fold egg yolks and flour mixture into the egg whites. Butter two 9-inch round cake pans and dust with flour. Divide batter between the pans.

Preheat oven to 350°F. Bake layers 30 minutes or until centers spring back when touched with finger. Cool in pans. (Centers of cakes may sink slightly.)

To prepare the custard filling, in small saucepan, mix egg yolks, butter, cornstarch, half-and-half, and sugar. Cook, stirring, over medium heat until mixture is smooth and thick. Remove from heat, cover, and cool. Stir in vanilla.

To assemble the cake, cut layers horizontally into 2 layers each. Place bottom layer on cake plate and spread with half of the custard. Top with next layer. Spread with the strawberry or apricot jam. Reserve a few of the nicest strawberries for garnish on top of the cake. Slice the rest and place on top of jam layer. Top with a third layer of cake. Spread with remaining custard. Top with remaining layer of cake.

No more than 1 hour before serving, whip cream and flavor with the powdered sugar and vanilla. Pile whipped cream on top of the cake and garnish with the reserved strawberries.

OPERA TORTE
(Operatårta)

$\mathcal{W}$hen the effect is dramatic, Scandinavians name their cakes accordingly. Delicate layers of sponge cake are filled with a vanilla cream and topped with almond paste in this cake, which is served as the final fancy course on the coffeetable.

❖ Makes one 9-inch torte

dry bread crumbs for coating pan
4 eggs
$\frac{2}{3}$ cup sugar
$\frac{1}{3}$ cup cake flour

FILLING

1 package unflavored gelatin
2 tablespoons sugar
2 cups whipping cream
1 egg yolk
1 teaspoon vanilla extract

ALMOND PASTE

1 cup blanched almonds
$\frac{2}{3}$ cup powdered sugar
1 egg white
powdered sugar for dusting cake

Butter a 9-inch springform pan and dust with dry bread crumbs. Preheat oven to 350°F.

Separate 3 of the eggs and put the whites into a clean, dry bowl. Beat whites until stiff but not dry; set aside.

In large bowl, beat the 3 egg yolks with 1 whole egg. Add the $\frac{2}{3}$ cup sugar and beat until light and lemon colored. Sift flour over the mixture. Add the beaten egg whites and fold everything together, using a rubber spatula, until dry ingredients and egg whites are blended. Turn into the prepared pan. Bake 25 to 30 minutes until cake springs back when touched.

For the filling, mix gelatin with sugar and 1 cup cream in a heavy saucepan. Heat, stirring, to simmering. Whisk the egg yolk in a little bowl. Whisk a bit of the hot cream into the egg. Return to the saucepan and cook over low heat 1 minute, stirring. Turn into a metal bowl and place over ice. Stir until cooled. Whisk in the remaining cream and whip until light and fluffy. Add the vanilla.

To prepare the almond paste, put almonds through a food chopper with the fine blade in place, or put into food processor with the steel blade in place and process until pulverized. Add the powdered sugar and egg white and blend until smooth and pasty. Chill. Place between sheets of plastic wrap and roll into a circle about 14 inches in diameter. Chill until ready to use.

Cut cake into 3 layers. Spread filling on two layers and stack. Add the third layer.

Peel off one sheet of the plastic wrap from the almond paste and center the paste on the cake, covered side up. Carefully peel off the second layer of plastic wrap. With hands dipped in powdered sugar, carefully press the almond paste onto the top and sides of the cake, and smooth. Dust with powdered sugar and chill until ready to serve.

KING HAAKON'S CAKE
(*Konge Haakon's Kake*)

*I*n Norwegian history there were seven kings and rulers named Haakon. The first was Haakon the Good, who grew up in England as a Christian and brought missionaries to Norway. He was followed by Haakon the Great, Haakon the Broad-Shouldered, and so on down to Haakon VII, who died in 1957. The last Haakon commanded the people's devotion and probably was the one for whom this cake is named. It is a universally popular cake in Norway and is traditionally decorated with almond paste, King Haakon's initials, and small Norwegian flags.

❖ Makes one 10-inch cake

6 eggs, separated
1 cup butter, room temperature
1 cup sugar
2 cups cake flour
1 teaspoon baking powder
$\frac{1}{2}$ cup milk

FILLING

1 cup whipping cream
2 teaspoons cornstarch
3 tablespoons sugar
3 squares unsweetened chocolate
3 egg yolks

ALMOND PASTE

1 cup blanched almonds
$\frac{2}{3}$ cup powdered sugar
1 egg white

FROSTING

1 cup whipping cream
2 tablespoons powdered sugar
$\frac{1}{2}$ teaspoon vanilla

Butter a 10-inch springform pan and dust with flour. Preheat oven to 350°F.

Separate the eggs and put the egg whites into a clean, dry bowl. With hand mixer, beat until whites are stiff but not dry. Set aside.

In a large bowl, using the same mixer without washing the blades, cream the butter and sugar. Add the egg yolks and beat until light and lemon colored.

Sift the flour and baking powder. Blend into the creamed mixture alternately with the milk and beat until smooth. Fold in the egg whites. Turn into the prepared pan and bake for 25 minutes or until center of cake springs back when touched. Cool.

To prepare the filling, combine the cream, cornstarch, sugar, and chocolate in a heavy saucepan. Stir over medium heat until chocolate is melted and mixture has thickened. Beat the egg yolks in a small bowl and add a little of the hot mixture to them. Stir until blended and return to the saucepan. Cook, stirring, over low heat for 1 minute longer. Remove from heat and chill.

To prepare the almond paste, put the almonds into a food processor with the steel blade in place, or grind through a food chopper with the fine blade. Add the powdered sugar, mixing well, and blend in the egg white until mixture is doughlike. Place between sheets of plastic wrap, flatten out to make a 10-inch round, and smooth out the edges. Chill.

To assemble, split the cake into 3 layers. Spread filling over the first and second layers and top with the third layer.

Remove the almond paste topping from refrigerator. Peel off one layer of the plastic wrap. Place over the cake with the covered side up. Remove the second piece of plastic wrap.

Before serving, whip the cream and sweeten it with the powdered sugar; blend in the vanilla. Spread over the sides of the cake.

Chill until ready to serve.

DANISH OTHELLO CAKE
(Otellokage)

$\mathcal{I}$ couldn't discover why Danes call this "Othello" cake, but it probably has a lot to do with their love of Shakespeare. The cake is dramatically layered with one good thing after another. The end result is anything but a tragedy except for its sinful richness!

❖ Makes 12 to 16 servings

3 whole eggs
1 cup sugar
1⅓ cups cake flour
2 teaspoons baking powder
¼ cup milk
2 tablespoons melted butter
1 tablespoon grated orange rind
2 tablespoons lemon juice

MACAROON LAYER

⅔ cup blanched almonds, toasted* and pulverized
⅓ cup powdered sugar
1 teaspoon baking powder
2 egg whites, stiffly beaten

FILLING

4 egg yolks
2 tablespoons sugar
1½ tablespoons cornstarch
1½ cups milk
1 teaspoon vanilla
½ cup whipping cream, whipped

CHOCOLATE ICING

4 ounces semisweet chocolate
2 tablespoons softened unsalted butter
¾ cup powdered sugar
2 tablespoons double-strength coffee
1 tablespoon dark rum

4 ounces (about $\frac{1}{2}$ cup) almond paste
1 egg white
$\frac{1}{2}$ cup powdered sugar
$\frac{1}{2}$ teaspoon almond extract

FROSTING

$1\frac{1}{2}$ cups whipping cream
2 tablespoons powdered sugar

To prepare sponge cake layers, in large bowl, beat eggs and sugar until light and lemon colored. Mix flour and baking powder together and fold into egg mixture with the milk. Last of all fold in the melted butter, orange rind, and lemon juice. Grease and lightly flour two 9-inch round cake pans. Divide batter between pans. Preheat oven to 350°F. Bake for 20 to 25 minutes or until cakes spring back when touched in the center. Cool in pans, then remove.

To prepare macaroon layer, stir almonds, sugar, and baking powder together; fold in the egg whites. Grease and flour, or line with parchment, a 9-inch round cake pan. Spread mixture in the pan and bake in a preheated 350°F oven for 20 to 25 minutes or until top feels dry.

To prepare vanilla custard filling, combine egg yolks, sugar, cornstarch, and milk in a heavy-bottomed saucepan. Cook over medium heat, whisking constantly, until mixture just comes to a boil and is thickened and smooth. Cover and cool. Add vanilla. When completely cool, fold in the whipped cream.

To prepare chocolate icing, in top of double boiler, or in bowl over water, melt chocolate. With a wooden spoon beat in the butter, sugar, coffee, and rum until mixture is glossy and smooth.

To prepare the optional almond paste decoration, mix the almond paste with the egg white, powdered sugar, and almond extract until mixture is a thick but pliable paste.

To assemble cake, place one of the sponge layers on serving plate. Top with half of the custard cream. Add the macaroon layer, and top with remaining half of custard cream. Top with second sponge layer. Spread top with chocolate icing.

If using the almond paste decoration, place almond paste mixture between sheets of plastic wrap and roll out to $\frac{1}{8}$-inch thickness. Cut a 1-inch strip and cut strip into pieces about $1\frac{1}{2}$ inches long. Shape into cornets and place in a ring around the center of the cake on top. Cut remaining almond paste into $\frac{1}{4}$-inch strips. Braid the strips using 3 at a time and place around the edge of the chocolate icing on top.

Whip cream and lightly sweeten with the powdered sugar. Frost the sides of the cake with cream. Refrigerate until ready to serve.

❖ To toast almonds, spread on a baking sheet. Place in oven set at 300°F. Bake 5 to 10 minutes until toasted.

ICELANDIC ALMOND CAKE
(*Möndlurkaka*)

*W*hen fresh strawberries are in season, this cake is luscious with berries between the layers. At other times, use homemade strawberry jam.

❖ Makes 12 to 16 servings

1 cup unsalted butter, room temperature
1 cup sugar
4 eggs, separated
1 teaspoon vanilla
1 cup blanched almonds, finely ground
1 cup cake flour
½ teaspoon baking powder

FILLING

½ cup strawberry jam, preferably homemade or
1 pint fresh strawberries, sliced

FROSTING AND DECORATION

1 cup whipping cream
2 tablespoons powdered sugar
fresh strawberries for garnish
toasted whole almonds for garnish *

Butter three 8-inch round cake pans and line bottom with parchment or waxed paper. Preheat oven to 350°F.

Cream the butter with the sugar. Add the egg yolks and beat until light and fluffy. Add the vanilla and almonds.

Sieve the cake flour and baking powder together into the bowl. Stir into the batter. Beat the egg whites until stiff and fold into the batter.

Divide batter among the cake pans. Bake for 30 minutes or until golden and cakes spring back when touched in the center. Cool 5 minutes, then invert onto cake racks and finish cooling on racks.

Spread strawberry jam between cooled layers. Or, spread 2 layers with sliced strawberries, covering the layers evenly and top with third layer. Whip the cream and sweeten with the powdered sugar. Spread cream over the top and sides of the cake. If you wish, put cream into a pastry bag and press swirls on top and sides of the cake. Decorate with fresh strawberries, arranging whole or halved fresh berries in the center of the cake and arranging toasted almonds around the edge. Or, sprinkle toasted almonds in the center of the cake and arrange whole berries around the edge. Refrigerate until ready to serve.

❖ To toast almonds, spread on a baking sheet. Place in oven set at 300°F. Bake 5 to 10 minutes until toasted.

CINNAMON LAYER CAKE
(*Kanellagkage*)

The layers of this rich cake are very thin and crisp. Although the recipe is Danish, similar cakes are popular in Sweden, Norway, and Finland. This is another cake that belongs on the Scandinavian coffeetable as the last course, which is always a fancy, filled cake.

❖ Makes 12 servings

½ *cup butter, room temperature*
⅓ *cup sugar*
1 *egg*
1½ *cups all-purpose flour*
1½ *teaspoons cinnamon*

FILLING

1 *cup whipping cream*
2 *tablespoons cinnamon-flavored liqueur or creme de cacao*
2 *tablespoons powdered sugar*

ICING

4 *squares (4 ounces) semisweet chocolate*
2 *teaspoons butter*
1 *tablespoon hot water*
½ *cup slivered almonds, toasted*❖

Butter three 8-inch round cake pans and line bottoms with parchment or waxed paper. Butter the paper and dust the sides and bottom with flour. Preheat oven to 425°F.

Cream the butter and sugar until light. Beat in the egg until mixture is fluffy. Blend in the flour and cinnamon. Divide mixture among the 3 prepared pans, spreading it evenly. Layers will be thin. Bake for 8 to 10 minutes until golden. Remove from pans while hot and cool on racks completely before filling and icing.

Whip the cream until stiff. Whip in the liqueur and powdered sugar. Divide the cream between 2 of the layers, stacking them. (Top layer will be iced.) Place in freezer for 30 minutes while preparing the icing.

To make the icing, melt the chocolate in a bowl over hot water. Beat in the butter and hot water.

Put the top layer on cake and pour the icing over it, smoothing it out and allowing it to drip down the sides of the cake. Decorate with almonds. Refrigerate until ready to serve.

◆ To toast almonds, spread on a baking sheet. Place in oven set at 300°F. Bake 5 to 10 minutes until toasted.

ICELANDIC TORTE
(*Vinarterta Hnodud*)

*T*his torte is the traditional celebration cake of Iceland. The layers are cookielike and are sandwiched together with jam and berries or with pureed cooked prunes.

❖ Makes one 8-inch torte

2½ cups all-purpose flour
2 teaspoons baking powder
⅔ cup sugar
1 cup firm butter
2 eggs

BERRY FILLING

¾ cup homemade-style strawberry jam
2 cups sliced fresh strawberries

PRUNE FILLING

1½ cups cooked and pureed prunes
3 tablespoons sugar
4 tablespoons butter

FROSTING

1 cup whipping cream
¼ cup powdered sugar
½ teaspoon vanilla extract

In a large bowl, mix the flour, baking powder, and sugar. Slice the butter into the mixture and, with a pastry blender or finger tips, or with a hand mixer at low speed, mix until the dough resembles coarse crumbs. Blend in the eggs and knead lightly to gather the dough. Divide into 4 parts.

Cover 2 baking sheets with parchment paper or grease and flour the sheets. Draw four 8-inch rounds on the paper. Preheat oven to 400°F.

On a lightly floured board, roll each part of dough out to an 8-inch circle. Transfer onto a prepared baking sheet. Pierce all over with a fork.

Bake for 15 minutes or until golden and crisp. (You may need to bake the layers in shifts. If so, refrigerate the unbaked layers until ready to bake.) Remove from baking sheet and cool on racks.

For jam-and-berry-filled torte, spread 3 of the layers with strawberry jam and cover jam with sliced fresh strawberries. Top with the fourth layer.

For the prune-filled torte, mix the pureed prunes, sugar, and butter until well blended. Spread 3 layers with the filling and cover with the fourth. Dust top of torte with powdered sugar.

Whip the cream and add the powdered sugar and vanilla extract. Pipe whipped cream onto sides and top of the torte.

SWEDISH CHOCOLATE LAYER CAKE
(*Chokladtarta*)

The layers for this nutty, rich layer cake are baked in a jelly roll pan and then cut into rectangles, which are stacked and filled with a chocolaty cream filling, then iced with a thin glaze and garnished with toasted nuts.

❖ Makes 12 to 16 servings

1¼ cups filberts, almonds, walnuts, brazil nuts, or a combination of these nuts, toasted*
6 tablespoons dark cocoa, preferably Dutch-processed
¾ cup butter, room temperature
1¼ cups sugar
4 eggs
breadcrumbs for coating pan

FILLING

1 cup whipping cream
2 egg yolks
¼ cup sugar
1 tablespoon all-purpose flour
4 ounces (4 squares) semisweet chocolate
2 tablespoons dark rum
½ cup cold, unsalted butter, sliced

GLAZE

2 cups powdered sugar
⅔ cup dark cocoa
3 tablespoons hot water
2 to 3 tablespoons dark rum
15 blanched and toasted filberts or almonds* for decoration

For cake layers, fit food processor with steel blade. Put nuts into the work bowl and process until pulverized or grind in a food chopper with a fine blade; add cocoa. In bowl, cream butter and sugar until light. Add eggs, one at a time, and continue creaming until very fluffy. Fold in the cocoa and nut mixture. Butter a 10 × 15-inch jelly roll pan and sprinkle with breadcrumbs. Turn batter into pan and bake at 350°F for 30 minutes. Cut crosswise into 3 layers, 5 × 10 inches each.

To prepare the filling, stir the cream, yolks, sugar, and flour together in a saucepan. Bring to a boil, stirring, and cook until thickened. Break up the chocolate and add to the hot mixture; let it melt into the cream. Stir to blend. Cool completely (place over ice water, stirring constantly, to speed cooling, if desired). With electric mixer, beat in rum and sliced butter until mixture is smooth and fluffy. To assemble chokladtarta, sandwich the cake layers together with the chocolate cream filling. Stack and chill until firm, about 2 hours.

To prepare chocolate glaze, mix powdered sugar, cocoa, water, and rum until icing is smooth. Ice the top and let the icing dribble down the sides of the cake. Decorate the top with toasted nuts. Chill until ready to serve.

◆ To toast nuts, spread on a baking sheet. Place in oven set at 300°F. Bake 5 to 10 minutes until toasted.

NORWEGIAN ALMOND RING CAKE
(*Kransekake*)

Kransekake is the celebration cake of Norway. It is made of almond macaroon rings ranging from about 10 inches in diameter to about 2 inches, stacked in order from the largest on the bottom to the smallest on the top, making an unusual pyramid of cookies. This is the Norwegian wedding cake, birthday cake, anniversary cake, or baptism cake. It can also be a Christmas cake, or a celebration cake for any other special occasion. The center of the cake is hollow; often a bottle of champagne is placed there when the cake is used for a wedding and the champagne saved for the couple's first anniversary. The cake is traditionally decorated with marzipan flowers or candies affixed to the sides with royal icing, or with little Norwegian flags. For a wedding, the cake may be topped with a beautiful rose. The rings are pressed from a pastry tube onto predrawn circles. You can buy kransekake cake forms in Scandinavian import outlets, which make the job much easier!

The traditional cake is made with ground almonds, egg whites, and powdered sugar. Another version is made of butter-cookie dough with almond paste, butter, sugar, egg yolks, and flour. Either version makes a towering cake that will serve about 50 guests (a 2- to 3-inch piece each). Traditionally, the cake is served with a rum cream pudding that is spooned from a cut-glass bowl onto dessert dishes beside the piece of cake.

❖ Makes 50 servings

TRADITIONAL ALMOND PASTE DOUGH

1 pound blanched whole almonds
1 pound powdered sugar
3 egg whites

ALMOND BUTTER-COOKIE DOUGH

2 cups unsalted butter
1 cup almond paste
2 cups powdered sugar
2 teaspoons almond extract
4 egg whites
$4\frac{1}{2}$ to 5 cups all-purpose flour

ICING

2 cups powdered sugar
1 egg white
$\frac{1}{2}$ teaspoon lemon juice

To make the traditional dough, grind the almonds, using the fine blade of a food chopper. Or, put almonds into the food processor with the steel blade in place and process until finely pulverized. Add the powdered sugar and egg whites, blending until the mixture is a thick paste. Place in a metal bowl over boiling water and stir until the mixture is tepid; this softens the mixture and makes it easier to press through a pastry bag.

Grease baking sheets generously and dust with flour. Mark off 18 rings starting at a diameter of 10 inches and making each subsequent ring $\frac{1}{4}$ inch less in diameter, down to 2 inches.

Or, generously grease and flour kransekake ring forms and pipe the mixture into the rings. Place on baking sheets.

Preheat oven to 300°F. Bake for 30 to 35 minutes or until golden. Remove rings from pans while still warm.

To make the butter-cookie dough, in a large mixing bowl, cream the butter, almond paste, and powdered sugar. Add the almond extract and egg whites and beat until smooth. Add the flour to make a stiff but workable cookie dough. Put dough into pastry bag or cookie press with a round tip.

Follow previous directions for shaping and baking.

To prepare the icing, mix together the powdered sugar, egg white, and lemon juice to make a thin icing. Put the icing into a pastry bag with a fine tip.

To assemble the kransekake, mount one ring upon the other, making a tower. Press icing through a pastry bag in a zig-zag pattern on each ring before adding the next. Use the icing to fasten decorations on the cake.

NORWEGIAN PRINCE'S CAKE
(*Fyrstekake*)

*A*lmond-filled butter pastry characterizes cakes that are in some way royal.

❖ Makes one 9-inch cake

$1\frac{1}{2}$ *cups all-purpose flour*
1 teaspoon baking powder
$\frac{1}{2}$ *cup sugar*
$\frac{1}{2}$ *cup plus 1 tablespoon butter, firm, but not hard*
1 egg

FILLING

1 cup unblanched almonds
1 cup powdered sugar
2 egg whites

In a mixing bowl, or in the food processor with the steel blade in place, combine the flour, baking powder, and sugar. Slice the butter and add to the flour mixture. Cut in using a pastry blender or on/off bursts of the food processor until the mixture resembles coarse crumbs. Beat in the egg and mix until a dough forms. Gather dough into a ball and chill.

To prepare the filling, pulverize the almonds in the food processor with the steel blade in place, or put through a food chopper with a fine blade. Blend in the powdered sugar and egg whites until mixture makes a firm dough. Wrap and chill.

Press $\frac{2}{3}$ of the chilled dough into a 9-inch ungreased cake pan, covering bottom and building up the sides of the pan to about 1 inch. Spread almond mixture over the dough.

On a floured board, roll the remaining dough out to $\frac{1}{8}$-inch thickness and cut into $\frac{1}{2}$-inch strips. Crisscross the strips over the filling, fastening them to the edges of the cake. The strips may break but, never mind, they will bake together and look fine. If you have dough scraps, roll into a thin strip and fasten around the top edge of the cake. Preheat oven to 375°F.

Bake for 25 to 30 minutes or until golden brown. Cool completely and cut into thin wedges to serve.

SWEDISH ALMOND BUTTER TORTE
(*Mazarin Torte*)

*T*his is a torte with a butter-rich almond crust, baked in a metal tart pan with an almond butter-cream filling.

❖ Makes 10 to 12 servings

$\frac{3}{4}$ *cup butter*
4 tablespoons powdered sugar
2 egg yolks
1$\frac{1}{4}$ cups all-purpose flour
$\frac{1}{8}$ teaspoon salt
$\frac{2}{3}$ cup unblanched almonds, pulverized

FILLING

2 eggs
$\frac{2}{3}$ cup superfine sugar
3 tablespoons softened unsalted butter
$\frac{2}{3}$ cup blanched almonds, pulverized
2 tablespoons any fruit-flavored liqueur, such as cloud-
    berry, lingonberry, or cranberry
powdered sugar

To prepare crust, in a mixing bowl, cream butter and powdered sugar; add egg yolks and beat until light. Stir in flour, salt, and almonds until mixture is stiff. Press together into a ball. Remove $\frac{1}{4}$ of the mixture. Shape remaining pastry into a ball and place between sheets of waxed paper. Roll out to make a circle 1$\frac{1}{2}$ inches larger than the diameter of a 10- to 11-inch metal tart pan with removable bottom. Peel off one sheet of waxed paper and place pastry, papered side up, into tart pan. Fit into edges carefully without stretching pastry. Remove top paper. With fingers, press pastry firmly onto sides and bottom and cut off excess pastry at top of the pan. Collect scraps and combine with the reserved pastry.

To prepare filling, beat eggs and sugar until light and fluffy; beat in the butter, almonds, and liqueur. Pour mixture into pastry-lined pan. Roll out scraps and cut into $\frac{1}{2}$-inch strips; place on top of filling in a latticework design. Do not worry about the top being perfect, as the pastry bakes into the filling, leaving only a pattern on top of the torte.

Preheat oven to 350°F. Bake for 30 to 35 minutes or until torte is golden. Dust with powdered sugar after cooling. Cut in wedges to serve.

SWEDISH MERINGUE TORTE
(Marängertorta)

*T*his cake is baked with meringue on top. After baking it is cooled and filled with a cream filling or fresh berries or both, then topped with whipped cream (and more berries if they are in season).

❖ Makes 12 servings

¾ cup butter
¾ cup sugar
6 egg yolks
1 teaspoon vanilla
½ teaspoon almond extract
1½ cups cake flour
1½ teaspoons baking powder
¼ teaspoon salt
½ cup milk

MERINGUE

6 egg whites
1 cup sugar
½ teaspoon vanilla
½ cup almonds, finely ground

FILLING

¼ cup cornstarch
1 cup sugar
dash salt
¼ cup water
1½ cups orange juice
¼ cup lemon juice
2 tablespoons grated orange rind
1 tablespoon grated lemon rind
4 egg yolks, beaten
1 pint fresh berries

1 cup whipping cream
2 tablespoons sugar
2 teaspoons vanilla
1 cup slivered almonds, toasted♦*
additional berries

Butter three 9-inch layer cake pans and line bottoms with parchment or waxed paper rounds. Butter again and dust with flour. Preheat oven to 350°F.

To prepare cake, cream butter and sugar; beat in the egg yolks until light and fluffy. Stir in the vanilla and almond extracts. Sieve the flour, baking powder, and salt into the creamed mixture and add the milk. Beat at low speed until blended, increase to high speed and beat for 2 minutes, scraping sides of bowl with spatula, until batter is light and fluffy. Divide batter among the 3 prepared cake pans and spread evenly.

To prepare the meringue, beat the egg whites until stiff. Gradually beat in the 1 cup sugar. Add the vanilla and fold in the almonds. Continue beating until the meringue stands in stiff peaks. Spread meringue evenly on tops of the cake batter, dividing it equally among the 3 pans. Bake for 35 to 40 minutes or until the cakes test done. Cool on racks. Remove from pans carefully.

To prepare the filling, combine the cornstarch, sugar, salt, and water in a saucepan. Add the orange juice, lemon juice, orange and lemon rinds. Cook over medium heat, stirring constantly until smooth and thickened, about 5 minutes. Stir a little of the hot mixture into the egg yolks. Return to the saucepan and cook over low heat for 3 minutes longer, stirring constantly. Remove from heat and beat until cool.

To prepare the topping, whip the cream until stiff; beat in the sugar and vanilla.

To assemble the torte, place 1 cake layer on a serving platter with the meringue side up. Cover with ⅓ of the filling. Add fresh berries if available, and top with the second layer, meringue side up, ⅓ of the filling, and berries. Repeat, placing third layer meringue side up. Pile whipped cream on top of the torte. Sprinkle with toasted almonds and decorate with fresh berries if desired. Refrigerate until ready to serve and cut into wedges.

♦ To toast almonds, spread on a baking sheet. Place in oven set at 300°F. Bake 5 to 10 minutes until toasted.

SWEDISH MOCHA MERINGUE TORTE
(*Mockatarta*)

*M*eringues make the layers in this cake. The filling is a coffee-flavored butter cream. Because the cake should be refrigerated at least a few hours before serving, you can make it a day in advance.

❖ Makes 12 to 16 servings

4 egg whites
½ teaspoon cream of tartar
1¼ cups sugar

FILLING AND FROSTING

½ cup double-strength coffee
1 cup light cream or half-and-half
3 egg yolks
1½ tablespoons cornstarch
1 cup unsalted butter, room temperature
1 cup powdered sugar
1 teaspoon vanilla extract

TOPPING AND DECORATION (OPTIONAL)

1 cup heavy cream
2 tablespoons powdered sugar
⅓ cup slivered almonds, toasted
⅓ cup coffee-filled candies

To prepare layers, in a large mixing bowl, beat egg whites until frothy; add cream of tartar and beat until stiff and meringuelike, adding sugar 1 tablespoon at a time while beating. Cover baking sheets with parchment paper, or grease and flour; with a pencil draw two 9-inch circles on the baking surface. Spread meringue evenly within the circles on the baking sheet. Preheat oven to 250°F and bake the layers 2 to 2½ hours or until layers are totally dry. If desired, you may make the layers the night before and leave them in the turned-off oven until morning after baking. Meringues will be a creamy yellow in color.

To prepare filling and frosting, mix coffee, cream, egg yolks, and cornstarch in a heavy-bottomed saucepan or in top of a double boiler. Cook over moderately high heat, beating at high speed with electric mixer until thick and smooth. Remove from heat, cover, and cool to room temperature. In small bowl, cream butter and sugar. Add vanilla extract and gradually stir in the thickened and cooled coffee mixture a tablespoonful at a time. Beat vigorously with electric mixer until smooth.

To assemble torte, place one meringue on serving plate. Spread 1 cup of the filling over the meringue. Top with second meringue. Spread remaining filling over the top. If desired, whip the cream and add the powdered sugar; spread around the edges of the torte. Garnish top with the toasted almonds and coffee-filled candies. Refrigerate 3 to 4 hours before serving.

◆ To toast almonds, spread on baking sheet. Place in oven set at 300°F. for 5 to 10 minutes until toasted.

FINNISH CRUSTLESS CHEESECAKE
(*Rahkapaistos*)

*T*his is a delicious soft, slightly sweetened cheesecake that does not have a crust. It borders on being a custard but has a texture similar to that of a classic cheesecake. Serve it in slender wedges, topped with fresh fruit or berries and thinned berry jam or softly whipped cream.

❖ Makes 10 servings

2 cups ricotta cheese or small-curd creamed cottage
  cheese
2 cups dairy sour cream
5 eggs
2 tablespoons sugar
2 teaspoons vanilla extract
fresh berries or jam
1½ cups whipping cream
2 tablespoons powdered sugar

Butter an 11-inch tart pan. Preheat oven to 350°F.

Combine the ricotta or cottage cheese, sour cream, eggs, sugar, and vanilla extract in the blender and process until smooth.

Pour mixture into the prepared pan and bake for 40 to 50 minutes or until just set. Serve warm or chilled, topped with fresh berries or berry jam thinned with a few tablespoons of fruit juice or fruit-flavored liqueur; or, whip the cream with the powdered sugar and spread on cake.

JAAKKO'S DREAM TORTE
(*Jaakon Unelmakääretorttu*)

*J*aakko Kolmonen is a chef on Finnish television. His rolled cake is delicate and simple to make. Use whatever fresh fruit or berries are in season. In Finland, it's likely to be wild strawberries in the spring-time, sun-drenched raspberries in the summer, and cloudberries later on in the fall. Finns often use a finely textured, fresh milk cheese called *rahka* in combination with whipped cream in cake fillings to stabilize the cream. Ricotta makes an acceptable substitute.

❖ Makes one roll serving 6 to 8

4 eggs
½ cup sugar
¾ cup all-purpose flour
1 teaspoon baking powder
powdered sugar

FILLING

1 cup ricotta cheese
1 cup whipping cream
¼ cup powdered sugar
1 teaspoon vanilla
4 cups fresh strawberries, blackberries, raspberries, cloudberries, or blueberries

Line a 15 × 10-inch jelly roll pan with parchment or waxed paper and butter bottom and sides of the pan. Dust with flour. Preheat oven to 375°F.

In the large bowl of an electric mixer, beat the eggs until foamy. Add the sugar gradually and continue beating until light and lemon colored, about 5 minutes at high speed. Sift the flour and baking powder together over the mixture and carefully fold in using a rubber spatula.

Turn mixture into the prepared pan and spread evenly to the edges and corners. Bake for 8 to 10 minutes until the top springs back when touched.

While cake is baking tear off a doubled length of paper toweling, folding it to about 18 inches in length. Generously dust the toweling with powdered sugar.

When cake is baked, loosen the edges and invert immediately onto the sugar-dusted towel. Peel off the parchment or waxed paper and roll up the cake, starting at a narrow end, rolling the towel into the cake. Allow to cool completely.

To prepare the filling, combine the ricotta and whipping cream in a bowl and beat at high speed until rather stiffly whipped. Blend in the powdered sugar and vanilla.

Carefully unroll the cake. Spread with the creamy mixture and berries. Roll up again. Place on serving plate and chill, covered, until ready to serve.

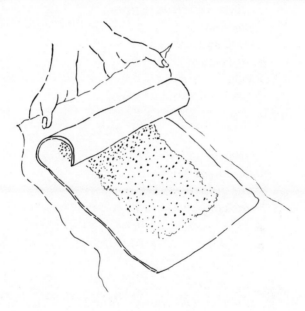

MANOR HOUSE APPLE TORTE
(Herregårdstarta)

The buttery crust holds in the juices of the apples; if you cut into this torte when it is still steaming hot, they almost burst out. It is, however, best to cool the torte before serving so flavors have time to meld. Select apples that are tart, flavorful, but not overly juicy. As is typical of many European apple tortes, there is no thickening agent mixed with the apples to cloud the rich flavors.

❖ Makes 12 servings

2½ *cups all-purpose flour*
1 *cup butter*
½ *teaspoon salt*
¼ *cup sugar*
1 *egg*
2 *tablespoons cold water*

FILLING

2 *pounds tart cooking apples, about 6*
½ *cup sugar*
½ *cup golden raisins*
½ *cup chopped toasted filberts**

TOPPING

⅓ *cup butter*
⅓ *cup brown sugar, packed*
¼ *cup chopped toasted filberts**
powdered sugar to dust over top (optional)
1½ *cups whipping cream*
2 *tablespoons powdered sugar*

Measure flour into mixing bowl or work bowl of food processor fitted with the steel blade. Cut butter into slices and rub into flour, or process until mixture is the texture of coarse crumbs. Add salt, sugar, egg, and water; mix or process until dough forms. Wrap dough in plastic and chill about 1 hour.

Preheat oven to 400°F. Divide dough into 2 parts and roll each part to make a circle 12 inches in diameter. Fit 1 circle into a lightly greased 10-inch springform pan, bringing up the edge inside the pan about 1 inch all around. Pare, core, and slice the apples. Lay in an even circle on top of the pastry in the pan, overlapping slices; make two layers of apples, and sprinkle each with half of the sugar, raisins, and nuts. Top with second round of pastry. Press pastry around edges to seal to the bottom layer of pastry.

Cream the butter and sugar for the topping and add the chopped nuts. Spread this over the top and pierce all over with a fork. Place pan on another rimmed pan to catch any butter that may ooze out between pieces of the springform pan. Bake for 45 to 50 minutes until golden brown. Cool to room temperature. Dust with powdered sugar if desired. Serve plain or softly whip the cream with the powdered sugar and spread over the torte.

❖ To toast nuts, spread on a baking sheet. Place in oven set at 300°F. Bake 5 to 10 minutes until toasted.

SWEDISH APPLE DUMPLING CAKE
(*Appelkäka*)

*T*his is a cross between a cake, a dessert, and a coffeecake. It is an interesting blend of almonds and apples in both flavor and texture.

❖ Makes one 9-inch square

4 large, tart cooking apples, pared
$\frac{1}{2}$ cup sugar
2 cups water
2 tablespoons fresh lemon juice
zwieback crumbs, vanilla wafer crumbs, or fine dry breadcrumbs
3 eggs, separated
$\frac{1}{2}$ cup butter
$\frac{2}{3}$ cup sugar
$\frac{1}{2}$ cup blanched almonds, ground or pulverized
$\frac{2}{3}$ cup all-purpose flour
2 teaspoons lemon juice

½ cup powdered sugar
2 to 3 tablespoons whipping cream
1 teaspoon almond extract

Cut the pared apples into halves lengthwise. Cut off the core and stem ends and scoop out the seeds using a melon baller or a round measuring spoon.

In a saucepan, combine the ½ cup sugar, water, 2 tablespoons lemon juice, and the apples. Bring to a boil, lower heat to simmering, and cook 8 minutes until the apples are just barely tender.

Butter a 9-inch square cake pan and dust it heavily with zwieback crumbs, vanilla wafer crumbs, or breadcrumbs.

Preheat oven to 350°F.

Drain the apples and place them with their cut sides down into the cake pan.

Separate the eggs and, with a hand mixer, beat the whites until stiff. Set aside.

In another bowl, without washing the beaters, cream the butter and ⅔ cup sugar. Add the egg yolks, ground almonds, flour, and 2 teaspoons lemon juice. Mixture will be stiff. Blend in the egg whites and spread mixture over the apples in the pan. Bake for 25 to 30 minutes until golden.

While cake bakes, mix the icing ingredients. Drizzle hot cake with the icing.

DANISH APPLE CAKE
(*Aeblekage*)

*B*y tradition, the Danish are connoisseurs of home baking. Even though they are known worldwide for rich and buttery Danish pastry, they do not limit themselves to just that. Apples are a favorite ingredient and theme for coffee and dessert cakes such as this one. Danish cakes are also pretty to look at. For instance, this one is a golden butter cake topped with apple halves that are sliced, kept intact, and pressed into the top of the dough before baking.

❖ Makes one 11-inch cake

$\frac{1}{2}$ cup butter, room temperature
$\frac{3}{4}$ cup sugar
3 eggs
1 teaspoon vanilla
$\frac{1}{4}$ cup milk
$1\frac{1}{2}$ cups all-purpose flour
$1\frac{1}{2}$ teaspoons baking powder
5 Granny Smith or Golden Delicious apples,
    pared and cored
2 tablespoons melted butter
2 tablespoons sugar

Butter an 11-inch tart pan with a removable bottom or a 9-inch square cake pan. Preheat oven to 375°F.

In a large bowl, cream the butter and sugar until blended. Add the eggs and vanilla and beat until light and fluffy. Blend in the milk. Combine the flour and baking powder and stir into the mixture to make a rather stiff batter. Spread in the pan.

Cut each apple in half, making the cut along the core. Place each half flat side down and make $\frac{1}{4}$-inch crosswise cuts from the rounded side toward the flat side of each half. Keep the slices together so that the shape of the apple is intact. Press whole apple halves, one at a time, flat side down into the dough in the pan, spacing them evenly. Brush with the 2 tablespoons melted butter and sprinkle with the 2 tablespoons sugar. Bake for 30 to 40 minutes or until golden and apples are tender when pierced with a skewer. Serve warm with ice cream.

SWEDISH APPLE CAKE
(*Sockerkaka med Äpplen*)

*C*akes ranging from sponge cakes with whole eggs or only egg yolks to rich pound-cakelike bases are favorites in all of the Scandinavian countries in the fall when tart apples are in season. One is hard pressed to pick out the very best recipe! This one is baked in a springform pan and has a topping of apples rolled in sugar and cinnamon along with sliced almonds.

❖ Makes one 10-inch round cake

> *vanilla wafer or zwieback crumbs*
> *⅔ cup butter, room temperature*
> *1 cup sugar*
> *4 eggs*
> *1¾ cups all-purpose flour*
> *1 teaspoon baking powder*
> *4 small tart apples, pared and cut into 8 sections each*
> *2 tablespoons sugar*
> *2 teaspoons ground cinnamon*
> *½ cup sliced almonds*
> *¼ cup simple syrup**
> *¼ cup light rum*
> *½ cup powdered sugar*
> *2 to 3 teaspoons rum or water*

Butter a 10-inch springform pan and sprinkle with vanilla wafer or zwieback crumbs. Preheat oven to 350°F.

In a large mixing bowl, cream the butter and sugar until blended. Add the eggs and beat until light and fluffy.

Combine the flour and baking powder. Mix into the creamed mixture until well blended. Turn mixture into the prepared baking pan.

Put the apples into a bowl and add the sugar and cinnamon. Toss until apples are coated with the mixture. Press into the cake batter. Sprinkle any remaining cinnamon mixture from the bowl over the top along with the sliced almonds.

Bake for 40 to 45 minutes until the cake tests done. Remove from oven. Heat the simple syrup to boiling and add the rum. Pour over the hot cake. Cool completely, then remove from the pan.

Mix the powdered sugar and rum and drizzle over the cake decoratively.

❖ To make simple syrup, heat ½ cup water to boiling. Add 1 cup sugar and 1 teaspoon light corn syrup. Boil 1 minute, stirring, until sugar is completely dissolved. Cool and store in a jar.

NORWEGIAN APPLE PIE
(*Eplepai*)

*A*lthough this is called a "pie" in Norway, we would think of it as a cake. Incredibly simple to make, it's a perfect last-minute dessert when fresh apples are in season.

❖ Makes one 9-inch pie

1 egg
¾ cup sugar
1 teaspoon vanilla extract
1 teaspoon baking powder
¼ teaspoon salt
1 teaspoon cinnamon
½ cup all-purpose flour
½ cup chopped almonds
3 medium-sized tart apples, pared, cored, and diced

TOPPING

1 cup whipping cream
2 tablespoons powdered sugar

Preheat oven to 350°F. Butter a 9-inch pie pan generously. Stir all the pie ingredients together in a bowl until blended. Mixture will be stiff. Spoon into the pie pan. Bake 30 minutes or until browned. To serve, cut into wedges. Whip the cream with the powdered sugar to accompany the cake or serve with ice cream.

DANISH CARROT CAKE
(*Dansk Ostekage*)

*A*lthough the name literally translates as "cheese cake," this cake is golden with shredded carrot and is topped with a cream cheese frosting.

❖ Makes 9 servings

¾ cup melted butter
¾ cup sugar
¾ cup finely shredded, pared carrot
½ teaspoon salt
1 teaspoon ground cinnamon
2 eggs
2 tablespoons aquavit or vanilla
1½ cups all-purpose flour
1½ teaspoons baking powder
½ cup golden or dark raisins

FROSTING

¼ cup butter, room temperature
1 (3-ounce) package cream cheese, room temperature
1 cup powdered sugar
½ cup slivered or sliced almonds, toasted❖

Butter an 8-inch square cake pan. Preheat oven to 350°F.

In a large bowl, beat the melted butter with the sugar, carrot, salt, cinnamon, eggs, and aquavit or vanilla until light. Mix the flour and baking powder and stir into the batter. Stir in the raisins. Pour into the prepared pan.

Bake for 30 to 35 minutes until the cake springs back when lightly touched in the center.

To make the frosting, beat the butter, cream cheese, and sugar until smooth. Spread frosting over the cake. With the tines of a fork, make a decorative pattern on the top of the cake. Sprinkle with the almonds.

❖ To toast nuts, spread on a baking sheet. Place in oven set at 300°F. Bake 5 to 10 minutes until toasted.

Pastries and Pies

*I*t was at Gustafson's Cafe and Bakery in Duluth, Minnesota, that I met the love of my life — flaky, buttery, almond-and-fruit-filled Danish pastries. Accompanying my father to Duluth was a special treat. He'd give me some money to shop for presents for my brothers and sisters at home, but the highlight of my shopping was the break I gave myself to enjoy a glass of milk and an almond Danish pastry. Gustafson's bakery was razed many years ago, but not from my memories!

Traveling in Scandinavia, I gathered more ideas to expand my repertoire, not only with different ways to fill and shape pastries, but with other wonderful choices. This chapter is filled with classics from Norway, Sweden, Iceland, and Denmark, as well as with some of my favorites from Finland.

I've included pancakes and waffles here, too, because they seem to fit this category of baking better than any other in the book.

CLASSIC DANISH PASTRY
(*Viennabrød*)

*K*nown as "Danish" the world over, except in Denmark, where it is "Vienna bread," this is the Danes' classic coffeebread. Light, buttery, only slightly sweet, and delicately perfumed with cardamom, the dough encases a small amount of well-flavored nut or fruit filling. This is the original method of preparing the basic dough; a soft yeasted dough is rolled out with a layer of butter, which when folded and rolled creates layers of flaky sweet pastry. A faster method follows.

❖ Makes about 24 servings

1½ cups chilled, unsalted butter
2 packages active dry yeast
½ cup warm water, 105°F to 115°F
½ cup heavy cream or undiluted evaporated
*   milk, warmed*
½ teaspoon freshly crushed cardamom seed (optional)
½ teaspoon salt
2 eggs, room temperature
¼ cup sugar
3¾ to 4 cups all-purpose flour

Slice butter into lengthwise pieces and place between sheets of plastic wrap. Roll out to make an 8-inch square. Refrigerate while preparing and chilling the yeast dough.

In a large bowl, dissolve the yeast in the warm water. Let stand 5 minutes. Add the cream or milk, cardamom seed if used, salt, eggs, and sugar. With a spoon, beat in 3 cups flour; continue beating until smooth and elastic. Stir in ½ cup more flour and beat again until smooth, about 2 minutes. Dough will be soft. Cover and chill at least 30 minutes or up to 8 hours.

Turn chilled dough out onto a floured board and roll out to make a 16-inch square. Unwrap chilled butter and place over half the pastry, Step 1. Fold uncovered half over the butter and press edges to seal together, Step 2. Roll dough out to make as large a square as possible, bursting bubbles as they show up and resealing holes. Fold into thirds, making 3 layers, Step 3. Dust with additional flour if necessary. Turn dough and roll again to make a long, narrow shape,

Step 4. Fold from the short sides into thirds; dough will end up about square. Repeat rolling out and folding the dough in the same manner 3 more times. Chill between steps if necessary to keep the dough cold and to keep the butter from melting. Chill 30 minutes before shaping. During the last chilling get out the baking sheets and fillings. (You may prepare the dough to this point a day in advance and finish shaping and filling it the next day.) For filling, shaping, and baking follow directions in the recipes that follow.

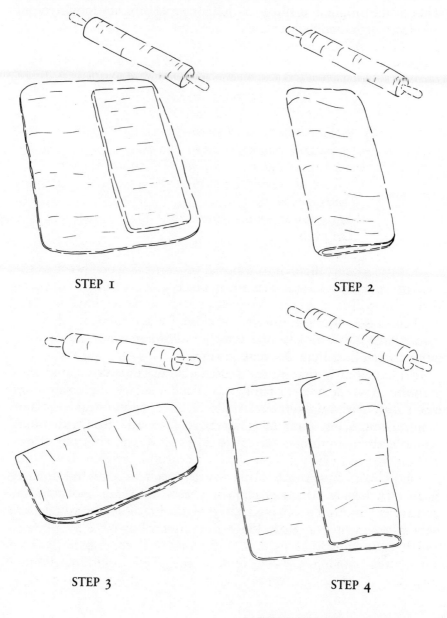

STEP 1

STEP 2

STEP 3

STEP 4

QUICK METHOD DANISH PASTRY
(*Viennabrød*)

*H*ere is a quick method for making Danish. Rather than folding and rolling a layer of butter into a yeast dough, the butter is first *cut into* the dough as in making pie crust. I like this method of making the dough and refrigerating it overnight. You can get by without the folding and rolling, but I like to do it a couple of times to flatten out the pieces of butter that are mixed into the yeast dough.

❖ Makes about 24 servings

$3\frac{3}{4}$ to 4 cups all-purpose flour
$1\frac{1}{2}$ cups chilled unsalted butter
2 packages active dry yeast
$\frac{1}{2}$ cup warm water, 105°F to 115°F
$\frac{1}{2}$ cup heavy cream or undiluted evaporated milk
$\frac{1}{2}$ teaspoon freshly crushed cardamom seed (optional)
$\frac{1}{2}$ teaspoon salt
2 eggs, room temperature
$\frac{1}{4}$ cup sugar

Measure $3\frac{1}{2}$ cups flour into a bowl, or into the work bowl of the food processor with the steel blade in place. Cut the butter into $\frac{1}{4}$-inch slices and add to the flour. Process or cut the butter into the flour until the butter is about the size of kidney beans.

In a large bowl, dissolve the yeast in the warm water. Let stand 5 minutes. Stir in the cream or milk, cardamom, salt, eggs, and sugar.

Turn the flour-butter mixture into the liquid ingredients, and with a rubber spatula mix carefully just until the dry ingredients are moistened. Cover and refrigerate 4 hours, overnight, or up to 4 days.

Turn dough out onto a lightly floured board; dust with flour. Pound and flatten to make a 16- to 20-inch square. Fold into thirds making 3 layers. Turn dough around and roll out again. Fold from the short sides into thirds. This should result in a perfect square. Repeat folding and rolling again if you wish. Wrap and chill the dough 30 minutes or as long as overnight. For filling, shaping, and baking, follow directions in the recipes that follow.

DANISH BIRTHDAY PRETZEL
(Fødselsdagskringle)

I have served this pretzel with birthday candles pressed into the top of the twist. It's perfect for a breakfast birthday party!

❖ Makes 1 large pretzel, 12 servings

1 recipe Danish Pastry, Classic or Quick Method

FILLING AND DECORATION

¼ cup soft butter
½ cup powdered sugar
1 cup almond paste
1 cup almonds, pulverized
½ cup raisins or currants
½ teaspoon almond extract
1 egg
1 slightly beaten egg white for brushing the pretzel
granulated or pearl sugar for topping
chopped almonds for topping

Cover 1 large baking sheet with parchment paper or lightly grease it.

Roll pastry out on a lightly floured surface to make a 12-inch square. Fold into thirds and roll out, stretching it as you are rolling it, to make a 24-inch-long strip. Fold into thirds again lengthwise and roll to flatten the layers together.

To prepare the filling, cream together the butter, powdered sugar, almond paste, pulverized almonds, raisins, almond extract, and egg to make a smooth paste. Spread filling down the length of the strip of dough. Roll up, jelly-roll fashion, from the long side to make a long, narrow roll. Pinch seam to seal.

Continue rolling the strip of dough to stretch it out to about 48 inches in length. Brush all sides of the roll with egg white and roll in sugar and chopped almonds until well coated on all sides.

Place roll on the parchment paper curved like a U, with the ends even as shown. About 5 inches from the ends, loop sides of the U around each other and tuck ends under the closed part of the U to make a simple pretzel shape. Let rise in a warm place about 40 minutes. It will not double. Preheat oven to 375°F. Bake for 20 to 30 minutes or until just golden. Do not overbake.

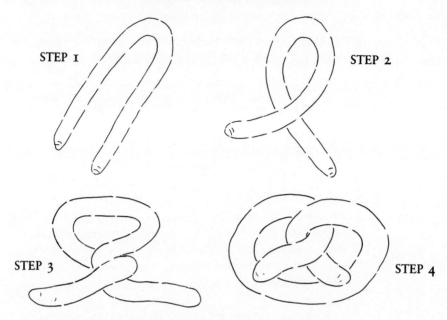

STEP 1

STEP 2

STEP 3

STEP 4

DANISH PASTRY BRAID
(*Wienerflåta*)

To make this mock braid, you start out with one batch of the basic Danish Pastry dough. The braid is shaped by slashing the edges of the rolled-out dough, and the resulting strips are folded over the filling.

❖ Makes 2 filled braids

1 recipe Danish Pastry, Classic or Quick Method

BUTTER CREAM FILLING

¼ *cup soft butter*
1 cup powdered sugar
1 teaspoon almond extract
1 cup pulverized almonds
1 (3-ounce) package almond paste
1 egg white

1 slightly beaten egg
2 tablespoons milk or water
pearl sugar or crushed sugar cubes for topping
chopped or sliced almonds for topping

ICING

1 cup powdered sugar
2 to 3 teaspoons warm water
½ teaspoon almond extract

Cover baking sheets with parchment paper or lightly grease and dust them with flour.

Divide chilled dough into 2 parts. Roll out each part to make a rectangle 12 × 6 inches. Place strips on prepared baking sheets.

To make the filling, cream the butter and sugar until light. Blend in the almond extract, almonds, almond paste, and egg white.

Spread filling down the length of the center of the strip. Cut slanting strips at ¾-inch intervals along both sides up toward the center using a fluted pastry wheel. Fold strips over the filling in a crisscross manner.

Preheat oven to 400°F.

Let rise for 15 to 30 minutes, just until the pastry appears puffy. It will not double. Beat the egg with the milk or water to make a glaze and brush the pastry lightly with it. Sprinkle with sugar and/or chopped almonds.

Bake about 15 minutes or until golden.

Frost, if desired, with almond water icing. Blend the sugar, water, and almond extract until smooth and thin enough to drizzle over the braids.

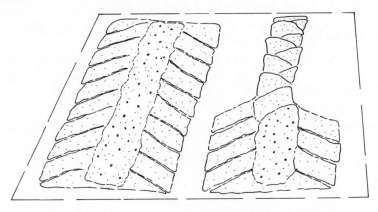

MAYOR'S BRAIDS
(Borgmästarfläta)

*E*ach of the strands in mayor's braids is stuffed with an almond filling.

❖ Makes 2 braids

1 recipe Danish Pastry, Classic or Quick Method

FILLING

$\frac{1}{2}$ *cup softened butter*
1 cup powdered sugar
$\frac{1}{2}$ *cup almond paste*
$\frac{1}{2}$ *cup almonds, pulverized*
$\frac{1}{2}$ *teaspoon almond extract*
1 egg white

GLAZE AND TOPPING

1 beaten egg
2 tablespoons granulated sugar
$\frac{1}{4}$ *cup sliced almonds*
powdered sugar

Cover 2 large baking sheets with parchment paper or lightly grease them.

Roll pastry out on a lightly floured surface to make an 18 × 14-inch rectangle. Cut in half lengthwise; cut each half lengthwise into thirds, making 6 strips in all.

Mix the butter, powdered sugar, almond paste, almonds, almond extract, and egg white until smooth and blended.

Spread $\frac{1}{6}$ of the filling down the center of each strip. Fold edges over to enclose the filling and pinch to seal.

Using 3 strips at a time, braid loosely with the seam side down. Place on the prepared baking sheet and seal both ends.

Let rise in a cool place for 30 to 45 minutes, or cover with plastic wrap and refrigerate overnight.

Preheat oven to 375°F. Brush pastries with beaten egg. Sprinkle with sugar and almonds. Bake 20 to 25 minutes or until puffed and golden. Sprinkle with powdered sugar and serve warm.

DANISH ENVELOPES
(*Konvolute*)

*E*nvelopes may be made as a large pastry that can be cut up for serving or as individual pastries.

❖ Makes 4 large pastries or 25 individual pastries

1 recipe Danish Pastry, Classic or Quick Method

FILLING AND DECORATION

1 cup raspberry or apricot preserves
½ cup almond paste
1 slightly beaten egg
powdered sugar

Cover 2 large baking sheets with parchment paper or lightly grease them. Roll pastry out on a lightly floured surface to make a 20-inch square. For large pastries, cut into 4 equal squares. Place on baking sheets.

Mix the preserves and almond paste until blended. Spoon ¼ of the mixture across the center of each of the squares. Fold over two opposite corners to partially cover the filling, and pinch together to fasten. Place 2 envelopes, 4 inches apart, on each prepared baking sheet. Let rise in a cool place for 30 to 45 minutes or cover with plastic wrap and refrigerate overnight.

Preheat oven to 375°F. Brush pastries with beaten egg. Bake 20 to 25 minutes or until puffed and golden. Sprinkle with powdered sugar and serve warm.

For individual pastries, cut rolled-out dough into 4-inch squares. Dot each square with the mixture of preserves and almond paste. Fold two opposite corners of each square over to partially cover the filling. Place on prepared baking sheets 2 inches apart.

Let rise in a cool place for 30 to 45 minutes, or cover with plastic wrap and refrigerate overnight. Bake at 375°F for 8 to 10 minutes until golden. Sprinkle with powdered sugar and serve warm.

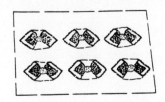

DANISH PECAN SNAILS
(*Snegler*)

*S*nails are usually filled with almond paste or a cinnamon and sugar mixture. Pecans are a Danish-American invention. And a good one!

❖ Makes 24 snails

1 recipe Danish Pastry, Classic or Quick Method

FILLING

½ cup softened butter
1 cup light or dark brown sugar, packed
1 cup finely chopped pecans
1 teaspoon cinnamon
1 slightly beaten egg

ICING

1 cup powdered sugar
3 to 4 teaspoons hot coffee

Place paper cupcake liners in 24 muffin cups.

Roll pastry out on a lightly floured surface to make a 20-inch square. Spread with the butter. Sprinkle with the brown sugar, pecans, and cinnamon.

Roll up jelly-roll fashion. Cut into 24 slices. Place slices with cut side up into each of the muffin cups.

Let rise in a cool place for 30 to 45 minutes, or cover with plastic wrap and refrigerate overnight.

Preheat oven to 375°F. Brush pastries with beaten egg. Bake 20 to 25 minutes or until puffed and golden.

Mix the powdered sugar with the coffee. Drizzle the icing over the hot pastries. Serve warm.

DANISH BEARCLAWS OR COCKSCOMBS
(*Kamme*)

*T*hese pastries have many names. Sometimes they're called "scrubbing brushes." Scandinavian-Americans are more likely to call these "bearclaws," but some Danes insist that they look like the comb on a rooster!

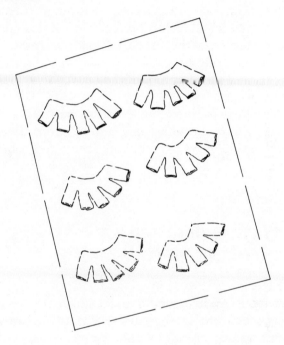

❖ Makes 16 bearclaws

1 recipe Danish Pastry, Classic or Quick Method

FILLING AND DECORATION

1 egg white
½ cup almond paste
¾ cup powdered sugar
1 slightly beaten egg to brush bearclaws
pearl sugar or crushed sugar cubes for topping
sliced almonds for topping

Cover 2 large baking sheets with parchment paper or lightly grease and flour them.

On a lightly floured surface, roll the chilled pastry out to make an 18 × 16-inch rectangle. Cut lengthwise into 4 strips.

In a small bowl, beat the egg white, add the almond paste and powdered sugar, and mix until smooth and blended.

Spread about 2 tablespoons filling down the center of each strip. Fold strips lengthwise to enclose the filling. Roll lightly to flatten and seal the edges. Cut each strip into 4-inch lengths. Make 7 cuts on each of the 4-inch lengths, cutting from the sealed edge toward the center. Place pieces on the prepared baking sheets, curving them slightly to separate the slits.

Let rise in a cool place until puffy, or cover with plastic wrap and refrigerate overnight.

To bake, preheat oven to 400°F. Brush pastries with beaten egg, then sprinkle generously with sugar and almonds. Bake 5 to 8 minutes until golden. Remove from baking sheets and cool on wire rack. Serve warm.

OLD DANISH CHRISTMAS KRINGLE
(*Dansk Smørekringle*)

*T*his legendary pastry symbolizes Danish *hygge,* or the "comfortable and good" life. It is always served at Christmas and Easter, as well as on special occasions and anniversaries. Although Danes use any fruit or nut filling in a *kringle,* almond filling is the favorite.

❖ Makes 1 large kringle

1 package active dry yeast
$\frac{1}{4}$ cup warm water, 105°F to 115°F
$\frac{1}{4}$ cup undiluted evaporated milk, room temperature
1 teaspoon freshly ground cardamom seeds (optional)
$\frac{1}{4}$ cup sugar
3 egg yolks
1 cup whipping cream
$3\frac{1}{2}$ cups all-purpose flour
1 teaspoon salt
$\frac{1}{2}$ cup butter, chilled

RAISIN-ALMOND FILLING

1½ cups water
1½ cups golden raisins
½ cup softened butter
½ teaspoon freshly pulverized cardamom seeds
2 cups powdered sugar
2 tablespoons heavy cream
½ cup chopped almonds

ALMOND FILLING

1 cup, about ½ pound, almond paste
½ cup finely chopped almonds
½ cup powdered sugar
1 egg white
1 teaspoon almond extract

PRUNE-PORT FILLING

1 (12-ounce) package pitted prunes
¾ cup sugar
⅓ cup red port wine

GLAZE AND TOPPING

1 slightly beaten egg white
pearl sugar or coarsely crushed sugar cubes or granulated sugar
sliced almonds

In a medium bowl, dissolve the yeast in the warm water. Let stand
5 minutes. Add the milk, cardamom, ¼ cup sugar, egg yolks, and
whipping cream. Set aside.

In a large bowl, or in the work bowl of a food processor with the
steel blade in place, combine the flour and salt. Cut in the butter until
butter pieces are the size of kidney beans or process. Add the yeast
mixture, mixing only until dry ingredients are moistened. Cover with
plastic wrap and refrigerate 12 to 24 hours. Meanwhile, prepare the
fillings and have them ready.

To make the raisin-almond filling, bring water to a boil; add the
raisins, let stand 5 minutes, and drain. Cool.

In a bowl, cream the butter until soft, and add the cardamom, powdered sugar, and enough cream to make a smooth, spreadable mixture. Add the raisins and chopped almonds.

To make the almond filling, break almond paste into pieces and blend with the almonds, powdered sugar, egg white, and almond extract to make a smooth paste. (This may be easiest to accomplish in the food processor.)

To make the prune-port filling, cook the prunes in water to cover until tender. Mash. Add the sugar and mix until dissolved. Stir in the port. Return to the pan and simmer until mixture is thick, about 5 minutes.

Turn dough out onto lightly floured board, and dust with flour. Using a rolling pin, pound dough until smooth and about $\frac{3}{4}$-inch thick. Roll out to make a 24-inch square. Fold dough into thirds to make a long and narrow strip. With rolling pin, roll again until about $\frac{1}{4}$-inch thick and about 36 inches long.

Spread the length of the roll up to 1 inch in from the edges with the filling. Roll up from the long side, enclosing the filling. Brush roll with egg white, then roll in sugar.

Cover a baking sheet with parchment paper or lightly grease and flour the sheet. Place the roll on the baking sheet in the shape of a large pretzel. Let rise in a warm place for 45 minutes. It will not double. Preheat oven to 375°F.

Brush kringle again with egg white and sprinkle with sliced almonds. Bake for 25 to 30 minutes or until golden.

DANISH RAISIN-ALMOND RING
(*Mandelkrans*)

*T*his method of folding and rolling Danish pastry is a little different from that for the Classic Danish Pastry but is another favorite formula for the dough.

❖ Makes 2 rings

2 packages active dry yeast
½ cup warm water, 105°F to 115°F
2 tablespoons sugar
3 eggs, beaten
¼ cup sour cream
2 tablespoons white wine
½ teaspoon salt
4 cups all-purpose flour
1 cup butter, firm, but not hard, sliced

FILLING

1 cup raisins
6 tablespoons sugar
½ cup unblanched almonds, pulverized
1 cup almond paste
grated rind of 1 lemon
2 egg yolks

ICING

1 cup powdered sugar
2 to 3 tablespoons hot water
1 teaspoon almond extract

In a large bowl, dissolve the yeast in the warm water. Let stand 5 minutes.

Add the sugar, eggs, sour cream, wine, and salt. Blend well. Mix in half the flour until batter is satiny. Add remaining flour to make a stiff, but soft, dough. Let stand 15 minutes, covered. Turn out onto a lightly floured board and knead until the dough is satiny and smooth. Let stand 15 minutes, again, covered.

On a lightly oiled surface, roll dough out as thin as possible, to about 20- to 22-inches square. Distribute the butter slices over half the dough. Fold unbuttered half over. Seal the edges. With hands, beat gently to remove any air bubbles. Fold dough to make a square. Place on a lightly oiled baking sheet and chill until firm, 1 to 2 hours.

On a lightly floured board, roll out chilled dough to about 20-inches square. Fold the 4 corners toward the center of the dough (just as an envelope is folded). Dust lightly with flour and roll out very thin. Repeat the folding and rolling 4 times. Chill if necessary between folding and rolling. Finally, cover and chill 30 minutes (or chill until the next day, if desired).

To prepare the filling, put the raisins into a blender or a food processor with the steel blade in place. Process or blend until chopped. Add the sugar, almonds, almond paste, lemon rind, and egg yolks. Process 30 seconds until blended, or turn the filling into a bowl and mix until well blended.

Butter two 5- to 6-cup tube pans and dust with flour.

With a knife, cut the chilled pastry square into 2 equal parts. Working with 1 part at a time (refrigerate the remaining part), roll out to make a long, narrow strip about 24 × 6 inches.

Spoon half the filling down the length of the strip. Brush edges with water, fold over, and seal. Place in one of the tube pans, sealing the ends together. Repeat with second half of the dough. Let rise, covered, until almost doubled. Preheat oven to 375°F. Bake 30 to 40 minutes until golden.

While rings bake, mix the powdered sugar with the water and almond extract to make a smooth, thin icing.

Invert rings from baking pan and cool on a rack. Drizzle with the icing.

DANISH FILBERT-BUTTER RING
(*Smorkage*)

First, a ring mold is lined with pastry, then the remainder of the pastry is filled with a filbert cream, rolled up, sliced, and placed in the pastry-lined pan. The baked ring is decorated with a thin rum icing.

❖ Makes 12 servings

2 cups all-purpose flour
4 tablespoons sugar
¾ cup unsalted butter, firm
1 package active dry yeast
¼ cup warm water, 105°F to 115°F
2 eggs, room temperature

FILLING

1 egg
¼ cup sugar
½ cup all-purpose flour
pinch salt
1 cup half-and-half or light cream
½ cup milk
1 teaspoon vanilla
½ cup filberts, toasted* and pulverized
1 tablespoon ground cinnamon

ICING

1 cup powdered sugar
about 2 tablespoons rum

In large mixing bowl, mix flour and 3 tablespoons of the sugar. Cut in butter until mixture resembles coarse crumbs. In small bowl, mix 1 tablespoon sugar, the yeast, and the warm water. Stir until yeast dissolves. Let stand 5 minutes until yeast becomes foamy. Beat eggs into yeast and then stir the liquid mixture into the flour mixture. Toss with spatula until mixture holds together in a ball. Cover and let rise until mixture is not quite doubled, 1 to 1½ hours.

Meanwhile, prepare the filling. In a heavy saucepan, beat egg with sugar until foamy; add flour, salt, cream, and milk. Cook and stir over medium heat until mixture is very thick. Cover and cool to room temperature. Add vanilla, filberts, and cinnamon.

Butter a 7- to 8-cup ring mold. Roll $\frac{1}{3}$ of the pastry out to make a round 16 inches in diameter. Make a small hole in the center of the pastry and lay it over the top of the buttered ring mold. Carefully fit and drape pastry into the ring mold, stretching the hole in the center out to the size of the center of the ring. Pastry will stretch and should hang over the edges by about $1\frac{1}{2}$ inches.

Roll out remaining pastry to make a 16-inch square. Spread with the filling evenly (it will be a thick coating). Roll up jelly-roll fashion. Cut into 12 parts and place the pieces cut side down in the pastry-lined ring mold. Lap the pastry lining over the rolls to enclose them. Let rise 1 hour or until pastry rises about 1 inch. Preheat oven to 350°F and bake for 30 to 35 minutes until golden. Cool in pan 5 minutes, then invert on rack. Mix the 1 cup powdered sugar with enough rum to make a smooth icing. Drizzle over the cooled cake.

❖ To toast nuts, spread on a baking sheet. Place in oven set at 300°F. Bake 5 to 10 minutes until toasted.

DANISH FRUIT-FILLED PACKETS
(*Spandauer*)

These may be shaped and filled as individual pastries or as larger ones that are cut into individual servings.

❖ Makes 4 large pastries or 25 small pastries

1 recipe Danish Pastry, Classic or Quick Method

FILLING

1 cup dried apricots or dried prunes
⅔ cup water
⅓ cup sugar
1 slightly beaten egg
sliced almonds

ICING

½ cup powdered sugar
2½ teaspoons milk

In a small saucepan, simmer the apricots or prunes in the water for 30 minutes, covered, until soft. Cool, mash or chop the fruit, add the sugar, and chill.

Cover two large baking sheets with parchment or lightly grease them. Preheat oven to 375°F.

For 4 large pastries, roll pastry out on lightly floured board to make an 18-inch square. Cut into 4 squares. Place 2 squares on each prepared baking sheet. Roll again lightly to bring the squares back to a 9-inch width.

Place ¼ of the filling on the top of each square. Fold the corners toward the center and press down well. Brush with egg. Sprinkle with sliced almonds. Let rise for 15 to 30 minutes until puffy. Bake for 15 to 20 minutes or until golden.

To make the icing, mix powdered sugar and milk until smooth. Drizzle or dot pastries while hot with the icing.

To serve, cut pastries into 4 quarters.

For 25 individual pastries, roll pastry out on lightly floured board to make a 20-inch square. Cut into 4-inch squares. Dot center of each square with filling. Fold in the four corners of each toward the center and press down well. Place on the prepared baking sheets. Brush with egg and sprinkle with sliced almonds. Let rise 15 to 30 minutes until puffy. Bake 8 to 10 minutes until just golden. Drizzle or dot pastries with the icing.

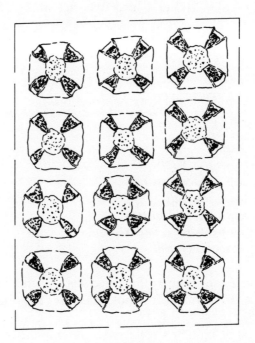

KARELIAN CHEESE-FILLED BUNS
(*Rahkapiirakat*)

*R*ahka is a fresh milk cheese somewhat similar to ricotta. These buns are served with coffee or as a dessert after a simple meal, such as a hearty soup. Buns made the same way are also filled with fresh blueberries (see following recipe).

❖ Makes 12 buns

1 package active dry yeast
$\frac{1}{4}$ cup warm water, 105°F to 115°F
$\frac{1}{2}$ cup milk, scalded and cooled to lukewarm
$\frac{1}{3}$ cup sugar
1 egg
$\frac{1}{2}$ teaspoon freshly ground cardamom (optional)
$\frac{1}{4}$ cup golden raisins
$\frac{1}{2}$ teaspoon salt
$\frac{1}{4}$ cup softened butter
$2\frac{1}{2}$ cups unbleached all-purpose flour

FILLING

$\frac{1}{2}$ cup ricotta cheese
3 tablespoons sugar
2 tablespoons lemon juice
grated rind of 1 lemon
$\frac{1}{4}$ cup raisins
1 egg
1 teaspoon vanilla extract

GLAZE

1 slightly beaten egg
2 tablespoons milk

In a large mixing bowl, dissolve the yeast in the water; add the milk. Let stand 5 minutes. Add the sugar, egg, cardamom if desired, raisins, and salt. Add the softened butter and 1 cup of the flour; beat until smooth and satiny. Gradually add the remaining flour, mixing until dough is smooth and satiny, not quite stiff enough to knead. Cover and let rise 1 to 2 hours until doubled.

Meanwhile, combine the cheese, sugar, lemon juice, lemon rind, raisins, egg, and vanilla extract.

Dust risen dough with flour. Shape into a ball, dusting with flour lightly, if necessary, to prevent stickiness.

Lightly oil a work surface. Turn dough out onto the work surface and divide into 12 parts.

Cover a baking sheet with parchment or lightly grease it. Roll dough into smooth balls and place on the baking sheet with the smooth side up. Let rise until puffy, 45 minutes to 1 hour. With a floured glass, as sketched, press an indentation into the center of each round of dough, and a rounded edge on each ball.

Preheat oven to 400°F.

Spoon the filling into the center of each bun, as shown. Beat the egg and milk to make a glaze and brush edges of the pastries with the mixture. Bake for 10 to 15 minutes or until golden brown.

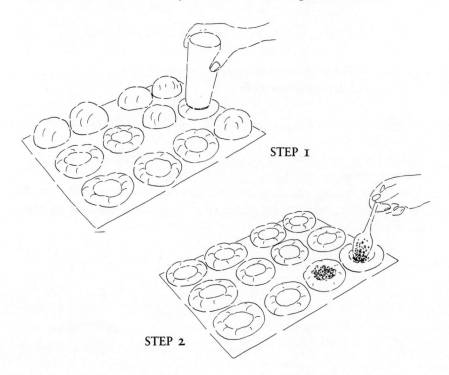

STEP 1

STEP 2

BLUEBERRY-FILLED BUNS
(*Mustikkapiiraat*)

*T*hese are wonderful made with fresh wild blueberries. The pastries are shaped exactly like the Karelian Cheese-Filled Buns.

❖ Makes 12 buns

1 recipe yeast dough for Karelian Cheese-Filled Buns

FILLING

1 pint fresh blueberries, preferably wild
1 tablespoon cornstarch
2 tablespoons sugar

GLAZE

1 slightly beaten egg
2 tablespoons milk

Prepare the yeast dough. Let rise and shape as directed for Karelian Cheese-Filled Buns.

Meanwhile, combine the blueberries, cornstarch, and sugar.

Preheat oven to 400°F.

Spoon the filling into the pastries. Beat the egg and milk together to make a glaze and brush edges of the pastries with the mixture. Bake for 10 to 15 minutes or until golden brown.

FINNISH BLUEBERRY SQUARES
(*Mustikkapiirakka*)

*I*n the summertime, when Finns spend a month or so at their summer cottages, they enjoy picking wild blueberries. This yeast-crusted blueberry pie is eaten for breakfast and with morning coffee.

❖ Makes one 15 × 10-inch open-faced pie, 12-16 servings

>1 package active dry yeast
>$\frac{1}{4}$ cup warm water, 105°F to 115°F
>1 egg
>$\frac{1}{2}$ cup sugar
>1 teaspoon salt
>$\frac{1}{2}$ cup milk, scalded and cooled to lukewarm
>$\frac{1}{2}$ cup softened or melted butter
>$3\frac{1}{4}$ cups unbleached all-purpose flour

>TOPPING

>4 cups fresh blueberries or frozen un-
>   sugared blueberries
>1 cup sugar
>1 tablespoon cornstarch

In a large bowl, dissolve the yeast in the warm water. Let stand 5 minutes. Add the egg, sugar, salt, and milk. Stir in the butter and 2 cups of the flour. Beat until smooth. Add the remaining flour and beat again until dough is stiff but smooth. Cover and let rise in a warm place until doubled, about 1 to 3 hours.

Preheat oven to 400°F. Grease one 15 × 10-inch jelly roll pan and dust with flour. Dump dough from bowl onto the prepared pan. With flour-dusted hands, press dough into the pan to line it evenly, pressing it enough so that it extends about 2 inches over the edges of the pan.

In a bowl, combine the blueberries and half the sugar with the cornstarch. Pour mixture onto the dough-lined pan in an even layer. Lift extended dough edges up over the berries to cover the berries, making an uneven edge.

Let rise 30 minutes. Preheat the oven to 400°F. Bake for 20 to 25 minutes until crust is golden and filling is bubbly. Serve from the pan cut into squares.

ICELANDIC SUMMER SKYR TART
(*Sumarterta*)

*S*kyr, a creamy dairy product, is soul food to an Icelandic! It is often served simply with sugar and cream as a pudding for dessert, and it is heavenly when topped with fresh berries in season. Depending on what part of this country you live in, you may or may not be able to obtain it, but sour cream or yogurt and cream cheese may be substituted. This tart or open-faced pie is based on an easy press-in pie crust that is baked until golden, then filled and topped with strawberries and toasted sliced almonds.

❖ Makes one 11-inch tart

1½ *cups all-purpose flour*
¼ *cup sugar*
¾ *cup softened butter*
1 *egg*

FILLING

2 *egg whites*
2 *tablespoons sugar*
1 *cup dairy sour cream or yogurt*
1 *(3-ounce) package cream cheese*

TOPPING

1 *pint fresh strawberries, cleaned and halved*
½ *cup sliced almonds, toasted*❖

Preheat oven to 425°F. Lightly butter and dust with flour an 11-inch tart pan.

In a large bowl, combine the flour, sugar, and butter; with a fork or electric hand mixer, blend until mixture resembles coarse crumbs. Stir in the egg.

Press the crumbly mixture into the prepared pan. Bake for 20 minutes or until golden. Cool.

To make the filling, whip the egg whites until frothy and beat in the sugar until mixture is stiff. Cream the sour cream or yogurt and cream cheese together until blended and smooth. Fold in the egg whites. Turn into the cooled crust.

Place berries on top of the tart with the cut sides down. Sprinkle with the sliced almonds. Chill until ready to serve, or about 1 hour.

❖ To toast nuts, spread on a baking sheet. Place in oven set at 300°F. Bake 5 to 10 minutes until toasted.

FINNISH APPLE PIE WITH CREAM CRUST
(*Omenapiirakka*)

*F*inns make pies without a special pan. The crust is simply rolled out on a baking sheet covered with parchment in the form of a square or round. The fruit is arranged on top and the edges lapped over the fruit. This pie also has a lattice top.

❖ Makes one 12-inch square

2¼ *cups unbleached all-purpose flour*
½ *teaspoon baking powder*
½ *teaspoon salt*
½ *cup soft butter*
1 *cup heavy cream*

FILLING

4 *to 5 tart apples, pared, cored, and sliced*
¼ *cup sugar*
1 *tablespoon all-purpose flour*
dash salt
½ *teaspoon cinnamon*

GLAZE

1 *egg*
2 *tablespoons milk*

In a bowl, combine the flour, baking powder, and salt. Cut in the butter until the mixture resembles coarse crumbs. Add the cream and mix to make a soft dough. Chill 30 minutes.

Preheat oven to 425°F. Grease and dust a baking sheet lightly with flour. Turn dough out onto the center of the sheet and roll out to make a 12-inch square. Trim edges to straighten. Reroll scraps on floured board.

Combine the apples, sugar, flour, salt, and cinnamon. Arrange the apples in rows over the crust, leaving about $1\frac{1}{2}$ inches empty at the edges. Cut rerolled scraps into strips and arrange across the filling, crisscrossing them. Turn edges up over the filling and seal the corners. Beat egg with milk to make a glaze and brush edges and lattice strips with the glaze.

Bake for 30 to 35 minutes or until golden.

BLUEBERRY SOUR CREAM PIE
(*Kermaviili-Mustikkapiiras*)

*T*his delicious pie with a buttery crust and a creamy filling is made in Finland with a special product called *kermaviili*. We used to make *viili* when I was a child, using a starter. Viili is a yogurtlike clabbered milk that is much more delicious (to a Finn) than yogurt. I sometimes *crave* the flavor of viili. The culture creates an incredibly silky sour milk. When added to rich, heavy cream, it makes a sour cream that is smoother than French crème fraîche and more tart than English double cream or Devon cream. The best substitute I can think of is to add fresh lemon juice to heavy whipping cream.

❖ Makes one 11-inch pie

$\frac{1}{2}$ *cup butter*
$\frac{1}{3}$ *cup sugar*
1 *egg*
1 *cup all-purpose flour*
$\frac{1}{2}$ *teaspoon baking powder*

FILLING

2 *tablespoons fresh lemon juice*
$1\frac{1}{2}$ *cups heavy or whipping cream*
2 *eggs*
$\frac{1}{4}$ *cup sugar*
1 *teaspoon vanilla*
$1\frac{1}{2}$ *cups fresh blueberries*
1 *tablespoon sugar*

Preheat oven to 375°F. Lightly butter and dust with flour an 11-inch tart pan or a 9-inch quiche pan.

Cream the butter and sugar together. Add the egg and beat until light. Add the flour and baking powder and mix to make a soft dough.

Turn the dough into the prepared pan and press to cover the bottom and sides of the pan, dusting hands and pastry with flour as necessary to prevent stickiness.

For the filling, mix the lemon juice with the cream. Whisk in the eggs, sugar, and vanilla. Turn the mixture into the pastry-lined pan. Sprinkle the blueberries over the top. Sprinkle the blueberries with the 1 tablespoon sugar.

Bake for 35 to 40 minutes or until the pastry is golden and the filling is set.

PURPLE PLUM TART
(*Plómukaka*)

*R*eykjavik bakeries display a variety of fruit-topped tarts in their windows. This one looks most appealing and can be made with any fresh plums in season.

❖ Makes one 12-inch tart

$\frac{1}{3}$ *cup sugar*
$\frac{1}{2}$ *cup butter*
1$\frac{1}{2}$ *cups all-purpose flour*
2 *tablespoons ice water*

TOPPING

1 *pound fresh purple plums, pitted and quartered*
$\frac{1}{4}$ *cup butter*
$\frac{1}{2}$ *cup all-purpose flour*
$\frac{1}{3}$ *cup brown sugar*

Preheat oven to 425°F. Cover a baking sheet with parchment paper.

Combine the sugar, butter, and flour in a mixing bowl. Blend with fork or electric mixer until the mixture resembles coarse crumbs. Toss with the ice water to moisten, and press dough together into a ball. Turn dough out onto parchment paper or an ungreased baking sheet. Roll out to a 13-inch round. Turn 1 inch of the outside edge over on itself to form a rim; pinch to flute. Arrange quartered plums on the pastry.

Combine remaining ingredients, blending until the mixture resembles coarse crumbs. Sprinkle over the plums. Bake for 20 to 25 minutes or until crust is golden and crumbs are browned. This is delicious served with vanilla ice cream!

GRANDMOTHER'S STRAWBERRY TART
(*Mansikkatorttu*)

*F*inns spend much of the summer at their country cottages, when both garden and wild strawberries are ripe. They serve uncomplicated foods, such as fish chowder made with freshly caught fish from the lake, raw vegetables, and a simply made fresh strawberry pie such as this one. When I was growing up on the farm in northern Minnesota, we picked wild strawberries by the quart, and my mother made tarts like this; she says her mother taught her to make it.

❖ Makes one 11-inch tart

$\frac{1}{2}$ *cup butter, room temperature*
$\frac{1}{2}$ *cup sugar*
1 egg
1$\frac{1}{3}$ cups all-purpose flour
1 teaspoon baking powder

FILLING

1 quart fresh strawberries
2 tablespoons cornstarch
$\frac{1}{2}$ *cup sugar*
2 tablespoons butter
1 tablespoon sugar to sprinkle over top

Preheat oven to 350°F. Lightly butter and flour an 11-inch tart pan or shallow quiche pan.

In a large bowl, cream the butter and sugar until blended. Beat in the egg. Mix the flour and baking powder together and add to the creamed mixture. Press $\frac{2}{3}$ of the mixture into the prepared baking dish, covering the bottom and sides, dusting with flour as necessary to prevent stickiness.

In a bowl, combine the strawberries with the cornstarch and sugar. Turn berries into the pastry-lined pan and dot with the butter.

Pinch off pieces of the remaining pastry and roll between hands and floured board into strips. Lay strips in a crisscross pattern on top of the strawberries. Sprinkle with the 1 tablespoon sugar. Bake for 25 to 30 minutes or until the pastry is golden brown.

FINNISH CHEESE PIE
(*Rahkapiirakka*)

*I*n Finland they use the fresh cheese called *rahka* in this pie. Ricotta or sieved cottage cheese comes close but does not really duplicate the unique flavor of rahka.

❖ Makes one 11-inch tart

¾ *cup butter*
⅓ *cup sugar*
1 *egg*
2 *tablespoons water*
1½ *cups all-purpose flour*
½ *teaspoon baking powder*

FILLING

1 *cup ricotta cheese or sieved creamy cottage cheese*
2 *tablespoons melted butter*
4 *tablespoons heavy cream*
4 *tablespoons sugar*
1 *teaspoon vanilla*
2 *eggs*
½ *cup raisins*

Preheat oven to 375°F. Lightly grease and dust with flour an 11-inch tart or a 9-inch quiche pan.

Cream the butter and sugar together. Add the egg and water, blending well. Add the flour and baking powder and mix until dough is stiff.

Turn ⅔ of the pastry into the prepared pan and press to cover the bottom and sides of the pan.

In a bowl, combine the cheese, butter, cream, sugar, vanilla, eggs, and raisins. Pour mixture into the dough-lined pan in an even layer. Roll out the remaining dough and cut into strips. Lay them in crisscross fashion over the cheese filling. Let rise 30 minutes.

Preheat the oven to 375°F. Bake for 20 to 25 minutes until crust is golden and filling is bubbly. Serve from the pan cut into squares.

BIRGITTE'S ORANGE TART
(*Orangekuchen*)

*B*irgitte is a home economist for the Danish cheese association. The Danes have produced fruit-flavored cream cheeses for several years and bake them into tarts and cheesecakes such as this one. The flavored cheese is not always available, so I went back to the recipe from which the inspiration for the flavored cheese originally came!

❖ Makes about 10 servings

1 cup all-purpose flour
⅓ cup sugar
6 tablespoons butter
1 egg yolk
1 teaspoon cold water

FILLING

1 (8-ounce) package cream cheese
1 tablespoon grated orange peel
½ cup freshly squeezed orange juice
3 eggs
3 tablespoons sugar
½ teaspoon vanilla
¼ cup finely chopped candied orange peel
½ cup slivered blanched almonds

Measure flour and sugar into a bowl, or into the work bowl of the food processor with the steel blade in place. Add the butter and cut in with a fork or process using on/off pulses until the pastry is the consistency of coarse crumbs. Mix the egg yolk and water and add to the dry ingredients. Blend until a dough forms. Chill 30 minutes.

Preheat oven to 400°F. Roll out pastry and fit it into an 11-inch round tart pan or into a 13 × 9-inch jelly roll pan. Bake for 15 minutes until edges begin to brown.

Meanwhile, in a large bowl, cream the cheese with the orange peel, orange juice, eggs, sugar, vanilla, and candied orange peel. Whip until light and fluffy. Pour into the partially baked crust and sprinkle with the almonds. Bake 35 minutes more or until tart is set and edges are golden.

ICELANDIC ALMOND TARTS
(*Saenskar Möndlukökur*)

*T*hese tartlets are baked in little fluted molds about 2 to 3 inches in diameter. Swedish sandbakkel tins work fine; otherwise, use small muffin tins (about ⅓ cup).

❖ Makes 20 tarts

1¼ cups all-purpose flour
¼ cup powdered sugar
½ cup firm unsalted butter
1 egg yolk
1 teaspoon lemon juice
1 to 2 tablespoons ice water

FILLING

½ cup unblanched almonds, pulverized
¼ cup butter
½ cup sugar
2 eggs
grated rind of 1 orange

FROSTING

½ cup powdered sugar
1 tablespoon water

Preheat oven to 400°F.

In large bowl, or in the workbowl of the food processor, combine the flour and powdered sugar. Slice the butter into the flour mixture and cut the butter in or process until the mixture resembles coarse crumbs. In a small bowl, combine the egg yolk, lemon juice, and 1 tablespoon ice water. Add to the butter mixture, mixing until dough forms. Divide dough into 30 parts. Press 1 part into each mold, pressing dough with finger and thumb to coat the inside of each mold evenly, making the dough thicker on the rims than on the bottom.

In a bowl, cream the pulverized almonds with the butter and sugar. Beat in the eggs until mixture is light and fluffy. Add the orange rind. Spoon mixture into the pastry-lined molds.

Place filled molds on a baking sheet and bake for 15 to 20 minutes until filling is set and pastry is golden.

To prepare the frosting, mix the powdered sugar with the water. Brush sparingly over the warm tarts. Let cool until frosting is set.

NORWEGIAN CREAM TARTS
(*Linser*)

*N*orwegians use heart-shaped tart pans for these tarts with a creamy filling and buttery double crust.

❖ Makes 18 tarts

2 cups all-purpose flour
¼ cup sugar
1 cup butter
2 egg yolks
2 tablespoons ice water

FILLING AND TOPPING

1 cup heavy cream
2 egg yolks
2 tablespoons sugar
1 teaspoon vanilla extract
1½ teaspoons potato flour or cornstarch
powdered sugar for topping

Combine the flour and sugar in a bowl. Cut in the butter until the mixture resembles coarse crumbs. Blend egg yolks and water. Sprinkle over the flour mixture and toss to moisten dry ingredients. Press together into a ball. Chill 30 minutes.

Preheat oven to 400°F. Lightly butter eighteen 2-inch, preferably heart-shaped, tart pans.

On a floured surface, roll out the dough and, using one of the tart pans as a cutter, cut 36 pieces to fit pans. Press half the pieces into the tart pans.

Mix all the filling ingredients together. Spoon into the pastry-lined tart pans and moisten pastry rims with finger dipped in water. Place remaining dough pieces over the filling. Trim edges and press to seal.

Bake for 15 to 20 minutes until golden. Dust baked tarts with powdered sugar.

BLUEBERRY TURNOVERS
(*Bláberjahorn*)

*T*hese Icelandic favorites are made from wild blueberries.

❖ Makes 25 turnovers

2½ cups all-purpose flour
3 tablespoons sugar
1 cup chilled butter
1 egg, beaten
2 teaspoons lemon juice
2 to 4 tablespoons ice water

FILLING

1½ cups fresh blueberries
1 tablespoon sugar
1 tablespoon cornstarch

GLAZE AND TOPPING

1 beaten egg
chopped almonds
pearl sugar or coarsely crushed sugar cubes

In a mixing bowl or in the workbowl of the food processor with the steel blade in place, combine the flour and sugar. Cut the butter into ½-inch dice and add to the flour. Cut butter into flour using a pastry blender or process using on/off pulses until butter is the size of peas.

In a small bowl, blend the egg, lemon juice, and 2 tablespoons water. Add to the flour mixture and mix just until flour is moistened and pastry holds together. Press into a ball. Chill if necessary.

Turn dough out onto lightly floured board and roll out to make a large square about 20 × 20 inches. Using a ruler as a guide, cut with pastry wheel into 4-inch squares. You will have 25 squares.

Preheat oven to 400°F.

Mix the blueberries, sugar, and cornstarch. Divide the blueberries among the squares. Fold over berries to make triangles, enclosing the berries. Place on ungreased baking sheet. Brush with beaten egg and sprinkle with chopped almonds and sugar. Bake 13 to 15 minutes until golden.

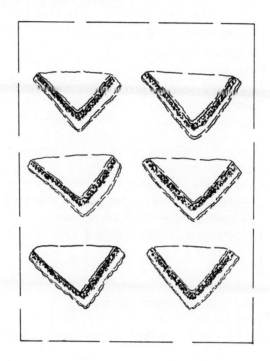

BUTTERY BERRY SQUARES
(*Marjapiirakka*)

*T*he blueberry is favored for this special pastry. However, sometimes lingonberries, strawberries mixed with chopped rhubarb, or chopped apples are used.

❖ Makes one 15 × 11-inch pan

2½ cups all-purpose flour
½ teaspoon baking powder
½ cup sugar
1 cup softened butter
1 egg
1 tablespoon lemon juice

FILLING AND TOPPING

2 cups fresh blueberries, lingonberries, or a
    mixture of sliced strawberries and chopped
    rhubarb, or diced fresh apple
4 tablespoons sugar (*more if using tart fruit*)
grated rind of 1 lemon
lemon juice to taste
2 tablespoons cornstarch
4 tablespoons sugar for topping

Preheat oven to 375°F. Lightly grease and flour a 15 × 11-inch jelly roll pan.

In a food processor or a large bowl, combine the flour, baking powder, and sugar. Blend in the butter with a pastry blender or use on/off pulses of the food processor until the mixture resembles coarse crumbs. Mix the egg and lemon juice. Add to the crumbly mixture, tossing to blend evenly, until dough will hold together. Chill 30 minutes, if necessary.

Reserve about ⅓ of the dough. Roll the remaining dough out to fit the jelly roll pan, covering the bottom and sides evenly. (This is a rather rich and crumbly dough, but just press to patch the pieces together in the pan.)

Combine the berries, sugar, lemon juice and rind, and cornstarch. Mix to blend well. Turn mixture into the pan and spread out evenly.

Roll out reserved dough and cut strips. Place strips in a crisscross fashion over the filling, sealing strips to the edges. Sprinkle top with additional 4 tablespoons sugar.

Bake for 25 to 30 minutes or until the crust is a light golden brown. Cut into squares to serve.

SWEDISH WELSH BREAD
(*Walesbröd*)

*T*his is a very popular pastry that is neither Swedish nor Welsh and is known as Swedish kringle to some Scandinavian-Americans, as Danish pastry to others, and to some as just Swedish coffeecake. In Sweden it is sometimes made into "Maria Pastries," but in that case the same elements are handled somewhat differently.

Walesbröd has a base of flaky pastry that is topped with choux, or puff, paste and baked. The baked pastry is iced with a powdered sugar and butter icing.

❖ Makes 2 pastries,
12 × 4 inches

1 cup all-purpose flour
6 tablespoons firm butter
2 to 3 tablespoons ice water

CHOUX PASTE

1 cup water
½ cup butter
1 cup all-purpose flour
3 eggs
1 teaspoon almond extract

ICING AND DECORATION

1 cup powdered sugar
2 tablespoons softened butter
2 to 3 tablespoons cream
1 teaspoon almond extract
about ½ cup toasted slivered almonds•

Measure the flour into a mixing bowl or workbowl of a food processor with the steel blade in place. Slice the butter and add to the flour. Cut in with pastry blender or process using on/off pulses until the butter is the size of peas. Add ice water and mix gently until flour is moistened. Press pastry into a ball. Divide dough into 2 parts. Roll each part out to make a 12 × 4-inch rectangle. Place on an ungreased baking sheet.

Preheat oven to 400°F.

In a saucepan, heat water and butter to boiling. Add the flour all at once and stir until smooth and stiff. Remove from heat and stir in the eggs one at a time, beating after each addition. Add the almond extract. Spoon or spread the mixture over the 2 pastry rectangles.

Bake for 30 to 35 minutes until puffed and golden. Do not overbake. Cool.

Mix powdered sugar, softened butter, and enough cream to make a smooth frosting. Add the almond extract. Drizzle over the top of the pastry and sprinkle with the slivered almonds.

❖ To toast nuts, spread on a baking sheet. Place in oven set at 300°F and bake 5 to 10 minutes until toasted.

SWEDISH MARIA PASTRIES
(*Mariabakelser*)

*T*his is a variation of Swedish Welsh Bread. The flaky pastry is cut into rounds, then each is topped with choux paste and baked. The puffs are filled with a cream filling and either frosted with a powdered sugar icing or simply dusted with powdered sugar.

❖ Makes 20 pastries

1 recipe Swedish Welsh Bread
1 recipe Choux Paste

FILLING

1 cup light cream
2 egg yolks
1 tablespoon sugar

1 tablespoon cornstarch
1 teaspoon unflavored gelatin
1 cup whipping cream, whipped
¼ cup sugar
1 teaspoon vanilla

FROSTING

1 cup powdered sugar
2 tablespoons softened butter
2 to 3 tablespoons cream
1 teaspoon almond extract

Prepare the pastry as directed in recipe for Swedish Welsh Bread. Chill pastry.

Prepare the choux paste as directed in recipe for Swedish Welsh Bread. Cool to room temperature.

To prepare the cream filling, combine the cream, egg yolks, sugar, cornstarch, and gelatin in a heavy saucepan. Heat, stirring, until mixture comes to a boil and thickens. Cool to room temperature.

Preheat the oven to 400°F.

Roll the pastry to about ⅛-inch thickness. Cut 3-inch rounds and place on ungreased baking sheets. Top each with a spoonful of choux paste. Bake for 20 to 25 minutes until puffed and golden.

Whip the cream and flavor with the sugar and vanilla. Fold whipped cream into the cream filling. Chill.

Mix powdered sugar, softened butter, and enough cream to make a smooth frosting. Add the almond extract.

Make a slit in the base of the pastries and pipe in the cream filling. Drizzle with the frosting or dust with powdered sugar. Serve immediately or chill until ready to serve.

ICELANDIC STONE CAKES
(*Stenkakor*)

*T*hese pancakes are named "stone cakes" because historically they are said to have been baked on hot stones. They're actually very light, since they are raised with yeast. You may wish to mix this batter the night before and refrigerate it, then bake the cakes the next morning for breakfast.

❖ Makes about 20 pancakes

1 package active dry yeast
1½ cups milk, heated to 105°F to 115°F
1 tablespoon sugar
1½ teaspoons salt
1 teaspoon freshly ground cardamom
1 egg
2 cups all-purpose flour
additional milk or water if necessary

In a large bowl, sprinkle the yeast over the warm milk, then sprinkle on the sugar. Let stand until yeast is dissolved into the milk. Add the salt, cardamom, egg, and flour. Whisk until smooth. Cover and let rise until bubbly. Or, cover and refrigerate until the next morning.

Heat pancake pan over medium-high heat and spread with butter. If batter is stiff, add milk or water to achieve pouring consistency. Spoon ¼ cup batter onto pan for each cake. Bake on both sides until golden. Serve hot with lingonberry jam and cream.

BLINIS
(*Linnit*)

*K*arelian Finns traditionally serve these yeast-risen pancakes with *mäteenmäti*, which is the roe of ling cod, on Shrove Tuesday, the day before Ash Wednesday and the beginning of Lent. They are often made with some buckwheat in the batter; then the name for them is *"tattariblinit."* They should be served with fresh caviar and sour cream, chopped onion, and a sprinkling of freshly ground allspice.

❖ Makes about 25 pancakes

½ package (1½ teaspoons) active dry yeast
¼ cup warm water, 105°F to 115°F
1 cup milk, scalded and cooled to lukewarm
2 cups all-purpose flour or 1½ cups all-
*   purpose flour plus ½ cup buckwheat flour*
2 tablespoons sugar
3 eggs, separated
6 tablespoons melted butter
½ teaspoon salt

In a large mixing bowl, dissolve the yeast in the warm water. Let stand 5 minutes. Add the milk, 1 cup of the flour, and sugar to the mixture. Cover and let rise in a warm place until foamy, about 30 minutes. Beat in the egg yolks. Stir in the butter, salt, and remaining flour, mixing well. Whip the egg whites until stiff and fold into the batter. Let rise in a warm place another 30 minutes.

Heat a *plette* pan (a pancake pan with 3-inch indentations) or a pancake griddle until a drop of water sputters on it. Coat with butter. Make small pancakes using 2 to 3 tablespoons of the batter for each cake. Bake on both sides until golden brown, about 2 minutes in all. Serve hot.

SWEDISH PANCAKES WITH LINGONBERRIES
(*Plättar*)

*T*hese are tender, crêpe-like pancakes. Start with the 2 cups of milk, but as you go along you will need to add more milk to the batter, which tends to thicken as it stands. If you do not have a special pancake pan with indentations about 3 inches in diameter, make the pancakes 6 inches in diameter, using an omelet or crêpe pan. In Sweden, this is a traditional Thursday evening dessert, which follows the traditional Thursday evening pea soup.

❖ Makes sixteen 6-inch crêpes
or thirty-two 3-inch pancakes

1 cup all-purpose flour
1 tablespoon sugar
¼ teaspoon salt
3 eggs
2 to 3 cups milk

TOPPING

lingonberry jam
1 cup whipping cream, whipped
2 tablespoons powdered sugar

In a mixing bowl, combine the flour, sugar, and salt. Mix the eggs and 2 cups of the milk together. Whisk the liquids into the dry ingredients until batter is smooth. Cover and let stand for 2 hours. Batter should be the consistency of thick cream. If it is thicker than that or if, while you are making pancakes, it becomes thicker, add more milk.

Heat a Swedish pancake pan, or a crêpe or omelet pan. Coat with butter. Beat the batter again and spoon a tablespoon of batter into each section of the pan. Tilt and turn pan to cover the bottoms of the indentations completely. Turn over and brown both sides. Remove onto warm platter and serve immediately with lingonberry jam and whipped cream, sweetened with the powdered sugar.

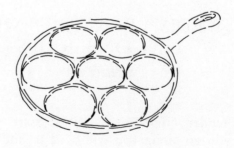

LISE'S DANISH PANCAKE BALLS
(*Aebelskiver*)

*F*or this recipe you need a Danish *aebelskiver* pan with round indentations. The pans are usually made of cast iron. My friend Lise uses a metal knitting needle to turn the aebelskiver over. Some people like to fill them with applesauce, while others prefer to leave them plain.

❖ Makes 20 pancakes

1 cup milk
$\frac{1}{2}$ cup melted butter
3 eggs, separated
2 tablespoons sugar
1$\frac{1}{2}$ cups all-purpose flour
2 teaspoons baking powder
applesauce (optional)
powdered sugar

Heat the milk to lukewarm. Whisk in the butter, egg yolks, and sugar. Turn into a bowl and add the flour and baking powder, whisking until well blended and no lumps remain. Whip the egg whites until stiff and fold into the mixture.

Heat aebelskiver pan over medium-high heat until a drop of water sizzles when dripped into the pan. Put about $\frac{1}{2}$ teaspoon butter into each indentation. Spread it around. Spoon in 1 tablespoon of the batter and let it cook about 30 seconds. If using applesauce, drop 1 teaspoon applesauce in the center and top with enough more aebelskiver batter to cover the applesauce. When the bottoms are browned, turn the cakes over and cook on that side until browned. Remove from pan and place on serving plate. Dust with powdered sugar.

ICELANDIC PANCAKES WITH WHIPPED CREAM
(Pönnukökur med Peyttum Rjóma)

*T*his Icelandic dessert is traditionally served with afternoon coffee or after a meal. I like them for brunch, too.

❖ Makes 10 to 12 pancakes

$1\frac{1}{4}$ to $1\frac{1}{2}$ cups milk
2 eggs, separated
2 tablespoons butter, melted
1 teaspoon vanilla
$1\frac{1}{2}$ cups all-purpose flour
$\frac{1}{4}$ teaspoon baking soda
$\frac{1}{4}$ teaspoon baking powder

TOPPING

preserves, jam, or jelly
1 cup whipping cream, whipped
2 tablespoons powdered sugar

In a bowl, mix together the milk, egg yolks, butter, and vanilla. Combine the flour, baking soda, and baking powder and mix into the liquids until blended. Beat the egg whites and fold into the mixture.

Heat a heavy skillet until a drop of water bounces off the surface. Butter the skillet. Bake thin pancakes using $\frac{1}{4}$ cup batter per cake until browned on both sides.

Spread with preserves, jam, or jelly, and whipped cream sweetened with powdered sugar. Fold into triangles and serve immediately.

BAKED PANCAKE
(*Pannukakku*)

5 June 2006 (Medric made it)

A puffy baked pancake is popular in all of the Scandinavian countries. The proportion of eggs to milk to flour varies according to individual tastes. Some people like a custardy pancake with less egg and milk in relation to the flour, and some like a heavier, rib-sticking variety. My personal favorite is this one, which turns out a crispy, high-sided, golden shell that is a perfect cradle for fresh fruit and whipped cream. It can also be served with just a squeeze of lemon and powdered sugar. The proportions are easy to remember and to scale up or down — an equal measure of flour, eggs, and milk with a touch of sugar and a touch of salt. For baking, a large, slope-sided paella pan or a large slope-sided frying pan with a handle that can go into the oven is ideal. Another option is to bake the pancake in four 9-inch pie pans.

❖ Makes 4 servings

$1\frac{1}{2}$ *cups all-purpose flour*
$1\frac{1}{2}$ *cups milk*
6 eggs
1 tablespoon sugar
1 teaspoon salt
about $\frac{1}{2}$ cup butter for the baking pan or pans

TOPPING

powdered sugar and lemon wedges or
1 cup whipping cream, whipped
2 tablespoons powdered sugar
fresh fruit

In a bowl, whisk together the flour, milk, eggs, sugar, and salt until no lumps remain. Let stand 30 minutes.

Preheat oven to 450°F. Put butter into 1 large (14- to 16-inch) slope-sided pan (with 4-quart capacity) or into four 9-inch pie pans and preheat in the oven until butter is melted. Brush entire pan with the butter. Pour in the pancake batter. Bake for 15 to 20 minutes until edges are puffed high and golden.

Serve immediately! The pancake will settle quickly, so have the eaters ready at the table. Sprinkle the pancake with powdered sugar and squeeze lemon over, or spoon fresh fruit onto individual servings and top with whipped cream sweetened with powdered sugar.

HEART-SHAPED CREAM WAFFLES
(*Våfflor*)

*T*he traditional Scandinavian waffle iron makes individual heart-shaped waffles. (A regular waffle iron may not be as attractive, but the waffles will taste just as good, although they may be slightly thicker and not quite so light.)

❖ Makes 4 servings

⅔ cup all-purpose flour
1 teaspoon freshly ground cardamom
3 eggs
¼ cup sugar
⅔ cup dairy sour cream
3 tablespoons melted butter
butter for brushing the iron
powdered sugar
jam or fresh berries to serve with the waffles
whipped cream to serve with the waffles (optional)

Stir flour and cardamom together and set aside. In small bowl of electric mixer, beat the eggs and sugar together at high speed for 10 minutes until mixture forms ribbons when beaters are lifted.

Sprinkle flour mixture over eggs; stir the sour cream until smooth and add to the mixture, folding until batter is smooth. Fold in the melted butter.

Place the waffle iron over medium heat and heat until a drop of water sizzles on the grid, turning over once to heat both sides. Brush the grids with butter and spoon in the batter. Bake, turning once, until golden brown, then remove from iron and sprinkle with powdered sugar. Serve immediately with tart lingonberry or other jam or fresh berries and whipped cream.

Or, bake waffles in a standard electric waffle iron as manufacturer of the iron directs.

SWEET CREAM WAFFLES
(*Våfflor*)

*H*ere is another favorite waffle recipe, which uses sweet, rather than sour, cream.

❖ Makes 4 servings

3 eggs
1 cup whipping cream
⅔ cup all-purpose flour
2 tablespoons water
3 tablespoons melted butter
butter for brushing the iron
jam or fresh berries to serve with the waffles
whipped cream to serve with the waffles (optional)

In small bowl of electric mixer, beat the eggs for 10 minutes at high speed until very light. Whip the cream and fold into the eggs. Sift the flour over and fold into the mixture along with the water and melted butter.

Place the waffle iron over medium heat and heat until a drop of water sizzles on the grid, turning over once to heat both sides. Brush the grids with butter and spoon in the batter. Bake, turning once, until golden brown, then remove from iron and sprinkle with powdered sugar. Serve immediately with tart lingonberry or other jam or fresh berries and whipped cream.

Or, bake waffles in a standard electric waffle iron as manufacturer of the iron directs.

FINNISH MAYDAY PASTRIES
(Tippaleipä)

*F*inns are quiet people. Even in an overcrowded trolley, the sound of a child whispering to its mother is audible. Soft music plays in the background as people bustle about doing their shopping at Stockman, the largest department store in Helsinki. If there are sounds of loud conversation on the streets, it is most likely to be that of American tourists, or a bus-load of American retired schoolteachers, not Finns. After a church service, the congregants quietly leave as the pastors scurry out the chancel door.

But on Mayday the whole country explodes into a steady roar. Oompah bands play in the parks and adults and children carry huge balloons sold by street vendors. May Day is the celebration of spring in Finland. Students at Helsinki University wear their coveted white caps and sing, dance, and have parties all night. At some time during the night, the mermaid at the end of the esplanade in Helsinki is crowned with a white cap, too.

Normally, nobody drops in on anybody for a visit, except on Mayday. On the first of May, *tippaleipä* and *sima*, a sparkling lemon drink, are on hand in every home for unexpected and expected guests. Tippaleipä is something like the Pennsylvania Dutch funnel cake. A thin batter is swirled into hot fat to make a pastry that resembles a bird's nest.

❖ Makes about 15 pastries

> 1½ teaspoons active dry yeast (½ package)
> 2 tablespoons warm water, 105°F to 115°F
> 1½ teaspoons sugar
> 1 cup milk, scalded and cooled to lukewarm
> 2 eggs
> ½ teaspoon salt
> 2 cups all-purpose flour
>
> hot fat for frying
> powdered sugar

In a mixing bowl, dissolve the yeast in the warm water and add the sugar. Let stand 5 minutes until foamy. Stir in the milk, eggs, salt, and flour. Beat until batter is smooth and satiny. Let rise in a warm place until bubbly, 45 minutes to 1 hour.

Heat fat to 375°F. (Salad oil, lard, or shortening may be used.) Pour about 1 cup of the batter into a small, heavy-duty plastic bag with a zip-type closure. With scissors, cut a tiny hole in the corner, about $\frac{1}{8}$ inch in diameter. Drizzle the batter into the hot fat, moving the bag in a continuous round to form a bird's nest shape about 3 or 4 inches in diameter. Fry 1 minute on each side. Remove from fat and drain on paper toweling. When cool, sift powdered sugar over pastries and serve warm.

Savory Pies and Filled Breads

$\mathcal{T}$he eastern edge of Finland, the province of Karelia, is the outer edge of Scandinavia; there, some of the most unusual baking, especially of savory pies, has been done for generations. Historically, rye and barley, fish, and summer berries were the staple foods. When potatoes were introduced, they produced abundantly. Rice and wheat were imported and could be stored so easily that they became staples, too.

In Karelian households, a simple pastry made of rye flour and water, rolled thin with a sloping pin, was probably first made with a filling of cooked mush of rye or barley and water. Today, a milky cooked rice or mashed potato filling is most often used. This pastry, *Karelian piirakka*, is served all over Finland and even in Finnish-American households, with an egg-butter, made simply of hard-cooked egg chopped into butter. The addition of salt was an extravagance in early days. These pies are delicious steaming hot from the oven, having been freshly brushed with buttery milk.

Kalakukko, a rye-crusted, fish-filled loaf is another creation that cannot be encountered anywhere in the world but eastern Finland. A thick rye crust, which is impervious to steam, encloses small fish and, after hours of slow baking, cooks the bones of the fish to tenderness.

Savory pies are found in the cuisine of most countries, and Sweden, Norway, and Denmark are no exception. Their pies, however, are more continental in nature than the Finnish variety and are usually encrusted in a puffy pastry rather than a rustic rye. I love them all!

CHEESE TARTLETS
(*Ostpastejer*)

Scandinavians take pride in their cheese-making abilities. Not only do they eat a great deal of cheese, but they have a great many ways of using it in their cooking. All the Scandinavian countries are very progressive in promoting their local cheeses. These little cheese-filled pastry shells are useful for snacks, entertaining, or to serve as an accompaniment for salads or soups.

❖ Makes 24 tartlets

1¼ cups all-purpose flour
½ cup butter
4 to 5 tablespoons ice water

FILLING

¼ cup crumbled blue cheese
½ cup shredded white cheese, Swiss,
    Gouda, or Edam
¼ cup cream
2 eggs
2 teaspoons lemon juice

Preheat oven to 425°F. Butter 24 miniature muffin tins.

Measure the flour into a mixing bowl or into the work bowl of the food processor with the steel blade in place. Cut the butter into slices and add to the flour. With pastry blender or on/off bursts of the food processor, blend the butter until the mixture resembles coarse crumbs. Add the ice water and gather dough into a ball. Chill 30 minutes.

To prepare the filling, mash the blue cheese and mix with the shredded cheese, cream, eggs, and lemon juice.

Roll dough out to about ⅛-inch thickness. Cut into rounds using a 3-inch cookie cutter. Fit rounds into the muffin tins.

Spoon filling into the pastry-lined cups.

Roll out pastry scraps and cut strips about ⅓-inch wide. Cross 2 strips over each tart. Bake for 15 to 20 minutes until golden. Allow to cool a few minutes before removing from the pans.

LEILA'S HAM PASTIES
(*Iltapalapasteija*)

*O*ur friend Leila Seppälä served these to us after a refreshing sauna. Finns might also serve these as a "salty piece" to go with afternoon coffee.

❖ Makes twelve 3-inch
or one 11-inch tart

1 cup all-purpose flour
¼ teaspoon salt
½ cup butter
4 tablespoons cold water

FILLING

2 eggs, beaten
1 cup half-and-half
1 cup shredded cheese
1 cup finely diced ham
1 small green bell pepper, seeded and diced
1 small red bell pepper, seeded and diced
salt and freshly ground black pepper
1 tablespoon prepared mustard

Combine the flour and salt in a mixing bowl. Cut in the butter until butter is the size of peas. Sprinkle cold water over to make a dough. Form into a ball, wrap, and refrigerate for 1 hour.

To prepare the filling, mix the eggs and half-and-half. Blend in the cheese, ham, green and red peppers, salt and black pepper to taste. Preheat oven to 425°F. Roll pastry out to ⅛-inch thickness and fit into 3-inch tart pans or into one 11-inch tart pan with a removable bottom. Brush the bottom of the pastry with mustard. Pour in the filling. Bake small tarts about 12 to 15 minutes until set. Bake the large tart for 30 to 35 minutes or until set.

KARELIAN RICE PASTIES
(*Karjalanpiirakat*)

*K*arelian rice pasties are popular throughout Finland and can be purchased fresh daily in bakeries and supermarkets. Although the most common version is made with a rice filling, a potato filling is also delicious.

❖ Makes 16 pasties

1 cup water
1½ teaspoons salt
1½ cups rye flour
1 cup all-purpose flour

RICE FILLING

1 cup water
3 cups milk
¾ cup rice
salt and butter to taste

POTATO FILLING

4 large potatoes (about 1 pound)
water
1 cup hot milk
salt, pepper, and butter to taste

GLAZE

1 cup milk, heated to boiling
¼ cup butter

EGG-BUTTER

2 hard-cooked eggs
1 cup firm butter

Mix together the water, salt, rye flour, and all-purpose flour to make a smooth dough. If necessary, add more water. Shape the dough into a rope about the thickness of your wrist. Cut into 16 equal portions. Shape the pieces into flat round cakes and roll each out to make a very thin circle about 6 to 8 inches in diameter. Set aside.

To prepare the rice filling, combine the water, milk, and rice in a heavy saucepan. Simmer for 1 hour or until rice has absorbed all of the liquid, taste, and add salt and butter.

To prepare the alternative potato filling, pare and cut up the potatoes. Place in a pot with water to cover. Cook until tender. Mash the potatoes and add the hot milk, salt, pepper, and butter to taste. Beat until light.

Cover baking sheets with parchment paper or lightly grease them. Preheat oven to 550°F.

Fill the center of each circle with the cooked rice or mashed potatoes and fold over about $\frac{3}{4}$ inch of the edges, pinching to crimp the edges, and shape an oval or round pie. Place pies on prepared baking sheets.

Mix the boiling milk and butter to make a glaze. Brush the pies with the mixture. Bake for 7 to 10 minutes. Brush again with the butter-milk mixture. Bake until tinged with gold. Remove from oven and brush again with the butter-milk mixture. Serve cooled. Pasties will soften as they cool.

To prepare the egg-butter, chop the hard-cooked eggs with the butter until blended. Pile into a bowl and offer as a topping or spread for the pasties.

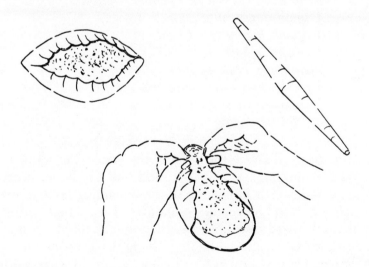

FRIED MEAT PIES
(*Lihapiirat*)

*P*ies like this are sold in cafés and kiosks in Finland. A variety of
different crusts are used, but my favorite is this yeast crust. In some
country kiosks, you can buy a meat pie that is split open and stuffed
with two *nakki* or frankfurters, Finnish fast food.

❖ Makes 12 pies

2 packages active dry yeast
$\frac{1}{4}$ cup warm water, 105°F to 115°F
1 cup milk, scalded and cooled to lukewarm
$\frac{1}{4}$ cup sugar
1 teaspoon salt
1 egg, beaten
$3\frac{1}{2}$ to 4 cups all-purpose flour

FILLING

2 tablespoons butter
$\frac{1}{4}$ cup chopped red bell pepper (optional)
1 small onion, minced
1 pound lean ground beef
1 teaspoon salt
$\frac{1}{2}$ teaspoon white pepper
1 hard-cooked egg, chopped
1 cup cooked rice
hot fat for frying

In a large bowl, dissolve the yeast in the water. Let stand 5 minutes. Add the milk, sugar, salt, egg, and half the flour; beat until
smooth and satiny. Stir in enough of the remaining flour to make a
stiff dough. Let stand, covered, 15 minutes. Turn dough out onto a
lightly floured board and knead until smooth, about 10 minutes.
Wash bowl, grease it, and add dough to the bowl, turning it over to
grease the top. Let rise until doubled, about 1 hour. Punch down and
let rise again for 30 minutes.

While dough rises, prepare the filling. Heat butter in a heavy
skillet. Add the red pepper, if desired, onion, and ground beef and

sauté until the meat is cooked through, stirring constantly. Add the salt, pepper, chopped eggs, and cooked rice. Cool.

Turn pastry out onto an oiled surface. Divide into 12 equal parts and roll each out to make rounds about ¼ inch thick. Put about 3 tablespoons of the filling in the center of each round. Moisten the edges and fold over into a half circle, sealing well. Place on a sheet of waxed paper dusted with flour.

Heat 2 inches of oil or fat for frying in an electric frying pan or pot to 375°F. Fry 2 to 3 pies at a time for 2½ to 3 minutes, or until golden, on each side. Turn only once. Drain on paper toweling. Serve hot.

POTATO-CRUSTED MEAT PASTIES
(*Pasteijat*)

*I*n a western province of Finland called Satakunta, meat pasties made with a potato crust are traditional. Sometimes they are made into a large pie that is cut up and served with sour cream as a main course. They are also excellent made into appetizer-size pies for a first course or party fare.

❖ Makes 16 pasties

2 cups all-purpose flour
½ teaspoon salt
¾ cup butter
¾ cup cooked, mashed potatoes or ¾ cup
    instant mashed potatoes and ¾ cup cold water

FILLING

3 tablespoons butter
2 medium-sized onions, minced
2 cups cooked meat (beef, venison, or ham),
    finely minced
½ cup sour cream
salt and pepper

GLAZE

1 egg, beaten

Mix flour and salt in large bowl. Cut in the butter until mixture resembles coarse crumbs. Blend in the mashed potatoes until dough forms. If using instant mashed potato flakes, add the dry potato flakes to the flour mixture. Blend in the cold water until dough holds together. Press dough into a ball and chill at least 2 hours.

Cover baking sheets with parchment paper or lightly grease them. Preheat oven to 425°F.

For the filling, melt butter in a heavy skillet; add the onions and sauté over medium heat until onions are soft. Blend onions with the meat. Add the sour cream and salt and pepper to taste.

On a floured board, cut dough into 16 equal parts. Roll each part out to make a 6-inch round. Spoon a heaping tablespoon of filling into the center of each round. Fold edges over the filling and seal. Brush with beaten egg and place on the prepared baking sheets. Bake for 15 minutes until golden. Remove from oven and cool. Serve warm or at room temperature. These are good served with mustard or horseradish sauce.

The pasties may be made ahead and frozen. To reheat, place on a baking sheet and into a 300°F oven for about 15 minutes until heated through.

RICE-FILLED POTATO PIES
(*Vatruskat*)

In the Finnish countryside of old, few exotic ingredients were available. But country cooks thought up many variations on the basic themes. These pies were made in eastern Finland, originally, with potatoes and rice as the two major ingredients.

❖ Makes 16 pies

1½ *pounds potatoes*
½ *to 1 cup all-purpose flour*
1 *egg*
1 *teaspoon salt*
melted butter to brush tops

FILLING

2½ *cups cooked rice*
¼ *to* ½ *cup melted butter*
salt to taste

Pare the potatoes and cut into small cubes. Put into a pot in salted water to cover and simmer until potatoes are soft. Drain. Turn potatoes into a bowl and allow to cool. Mash and mix the flour, egg, and salt into the cooled mashed potatoes.

Mix the filling ingredients together and hold in another bowl.

Cover a baking sheet with parchment paper or grease it generously. Preheat oven to 450°F.

Divide the potato mixture into 16 parts. In floured palm of your hand, or on a floured board, pat out 1 part at a time to 4-inch diameter. Place a heaping tablespoonful of the rice mixture in the center of the circle. Fold over to enclose the rice and place on the parchment paper. Repeat with the remaining portions of potato and rice. With fingers, crimp the edges of the half circles.

Brush with melted butter and bake 15 minutes until browned. Brush again with melted butter and serve hot.

❖ Some potatoes will soften in the mixture faster than others, and you may need to add more flour.

ICELANDIC FILLED HORNS
(*Fyllt Horn*)

$\mathcal{S}$erve these ham-filled crescent rolls for lunch with soup or with a salad.

❖ Makes 16 rolls

3 to 3½ cups all-purpose flour
¼ cup softened butter
1 teaspoon salt
1 teaspoon sugar
1 package active dry yeast
1 cup water, 105°F to 115°F

FILLING

6 ounces fully cooked ham, turkey ham, or smoked turkey breast
1 (3-ounce) package cream cheese
2 tablespoons chopped chives

GLAZE

1 egg
1 tablespoon water
caraway seeds

In a mixing bowl, blend 3 cups of the flour with the butter and salt until the mixture resembles coarse crumbs. In a measuring cup, dissolve the sugar and yeast in the warm water. Let stand 5 minutes until yeast foams. Stir the yeast mixture into the crumbly mixture until a smooth dough forms. Beat well. Let stand 15 minutes, covered.

To make the filling, grind the ham or put into the food processor with the steel blade in place and process until ground. Mix with the cream cheese and chives.

Cover 2 baking sheets with parchment paper or lightly grease them.

Divide the dough into 2 parts. On a lightly oiled surface, roll out 1 part to make a 14-inch circle. Let rest a minute, then cut into 8 equal pie-shaped wedges. Spoon a heaping tablespoonful of the ham mixture onto the wide end of each piece of dough. Starting from the wide end, roll up, encasing the filling, to make a crescent shape. Place on parchment-covered baking sheets.

Let rise in a warm place until puffy, about 45 minutes.

Preheat oven to 450°F. Mix the egg and water to make a glaze. Brush the crescents with the glaze and sprinkle with the caraway seeds. Bake 10 minutes or until golden.

CHANTERELLE PIE WITH SOUR CREAM PASTRY
(*Kanttarellipiirakka*)

*F*inns are avid mushroom collectors. There is usually at least one person in the family who loves wild mushrooms and can identify several varieties. Finns eat what they can fresh and dry the rest for enjoying all year. There are chanterelles of many varieties in the Finnish forests, and we enjoyed both large and little pies filled with tasty black chanterelle, brown chanterelle, and golden chanterelle fillings. Fresh commercial mushrooms make an acceptable substitute for the chanterelles, which can be expensive and difficult to find.

❖ Makes 8 main-dish servings

2½ cups all-purpose flour
2 teaspoons baking powder
½ teaspoon salt
1 cup butter, room temperature
1 cup sour cream

FILLING

4 cups finely chopped chanterelles* or fresh commercial
*   mushrooms, or a combination of the two*
½ cup minced onion
1 (8-ounce) package cream cheese
salt and pepper to taste

1 egg, beaten
3 tablespoons milk

Measure the flour, baking powder, and salt into large bowl of electric mixer. Add the butter and mix into the dry ingredients at low speed until mixture resembles coarse crumbs. With wooden spoon, stir in the sour cream until a soft dough forms. Do not overblend or dough will be tough. Wrap and chill 1 to 2 hours.

For the filling, turn the mushrooms and onion into a large skillet. Turn heat onto high and stir and cook until both the mushrooms and onions are soft and lightly browned. Remove from heat and cool. Cut the cheese into cubes and mix into the mushroom filling. Taste and add salt and pepper.

Preheat oven to 400°F.

Roll $\frac{3}{4}$ of the pastry out to make a round to fit a 9-inch tart pan. Fit pastry into the pan and trim the edges. Fill with the mushroom mixture. Roll out the remaining pastry. Cut into strips and weave the strips over the filling. Pinch to seal to the edges of the bottom crust.

Mix egg and milk and brush pastry with mixture. Bake for 25 minutes or until golden. Serve warm or at room temperature cut into wedges.

❖ You may use dried chanterelles; reconstitute according to directions on the package to make 4 cups, including the liquid.

MUSHROOM PIE WITH POTATO PASTRY AND PEARL BARLEY
(*Sienipiirakka*)

*F*inns combine fresh mushrooms with grains to make a wonderful main-dish pie. Most cooks have a wide variety of wild mushrooms, which they have gathered and dried, including brown, yellow, and black chanterelles and a host of others. Reconstituted, the dried mushrooms are used often in main-dish pies. You can use commercial mushrooms, or you can use any variety of dried and reconstituted mushrooms.

❖ Makes one 8 × 10-inch pie

$1\frac{1}{2}$ cups all-purpose flour
1 teaspoon baking powder
$\frac{1}{4}$ teaspoon salt
$\frac{1}{2}$ cup softened butter
$\frac{3}{4}$ cup cold mashed potatoes or $\frac{3}{4}$ cup instant
    mashed potatoes and $\frac{3}{4}$ cup cold water

FILLING

2 tablespoons butter
4 cups fresh or reconstituted
    (including liquid) dried mushrooms, chopped
1 large mild onion, chopped
1 cup cooked pearl barley
$\frac{1}{2}$ cup sour cream
2 eggs
1 teaspoon salt
$\frac{1}{8}$ teaspoon ground allspice

Combine the flour, baking powder, and salt in a large bowl or in the work bowl of the food processor with the steel blade in place. Add the butter and blend or process until the mixture resembles coarse crumbs. Mix in the mashed potatoes until a dough forms. If using instant mashed potato flakes, add the dry potato flakes to the flour mixture. Blend in the cold water until the dough holds together. Gather dough into a ball and chill for 30 minutes.

In a large, heavy skillet, melt the butter; add the mushrooms and onions and cook over high heat until onion is soft, mushrooms are cooked, and pan liquids have evaporated. Mix in the barley, sour cream, eggs, salt, and allspice. Bring to a simmer. Remove from heat and cool.

Cover a baking sheet with parchment paper. Preheat oven to 450°F.

On a lightly floured board, roll out half the pastry to fit an 11-inch quiche or tart pan.

Turn the mushroom mixture into the pastry-lined pan. Roll out the remaining pastry to $\frac{1}{8}$-inch thickness. Cut into strips about $\frac{3}{4}$ inch wide. Place strips over the mushroom filling, making a latticework top. Pinch edges to seal.

Bake for 25 to 30 minutes or until pastry is golden and filling is set.

FINNISH CABBAGE PASTY
(*Kaalipiirakka*)

*T*his is an old-fashioned country pie, served as a main dish. It is important that the cabbage be slowly sautéed to produce a sweet and succulent flavor. *Kaalipiirakka* is usually served warm, spread lightly with butter. It is often served with a glass of milk or a mug of beer as an after-sauna snack.

❖ Makes 8 servings

3 cups all-purpose flour
1 cup butter
1 egg
1 tablespoon vinegar
4 to 6 tablespoons ice water

FILLING

$\frac{1}{4}$ cup butter
1 medium to large head cabbage, about 4 pounds
3 tablespoons dark corn syrup
2 tablespoons vinegar
1 teaspoon salt
$\frac{1}{4}$ teaspoon ground allspice

1 slightly beaten egg
2 tablespoons milk

Measure the flour into a large bowl or into the work bowl of the food processor with the steel blade in place. Cut the butter into small pieces and add to the flour. Cut in or process until butter is about the size of split peas. Mix the egg, vinegar, and 4 tablespoons ice water. Sprinkle the flour mixture with the egg mixture and mix quickly until a dough forms. Press into a ball and chill. (You can make the pastry a day ahead if you wish.)

Because the cabbage is so bulky, you may wish to work with two large skillets at once to make the filling, or make the filling in two batches. In a large skillet, melt 2 tablespoons of the butter. Add half the cabbage and cook over medium heat until the cabbage shrinks down, then increase heat to high and cook, stirring, until the cabbage is browned but not burned. This will take about 30 minutes per batch. Cook away the watery liquid that forms. When cabbage has shrunk down, you can combine the two mixtures into one pan. Add the corn syrup and vinegar. Stir to blend. Remove from heat and cool. (You can make the filling a day ahead.)

Preheat oven to 425°F. Butter and flour a 13 × 9-inch jelly roll pan or another large, shallow casserole or baking pan. Divide pastry into 2 parts. On a floured board, roll out to fit the pan. Spoon the filling into the pastry-lined pan. Roll out the remaining crust to fit the top of the pie. Place on top of the filling and seal the edges well.

Brush top of pie with the egg mixed with milk. With fork, make vent holes in the top of the pie. Bake for 30 minutes or until golden.

FINNISH ONION PIE
(*Sipulipiirakka*)

*T*his yeast-crusted onion pie can stand on its own as a main dish. It is not vegetarian, however, because it does include bits of ham.

❖ Makes one 10-inch pie

1 package active dry yeast
¾ cup water, 105°F to 115°F
½ teaspoon salt
2 tablespoons oil or melted butter
1½ cups all-purpose flour

FILLING

1½ pounds sweet onions
¼ pound smoked ham, cut into ½-inch dice
1 cup sour cream
4 eggs
salt
1 tablespoon caraway seeds

In a large bowl, dissolve the yeast in the warm water. Let stand 5 minutes. Add the salt, oil or butter, and flour and beat until dough is smooth and satiny. Cover and let rise for 1 hour until doubled.

Cut the onions into thin slices. Place in a heavy frying pan along with the ham and cook over low heat until onions are soft, about 15 minutes. Remove from heat and stir in the sour cream, eggs, salt to taste, and caraway seeds.

Butter a 10-inch pie, quiche, or tart pan. Preheat oven to 400°F.

On a lightly floured board, roll out the pastry to fit the prepared pan. Turn the filling into the lined pan.

Bake for 35 to 40 minutes until the crust is browned and pie is set.

VEGETARIAN PIE
(*Kasvispiirakka*)

I first tasted this wonderful main-dish pie in the test kitchens of the Vaasan Mylly flour mill in Helsinki. Home economists there revise and update country classics for use in today's modern kitchens.

❖ Makes one 11-inch pie

2½ *cups all-purpose flour*
2 *teaspoons baking powder*
1 *teaspoon salt*
¾ *cup firm unsalted butter, sliced*
1 *cup sour cream*

FILLING

3 *tablespoons butter*
6 *cups shredded fresh vegetables such as leeks, carrots,*
celery, parsnips, and cabbage, in any combination
1½ *cups cooked rice*
¼ *cup cream*
1 *teaspoon oregano*
salt to taste
1 *cup shredded mild cheese such as Edam or Gouda*

GLAZE

1 *slightly beaten egg*
1 *tablespoon water*

Measure the flour, baking powder, and salt into a large bowl or into the work bowl of the food processor with the steel blade in place. Add the butter and cut in using a pastry blender or on/off bursts of the food processor until the butter is in pieces the size of split peas. Add the sour cream and mix until dough forms. Gather dough together into a ball, wrap, and refrigerate for 30 minutes.

To prepare the filling, heat the butter in a large, deep skillet or wok. Add the vegetables and cook over high heat, stirring and tossing constantly until vegetables wilt, about 5 minutes. Remove from heat and mix in the rice, cream, oregano, salt, and cheese.

Preheat oven to 400°F.

On a lightly floured board, roll out $\frac{3}{4}$ of the pastry to make a round to fit a 10-inch pie pan or quiche pan.

Fill the pastry with the vegetable mixture.

Roll out the remaining pastry. Cut into $\frac{1}{3}$-inch-wide strips and arrange the strips crisscrossed over the top to make a latticework top. Seal at the edges. Brush with the egg and water mixed together.

Bake for 25 minutes or until golden.

FINNISH FISH PIE
(*Silakkapiirakka*)

*F*inns make this pie with a small member of the herring family called *silakka*. We do not have a comparable fish, but after some experimenting I've decided that cod, haddock, or any other simple nonfatty fish is an excellent substitute.

❖ Makes 6 servings

2 cups all-purpose flour
½ teaspoon salt
¾ cup butter
¾ cup cooked, mashed potatoes or ¾ cup
    instant mashed potatoes and ¾ cup water

FILLING

4 hard-cooked eggs, chopped
1 cup cooked rice
1 pound filleted fresh herring or smelts, or
    codfish or haddock fillets
1½ teaspoons salt
½ teaspoon white pepper
2 tablespoons chopped fresh or dried dill weed
½ cup heavy cream
1 egg, beaten

GLAZE

1 egg, beaten

SAUCE

½ cup melted butter
¼ cup chopped fresh dill or 2 tablespoons dried dill weed
2 tablespoons fresh lemon juice

Mix flour and salt in large bowl. Cut in the butter until mixture resembles coarse crumbs. Blend in the mashed potatoes until dough forms, or mix instant dry potatoes with flour and add water to make a stiff dough. Press together into a ball and chill 30 minutes.

Butter a 9-inch pie pan or quiche dish. Preheat oven to 350°F.

Divide the pastry into 2 parts and roll out 1 part to fit the prepared baking pan.

Combine the eggs and rice. Put half the mixture into the pastry-lined pan. Arrange the fish evenly over the egg-rice layer. Sprinkle with the salt, pepper, and dill. Top with the remaining egg-rice mixture. Mix the cream and egg and pour over the filling.

Roll out the second half of the pastry and place over the fish filling. Seal the edges and pierce holes in the top. Brush with beaten egg. Bake for $1\frac{1}{2}$ hours, or until pastry is golden.

To prepare the dilled butter, combine the melted butter with the dill and lemon juice. Keep warm until ready to serve. Spoon over individual servings of the pie.

FINNISH FRESH SALMON PIE
(*Lohipiirakka*)

$\mathcal{S}$almon pie is a favorite Finnish company dish and is commonly found on fancy restaurant menus in Finland.

❖ Makes 6 servings

2¼ *cups all-purpose flour*
1 *teaspoon baking powder*
½ *teaspoon salt*
1 *cup unsalted butter*
½ *cup heavy cream*

FILLING

1 *pound fresh salmon fillets, skin removed*
5 *tablespoons butter, melted*
3 *cups cooked rice*
salt to taste
fresh dill, chopped

GLAZE

1 *egg*
1 *tablespoon water*

SAUCE

½ *cup melted butter*
2 *tablespoons fresh lemon juice*
¼ *cup chopped fresh dill or 2 tablespoons dried dill weed*

Measure the flour, baking powder, and salt into a mixing bowl or work bowl of food processor with the steel blade in place. With a pastry blender or fork, or using on/off pulses on the food processor, blend in the butter until the mixture resembles coarse crumbs. Gently mix in the cream; gather the dough together into a ball; wrap and refrigerate 30 minutes.

Preheat the broiler and place the salmon on a baking sheet covered with foil. Broil 5 inches from the source of heat for 5 minutes on each side, brushing both sides with the melted butter. Cool. Carefully cut the fish into ½-inch slices.

Mix the remaining butter with the rice; season with salt and fresh dill.

Cover a baking sheet with parchment paper. On a lightly floured board, roll out the dough to a rectangle and trim to measure 12 × 16 inches. Place on baking sheet. Spread half the rice mixture down a 3-inch-wide strip the length of the pastry. Top rice with fish slices. Top fish with the remaining rice. Lift pastry up over the filling, moisten the edges, and seal. Turn over so that seam side is down.

Mix the egg and water to make a glaze and brush pastry with the mixture. Decorate with the pastry trimmings cut into shapes and pierce pie with a fork to make steam vents.

Preheat oven to 400°F. Bake for 25 to 30 minutes or until golden. Serve slices of the piirakka with a sauce made by mixing the melted butter, lemon juice, and fresh dill.

FINNISH EVERYDAY SALMON PIE
(*Lohipiiras*)

*T*his is an "everyday" pie, as it is filled with canned salmon, rather than fresh, and hard-cooked eggs, both staples of a Finnish larder. The pastry in this pie is shortened with oil; however, you may use the butter crust from the previous recipe.

❖ Makes 4 to 6 servings

2 cups all-purpose flour
1 teaspoon baking powder
$\frac{1}{2}$ teaspoon salt
$\frac{1}{2}$ teaspoon sugar
$\frac{1}{3}$ cup salad oil
1 tablespoon fresh lemon juice
2 to 4 tablespoons cold water

FILLING

2 (15- or 16-ounce) cans pink or red salmon
2 eggs, hard-cooked
chopped fresh dill to taste
1 cup shredded Swiss, Gouda, or Edam cheese

GLAZE

1 egg
1 tablespoon water

Measure the flour, baking powder, salt, and sugar into a bowl. Stir together the oil, lemon juice, and 2 tablespoons water. Stir the liquids into the dry ingredients, using a fork, until a dough forms; add more water if necessary. Gather into a ball and chill 30 minutes.

To prepare the filling, drain the salmon and remove the skin and bones. Flake the salmon. Slice the eggs.

Cover a baking sheet with parchment paper. Preheat oven to 425°F.

Roll out $\frac{2}{3}$ of the pastry to make a 12-inch square. Place on the parchment-covered baking sheet. Fold $\frac{1}{2}$ inch of the pastry toward the center all around the pastry to make a rim. Top the pastry with an even layer of flaked salmon and eggs, sprinkle with dill, then sprinkle the cheese over all.

Roll out the reserved pastry. Cut into thin strips and place over the filling in a crisscross fashion to make a latticework top. Brush with the mixture of egg and water.

Bake for 20 to 25 minutes until golden.

SALMON PASTIES
(*Lohipasteijat*)

*N*ot just for company, these pasties are often served after sauna with a glass of milk, lemonade, or a mug of beer. I think they make perfect appetizers for a party, as you can assemble them ahead, refrigerate or freeze them, and bake them just before serving.

❖ Makes 48 pasties

> *3 cups all-purpose flour*
> *2 teaspoons baking powder*
> *1 cup butter, room temperature*
> *1 egg*
> *1 tablespoon lemon juice*
> *4 to 6 tablespoons ice water*

FILLING

> *$\frac{1}{3}$ cup cooked rice*
> *1 ($6\frac{1}{2}$-ounce) can skinless, boneless salmon, drained*
> *1 hard-cooked egg, chopped*
> *$\frac{1}{4}$ cup heavy cream*
> *1 teaspoon dill weed*
> *salt and white pepper*

Mix the flour with the baking powder in a bowl. Blend in the butter, using an electric mixer or a fork, until the mixture resembles coarse crumbs. Mix together the egg, lemon juice, and ice water. Sprinkle mixture over the dry ingredients and mix quickly to make a dough. Press into a ball and chill 30 minutes.

Roll dough out to make a rectangle about 20 inches square. Fold into thirds. Roll again as thin as possible and fold into thirds in the opposite direction from the first folding. Chill again for 30 to 60 minutes.

To prepare filling, in a small bowl, with a fork, stir the rice with the salmon and eggs. Blend in the cream, dill, and salt and white pepper to taste.

Preheat oven to 400°F.

Roll out the pastry to $\frac{1}{8}$- to $\frac{1}{4}$-inch thickness. With a round cutter, cut out 3- to 4-inch circles. Put a teaspoonful of filling in the center of each circle. Moisten the edges and fold into half circles, sealing the edges. Place on a parchment-covered or an ungreased cookie sheet. Bake for 10 to 15 minutes or until golden. Serve warm.

These may be made ahead and frozen unbaked. To bake after freezing, place on cookie sheet directly from freezer and bake. Baking time may be 2 minutes longer when frozen.

LIISA'S CHRISTMAS PIE
(*Liisan Joulupiirakka*)

*L*iisa lives in Jyväskylä and serves this fancy decorated pie on Christmas Eve with either creamy potato soup or fish stew. The pie is filled with smoked fish or ham, and sometimes she makes one of each kind.

❖ Makes 8 servings

¾ *cup dry potato flakes*
½ *teaspoon salt*
1 *teaspoon baking powder*
2¾ *cups all-purpose flour*
1 *cup firm butter*
1 *to* 1¼ *cups ice water*

SMOKED FISH FILLING

1 *pound smoked whitefish, salmon, or lake trout, boned and skinned*
1 *cup cooked medium-grain rice*
3 *hard-cooked eggs, finely chopped*
2 *to* 3 *teaspoons dill weed or fresh dill*
fresh lemon juice to taste
black and/or white pepper
½ *cup heavy cream*

HAM FILLING

12 *ounces cooked ham, finely ground*
1 *egg*
2 *tablespoons all-purpose flour*
1 *cup shredded Swiss, Gouda, or Edam cheese*
¾ *cup cream*
2 *teaspoons oregano*

GLAZE

1 *egg, beaten*
1 *tablespoon water*

Combine the potato flakes, salt, baking powder, and flour in a bowl, or in the food processor with the steel blade in place. Slice the butter into the dry ingredients and cut in using a pastry blender or a fork, or using on/off pulses of the food processor, until butter is in pieces the size of split peas. Add ice water just until dry ingredients are moistened. Gather into a ball and chill.

To prepare the smoked fish filling, flake the fish into a bowl. Mix in the rice, eggs, dill weed, and lemon juice, and pepper to taste. Blend in the heavy cream. Chill until ready to use.

To prepare the ham filling, mix together the ham, egg, flour, cheese, cream, and oregano and chill.

Cover a baking sheet with parchment paper or brown paper. Butter the brown paper. Preheat oven to 400°F.

Divide dough into 2 parts. Roll each part out to make a circle 10 inches in diameter. Trim edges and save trimmings for decorations.

Lift one of the dough circles onto the covered baking sheet. Spread one of the fillings in an even layer over the pastry on the baking sheet. Cover the filling with the second pastry circle, enclosing the filling. Mix the egg and water to make a glaze and brush the edges so the pie will be well sealed. Press the edges together to seal. Brush top of pie with the glaze. Roll out dough scraps and cut strips, hearts, and stars to decorate the top of the pie. Brush again with the glaze. With a toothpick, make evenly spaced holes in the top of the pie to vent.

Bake until golden, about 30 minutes. Serve either warm, at room temperature, or chilled.

FINNISH FISH-FILLED "ROOSTER"
(*Kalakukko*)

*T*his is one of the most unusual and identifiably Finnish traditional dishes. In the eastern provinces of Finland, where the fishing is good, there are abundant small, freshwater herrings called *muikku*. They are bony little fish and practical cooks discovered generations ago that, when baked for a long time in a rye crust, the bones get soft and the flavors blend, resulting in a delicious dish. You can purchase authentic *kalakukko,* freshly baked, in the open market at Kuopio in the eastern part of the country, where the dish originated. Jaakko Kolmonen, Finland's television chef, illustrates in one of his books three different ways to cut the loaf. One is to cut a lid in the top and scoop out the cooked fish, eating it with pieces of the crust broken away and dipped in butter. A second is to cut the whole loaf as you would a slice of bread, revealing a mosaic cross section of fish and bacon encircled with the rye crust, and the third is to cut the loaf into pie-shaped wedges. In all cases, the fish is to be served with melted butter and cooked new potatoes, cucumbers, and tomatoes.

Why the name "rooster"? It is the literal translation from the Finnish. Just why the ancient Finns named it this way is left to conjecture. Some say it is because the filled bread isn't baked but is "hatched" at a low temperature.

Making the kalakukko requires time. The rye crust is often "soured" overnight. If you are a baker with sourdough starter on hand, use a portion to enhance the flavor of the crust. The crust is filled, then baked for 4 to 5 hours at a low heat. It is then wrapped in foil or paper and allowed to steam another hour. So plan accordingly!

If you like the smoky taste of bacon, use hickory-smoked bacon. If you prefer, you may use unsmoked, sliced sidepork, which is a little harder to find but more authentic. Domestic herring, codfish, haddock, or any nonfatty fish can be substituted for the herring.

❖ Makes 1 loaf

$\frac{1}{2}$ cup sourdough starter (optional)
1 package active dry yeast
2 cups warm water, 105°F to 115°F
1 teaspoon salt
4 cups dark rye flour
2 to 3 cups bread flour or unbleached all-purpose flour

FILLING

2 pounds small fresh herring, or 2 pounds codfish or
   haddock fillets, or other nonfatty fish, filleted
1 teaspoon salt
1 pound thickly sliced sidepork or bacon

GLAZE

$\frac{1}{2}$ cup melted butter
$\frac{1}{2}$ cup water

In a large mixing bowl, stir together the sourdough starter, if using, dry yeast, and warm water. Let stand 5 minutes. Add the salt and half the rye flour and 1 cup of the bread flour. Beat well. Cover and let sour overnight or 8 to 12 hours if using sourdough starter. Otherwise, continue with the recipe.

Stir in the remaining rye flour and add enough bread flour to make a stiff dough. Sprinkle board with flour and turn dough out onto the board. Knead for 10 minutes or until smooth. Wash bowl, grease it, and place dough in the bowl, turning over to grease top. Cover and let rise for 1 hour. It will not double.

To prepare the filling, wash and dry the fish. Sprinkle with salt. Separate the bacon slices.

Turn dough out onto lightly oiled surface and roll or pat out to a 12- to 14-inch circle.

In the center of the circle, layer bacon and fish, leaving 3 inches free of filling all around. First, lay one-quarter of the bacon slices all in one direction. Place one-third of the fish over the bacon, all in the same direction but across the bacon. Again lay the bacon slices over the fish and repeat with the fish layer going in the opposite direction. Continue layering, ending with the bacon. Lift the uncovered rye dough up over the fish and bacon to enclose it completely to make an oval-shaped pie. Brush edges with water and seal well so juices cannot escape. Brush all sides with a mixture of butter and water.

Preheat oven to 450°F.

Cover a baking pan with a generous double thickness of foil. Lightly grease the foil. Place the loaf with the seam side down on the foil. Bake for 1 hour. Reduce oven temperature to 300°F. Brush again with butter and water and lift the foil over the rooster and seal by folding foil into a seam. Return to oven and bake 3 hours longer. Turn oven off. Leaving the rooster in the foil, wrap in several layers of brown paper (grocery store bags work fine). Place on a pan in the turned-off oven and let "hatch" 6 hours or overnight. Serve at room temperature, cut into slices, or cut a lid off the top and scoop out the fish.

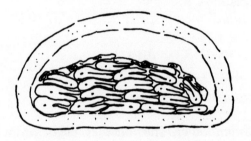

BEEF AND PORK "ROOSTER"
(*Lihakukko*)

*T*his is made like the fish-filled version, but with just beef and pork, salt and pepper. Use a tough cut of meat, such as beef stewing meat, which will cook to succulent tenderness in the rye crust.

❖ Makes 6 to 8 servings

1 package active dry yeast
2 cups warm water, 105°F to 115°F
1 teaspoon salt
4 cups dark rye flour
2 to 3 cups bread flour or unbleached all-purpose flour

FILLING

1 pound sliced beef stewing meat, chuck
    or bottom round
¾ pound pork leg or loin, fairly lean,
    but with some fat
1 teaspoon salt
½ teaspoon white pepper

GLAZE

2 tablespoons melted butter
hot water

In a large mixing bowl, stir together the dry yeast and warm water. Let stand 5 minutes. Add the salt, half the rye flour, and 1 cup of the bread flour. Beat well. Cover and let rise 1 hour.

Stir in the remaining rye flour and add enough bread flour to make a stiff dough. Sprinkle board with flour and turn dough out onto the board. Knead for 10 minutes or until smooth. Wash bowl, grease it, place dough in the bowl, and turn over. Cover and let rise 1 hour. It will not double.

Turn dough out onto lightly oiled surface and roll or pat out to a 12- to 14-inch circle.

In the center of the circle, make a pile of the beef and pork and sprinkle with salt and pepper. Fold the edges over the filling to make an oval-shaped pie. Seal with water. Brush all sides with a mixture of butter and water.

Preheat oven to 450°F.

Cover a baking pan with a generous double thickness of foil. Lightly grease the foil. Place the loaf with the seam side down on the foil. Bake for 1 hour. Reduce oven temperature to 300°F. Brush again with butter and water, lift the foil over the rooster, and seal by folding foil into a seam. Return to oven and bake 1½ hours longer. Turn oven off. Leaving the rooster in the foil, wrap in several layers of brown paper (grocery store bags work fine). Place on a pan in the turned-off oven and let "hatch" 6 hours or overnight. Serve at room temperature, cut into slices, or cut a lid off the top and scoop out the filling.

DANISH HAM BAKED IN A BLANKET
(*Skinke I Sengetaeppe*)

*T*he Danes are not the only ones who bake ham in a blanket, but this is an especially tasty version. This is a wonderful centerpiece for a festive buffet meal for a crowd.

❖ Makes 30 to 40 servings

12-pound boneless, smoked, fully cooked ham
½ cup Dijon-style mustard
½ cup honey

PASTRY

9 cups all-purpose flour
6 teaspoons baking powder
2 teaspoons salt
1 teaspoon sage leaves, ground
1½ cups unsalted butter
2 cups milk

GLAZE

1 egg, beaten
1 tablespoon water

$\frac{1}{2}$ *cup water*
$\frac{1}{2}$ *cup honey*
1 teaspoon freshly pulverized cardamom seeds
6 large, fresh mint leaves
$\frac{1}{4}$ *teaspoon salt*
$\frac{1}{2}$ *cup port wine*

Preheat oven to 350°F. Score the fat on the ham and place the ham in a shallow baking pan with the fat side up. Rub ham with mustard and brush with honey. Bake 10 minutes per pound until warmed through, about 2 hours. Remove from the oven.

Increase oven temperature to 450°F.

To prepare the crust, mix the flour, baking powder, salt, and sage in a large bowl. Cut in the butter until butter is the size of split peas. Add the milk and mix until dough forms. Gather into a ball and knead 2 to 3 turns to mix.

Roll the dough out until it is large enough to cover the ham. Place the dough on the ham and wrap around the ham, pinching the edges together, and trim edges.

Mix the egg and water to make the glaze. Brush the pastry with the glaze. Roll out scraps and make cutouts to decorate the top of the ham. Brush with the glaze again. Pierce with a fork to make vents.

Bake for 1 hour or until the crust is golden brown and crunchy. Meanwhile, make the sauce.

In a saucepan, mix the water, honey, and cardamom seeds and simmer over low heat 5 minutes. Chop the mint leaves and add to the honey mixture along with the salt; simmer 2 minutes more. Remove from heat and let cool to room temperature.

When ready to serve, add the port wine and mix well. If sauce is too thick, add a little more wine and mix again.

SWEDISH HAM PIE WITH MUSHROOM SAUCE
(*Skinkpastej*)

*T*his is a wonderfully rich company dish served with a savory mushroom sauce. You may substitute 1 pound of frozen puff pastry for the homemade. When you purchase the flour for this recipe, check the nutritional label to be sure it has no more than 11 grams of protein per cup, to get the tenderest results. It might seem strange to have brandy or cognac in the pastry, but it tends to soften and tenderize the final product.

❖ Makes 6 servings

> 1 recipe Puff Pastry (recipe follows) or 1 pound frozen
>   puff pastry
>
> ½ pound smoked fully cooked ham
> ½ pound lean veal or extra-lean ground beef
> 2 cups fresh bread crumbs
> 1 cup heavy cream
> 4 eggs, separated
> ½ teaspoon salt (optional)
> ¼ teaspoon pepper
> 1 tablespoon water

SAUCE

> 1 cup fresh white mushrooms or reconstituted dried
>   wild mushrooms, such as chanterelles, or morels
> 2 tablespoons butter
> ½ cup beef stock
> 2 tablespoons brandy or cognac
> 1 cup heavy cream
> salt and white pepper to taste

Prepare the pastry or have frozen puff pastry ready.

Put the ham and the veal through a food chopper, using the finest blade, or cut into cubes and place in food processor. Process, using the steel blade, until ham and veal are minced.

In a large bowl, combine the bread crumbs and cream. Mix in 3 of the egg yolks and blend in the minced meats, salt, and pepper. Whip the 4 egg whites until stiff, and mix with the meat mixture.

Roll $\frac{3}{4}$ of the puff pastry out to fit a 9 × 5-inch loaf pan or oblong terrine, about 2-quart capacity, leaving a generous edge of dough all around the top. Fill with the meat mixture. Roll out remaining dough and place on the top. Moisten edges and seal. Crimp edges decoratively. Pierce or slash the top of the pastry to allow steam to escape. If there are any scraps of dough, you may use them to decorate the top of the pie.

Mix the remaining egg yolk with 1 tablespoon water and brush the pie generously around the crimped edge. Also use the mixture to "glue" fancy cutouts onto the top if desired.

Preheat oven to 375°F. Place pan on a larger pan (to prevent dripping in the oven) and bake 1 to $1\frac{1}{4}$ hours, or until pie is golden and the meat is done. Remove and let stand a few minutes before serving. Serve with the mushroom sauce.

To prepare the mushroom sauce, chop the mushrooms. Heat butter in a heavy skillet and add mushrooms. Sauté over high heat until mushrooms are browned and liquid has evaporated. Add the beef stock and brandy and simmer 5 minutes. Add the cream and simmer 5 minutes longer until sauce is thickened. Taste and add salt and pepper.

PUFF PASTRY

1 cup unsalted butter
2 cups all-purpose flour
½ cup ice water
1 tablespoon salad oil
¼ cup brandy or cognac

Slice the butter into ½-inch slabs and place between sheets of plastic wrap, close together. With rolling pin, roll lightly to join the pieces. Roll butter to about a 7- to 8-inch square.

Add the ice water, salad oil, and cognac to the flour to make a stiff dough. Knead on a slightly floured board until smooth and elastic, about 2 minutes. Cover and let stand a few minutes. Roll out to make a rectangular shape ¼-inch thick, about 16 × 12 inches.

Place butter in the center of the lower half of the pastry. Sprinkle lightly with flour; fold upper half of pastry over the butter and press edges firmly together. Fold the right end of the pastry over the butter and the left end under it; press edges to seal. Cover and let stand 5 minutes. Roll out to about a 12-inch square and fold into thirds. Turn it halfway around and roll out just enough to seal the layers and fold into thirds to make a square. Repeat rolling out and folding in thirds 2 more times, ending with a square. If necessary, refrigerate between folding and rolling. (The necessity to refrigerate depends on how warm the dough becomes and how hot it is in the kitchen.) Chill dough before finally rolling out for pastry.

LAMB AND ONION PIROG
(*Lammaspiirakka*)

*T*his Finnish specialty is served as a main dish. Make the filling for the *pirog* the day before you plan to make the crust and assemble it for baking. It can be served either hot, cooled, or chilled. Horseradish sour cream sauce makes an excellent accompaniment.

❖ Makes 6 to 8 servings

¾ *cup warm water, 105°F to 115°F*
1 package active dry yeast
½ *teaspoon salt*
1 tablespoon brown sugar
1 tablespoon caraway seeds
3 eggs
½ *cup softened unsalted butter*
1 cup dark rye flour
2 to 2½ cups all-purpose flour

FILLING

1 tablespoon butter
2 to 3 large onions, chopped
2 tablespoons all-purpose flour
1 tablespoon dried dill weed
½ *cup sour cream*
1½ pounds ground lean lamb
2 eggs
1 teaspoon salt
½ *teaspoon freshly ground black pepper*

GLAZE

1 egg, beaten
2 tablespoons water

SAUCE

¼ *cup freshly grated horseradish*
½ *cup sour cream*
salt to taste

Measure water into a large bowl and add yeast, salt, and brown sugar. Let stand 5 minutes until yeast foams. Stir in caraway seeds, eggs, and butter. Add rye flour and beat well. Stir in enough all-purpose flour to make a stiff dough. Turn out onto floured board and knead until smooth and elastic, about 10 minutes. Place dough in greased bowl and turn over once to grease top of dough. Cover and let rise in a warm place until dough is approximately doubled in volume, about 1 hour.

Meanwhile, prepare the filling. Melt butter in large, deep skillet and add onions; cook over medium to low heat, covered, for 20 minutes, until onions are very soft but not browned. Remove cover and cook until liquid has evaporated, stirring constantly; add the flour and dill weed. Stir until blended and cook for 2 to 3 minutes longer. Stir in the sour cream, and cook, stirring, until mixture bubbles and is blended. Pour into a large bowl and cool.

Combine cooked mixture with the ground lamb, eggs, and salt and pepper.

Turn dough out onto lightly oiled surface. Knead lightly to expel air bubbles. Roll dough out to make a rectangle 10 × 18 inches. Butter a 9 × 5-inch loaf pan or 2-quart terrine and place dough in the pan, fitting it across the bottom and sides and allowing an overhang. Spoon lamb filling into the dough-lined pan. Fold over-hanging dough over the top and crimp to seal. With tip of knife or fork, make 2 or 3 vent holes in the top of the pirog. Mix egg and water to make a glaze and brush top of loaf with the glaze. Let rise about 30 minutes until crust appears puffy.

Preheat oven to 350°F. Bake pirog for 50 minutes or until golden. Mix together sour cream and horseradish and season with salt to taste. Slice the pirog and serve with the sauce.

SWEDISH BEEF AND HAM PIE
(*Köttpudding*)

*T*his Swedish country-style pie makes a sophisticated company main dish.

❖ Makes about 8 servings

1½ *cups all-purpose flour*
1 *teaspoon salt*
⅓ *cup firm lard or* ½ *cup butter*
1 *egg*
2 *teaspoons cider vinegar*
1 *to 3 tablespoons ice water*

FILLING

1½ *pounds beef sirloin*
1 *pound fully cooked smoked ham*
½ *pound fresh mushrooms*
2 *tablespoons butter*
¼ *cup all-purpose flour*
¾ *teaspoon salt (optional)*
½ *teaspoon pepper*
1 *cup beef broth or bouillon*
¼ *cup brandy or dry sherry*

Measure flour and salt into a mixing bowl or into the work bowl of the food processor with a steel blade. Chop lard into 1-inch chunks and add to the flour. Cut in with a pastry blender or fork or process until the fat is in pieces the size of split peas. In a small bowl, beat together the egg, vinegar, and 1 tablespoon ice water. Add the liquid to the dry ingredients, tossing until the pastry comes together into a ball. Knead 2 or 3 turns just until pastry is pressed together. Wrap and chill 30 minutes.

Cut the sirloin and ham into 1-inch cubes. Clean the mushrooms and cut off the stems; chop the stems but leave the caps whole. Heat the butter in a heavy skillet; add the sirloin and brown over high heat for 2 to 3 minutes until meat is browned but still pink in the center. Turn into a 2-quart casserole. Add the ham to the skillet and brown 2 to 3 minutes until heated through. Add to the beef in the casserole.

Add the mushroom caps to the butter in the frying pan and brown. Add mushrooms to the meat. Sauté the chopped mushroom stems in the pan and sprinkle with flour, season with salt and pepper, stir, and add the beef broth; simmer 3 minutes until thickened. Add the brandy or sherry. Pour into the casserole over the mushrooms and meat.

Preheat oven to 450°F.

On a lightly floured board, roll out the chilled pastry to fit the top of the dish. Crimp the edge of the pastry to the edge of the casserole. Cut decorative steam vents in the top. Bake until crust is golden and filling bubbles, about 20 to 25 minutes. Serve immediately.

FINNISH MINER'S PASTIES
(*Lihapasteijat*)

*F*inns who settled in northern Minnesota on what is called the "Iron Range" and those who settled in Michigan's Upper Peninsula in "Copper Country" carried meat pies like these in their lunchpails every day into the depths of the mines. The pasties were baked fresh in the morning and wrapped so they would stay hot until lunchtime. The original Finnish version included only beef, potatoes, and onions. I prefer to add carrots as well. I was discussing pasties one day with women from the Iron Range, and found that some miners' wives baked an apple filling into one end of the pasty to make a complete meal. I tried it and thought it worked surprisingly well. The recipe that follows this one includes the option of adding an apple filling as a novelty. With or without the apples, these make excellent picnic pies!

❖ Makes 8 servings

1 cup lard or shortening
1¼ cups boiling water
1 teaspoon salt
4½ to 5 cups all-purpose flour

4 medium potatoes, pared and diced into ½-inch pieces
1 cup raw carrots, diced into ½-inch pieces
1 large onion, chopped
1 teaspoon salt
½ teaspoon freshly ground pepper
1½ pounds top round of beef, cut into ½-
*   inch pieces*

Mix lard or shortening with boiling water and salt in mixing bowl; stir until lard is melted. Add flour to make a stiff dough. Chill 1 hour or more. Divide into 8 parts. Roll each part out to make a circle about 10 inches in diameter.

Preheat oven to 350°F. Cover baking sheet with parchment paper, or lightly grease and flour the baking sheet.

Toss potatoes, carrots, onion, salt, pepper, and beef together in bowl. Put 1 cup of the mixture on one side of each pastry circle. Lift other side of the pastry over to cover the filling, making a half circle. Crimp the edges and pierce the top of the pastry to make steam vents. Place on prepared baking sheet.

Bake pasties 1 hour or until golden. Serve hot, cooled to room temperature, or refrigerate or freeze. Reheat before serving if chilled or frozen, about 15 minutes in a 300°F oven or until heated through.

MEAT AND APPLE PASTIES
(*Lihaomenapasteijat*)

❖ Makes 8 servings

1 recipe Finnish Miner's Pasties, including meat filling

APPLE FILLING

4 medium apples, pared, cored, and sliced into 12
  wedges each
2 tablespoons sugar
2 teaspoons all-purpose flour
$\frac{1}{2}$ teaspoon cinnamon
$\frac{1}{8}$ teaspoon salt

Preheat oven to 350°F. Cover baking sheet with parchment paper or lightly grease and dust with flour.

Prepare the pastry as directed. Divide chilled dough into 8 parts and roll each part out to make an oval 11 inches long and 8 inches across.

Combine meat filling ingredients. Put 1 cup of the filling on one end of the pastry oval in the center, leaving the other end for the apple filling, and leaving about 2 inches uncovered at the edges of the pastry.

In another bowl, combine apples, sugar, flour, cinnamon, and salt. Arrange 6 apple wedges in a little pile on the empty side of the pastry oval, next to the meat and potato filling.

Gently lift pastry edge up around meat and apple filling. Pinch seam firmly lengthwise across the top of the pastry, to make a seam that is about $\frac{1}{2}$ inch tall. Pinch with two fingers and thumb to make a pretty ropelike design. Repeat for all of the 8 pasties. Place a toothpick on the end of the pasty designating the apple end of the filling. Arrange pasties on baking sheet. Bake for 1 hour or until golden. Serve hot, cooled to room temperature, or refrigerate or freeze. Reheat before serving if chilled or frozen, about 15 minutes at 300°F.

Index

BEATRICE OJAKANGAS has written more than a dozen cookbooks, including *Whole Grain Breads by Machine or Hand* and *The Finnish Cookbook*, and has contributed to such magazines as *Gourmet, Bon Appétit, Woman's Day, Sunset,* and *Country Living*. She lives in Duluth, Minnesota.